To Whom Shall We Go?

To Whom Shall We Go?

Inspirational Thoughts on God's Word

By
Richard A. Collings

E-BookTime, LLC
Montgomery, Alabama

To Whom Shall We Go?
Inspirational Thoughts on God's Word

Library of Congress Control Number: 2006930342

ISBN: 1-59824-297-0

First Edition
Published July 2006
E-BookTime, LLC
6598 Pumpkin Road
Montgomery, AL 36108
www.e-booktime.com

Unless otherwise noted, all biblical quotations are from The New American Bible, © 1970, Confraternity of Christian Doctrine.

"Lord, to whom shall we go?
You have the words of eternal life."

John 6:68

Contents

Contents

Contents

Contents

1

Philosophers take great care in explaining the powerful paradigm shifts in the history of thought. However, they often ignore the greatest words which can change a person forever, the words spoken by Jesus of Nazareth who said, "I am the way the truth and the life." (John 14:6) Those few words contain more power to change us than all of man's philosophy.

In order to understand the impact of those words of Jesus, we need to seek him with the same passion that scholars seek knowledge. God's word says, "Seek me with all your heart" (Jeremiah 29:13) and if we do, we find him in our heart. If we seek truth as fervently as prospectors seek for gold, we will encounter truth in the person of Jesus. When Jesus said "Follow me," (Mark 2:14) he meant accompany me. Go where I go and do what I do. We tend to follow him from afar and are satisfied with that, which is but a pale imitation of what he meant. To accompany Jesus means to go with him to the cross where we put to death the illusions of our feeble faith.

To follow Jesus is to accompany him into the desert where absorbed in prayer we confront our weaknesses and our pride. Stripped of our false sense of self we see anew the image of God in which we were created, but which our sins have sullied and hidden from us. In the presence of Jesus we are bathed in his love and forgiveness and are empowered to become the children of God that we were created to be (John 1:12). It is then that we can listen with a new awareness to the message that he is the one who baptizes with the Holy Spirit and fire.

Such a baptism of Spirit and fire releases us to serve the Kingdom of God which is in our midst and within our being. We are set free to love God and neighbor, to serve God and neighbor, and to proclaim that the Kingdom of God is at hand for everyone. It is an open Kingdom, vast and forever peaceful, where the only barrier to entry is unbelief. Jesus mentioned the Kingdom more than anything else. Many parables and illustrations teach us that God's Kingdom is a gift and that there is a place in it for everyone who seeks it. It is a gift of unparalleled beauty, a gift of real grace, a gift of God's love to His children.

The secret of the Kingdom is revealed to children and to those who receive it as a child with open hearts and open minds. Jesus told us that only those with childlike faith can enter the Kingdom of God - something that seems to allude the clever and the learned. To be childlike means to have no personal agenda, no ego to promote, and to accept what Jesus said and act upon it. After all, Jesus changed the world forever. His message is the greatest revolution. What he promised to those who believe in him is the mightiest paradigm shift of all: he promised eternal life, which begins in this world and is God's life within his followers for all eternity.

2

God is not indifferent to our sorrow or blind to the misery in the world. When we suffer God experiences our suffering. Psalm 10:14 explains how our Heavenly Father does not forget the afflicted:

> You do see, for you behold misery and sorrow
> taking them in your hands.

In God's hands pain and suffering are healed of their intensity and venom and become holy. In the Psalms his word reminds us that not only is he close to the broken hearted, but he also heals their hearts. He has compassion on the lowly and the poor and he does not ignore the cry of the lonely and forsaken. The prophet Isaiah proclaimed that God dwells with the poor and the rejected to revive their failing hearts. (Is.57:15) The Hebrew Bible promises many times that the Lord takes care of the orphans and widows. It also commanded the Lord's people to make provision for the alien and the poor.

Scripture makes it crystal clear that God takes delight in his people (Ps. 149), and that he loves them with an everlasting love. For example: in the Song of Songs, the Lord has inspired a love song of sublime beauty, words of passionate intensity describing the marriage of God with his bride, the people of God. As St. Gregory of Nyssa noted, the bride is beautiful because "he made me beautiful through his love, by [replacing] his beauty for my deformity." Surely that is what Jesus has done for the whole world - by his death on the cross he wiped away our sin and made us by his grace capable of living in a renewed image and likeness of our Heavenly Father.

The Song of Songs is so redolent with God's love that one great preacher gave 86 sermons on the Song and did not get past chapter two. He was overcome from the very beginning of the poem by the thought that the Creator of the whole universe loved him with such intensity. He has the same love for all of us. Moses Maimonides in writing about the Song of Songs said that love not reverence is the highest relationship we can have with God. He noted that when a man loves a woman he cannot get her out of his mind and we should love God in the same way.

It is often difficult to meditate on God's love for us. We often think we are unlovable. We are so sure of our unworthiness that we can readily see his love for saints and martyrs and never contemplate that we are called to be like them. But God's word tells us with great authority and certainty that He loves us so much that he gave his only son, that whoever believes in him may have eternal life. Isn't that being loved as a saint? The Father esteems us because he believed that we are worth the gift of his son. And Jesus the Son of God loves us so much that he gave his life for us.

3

The first recorded words of Jesus in the gospel of Luke tell of
Jesus' desire to be among the things of his father. Luke's last
recorded words of Jesus spoken as he was dying on the cross are
his desire to put everything into his Heavenly Father's hands.
The words spoken by Jesus in the very middle of Luke's gospel
encourage us not to be afraid because his Father is pleased to
give us the Kingdom of Heaven. Thus, the Father takes center
stage in the gospel of Luke.

It is Luke's gospel which teaches us that our Father knows
everything we need, and when we seek his Kingdom first above
all else, then everything we need will be given to us. Luke
reports that Jesus said if we who are sinners know how to care
for our children, then how much more will our Father in heaven
care for us by giving us the Holy Spirit when we ask.

Perhaps the greatest teaching on the Father in Luke's gospel is
his portrayal of the Father in the parable of the Prodigal Son. A
father had two sons whom he loved. One son stayed home to
farm the land, while the younger son took his inheritance and
went off to a distant land where he squandered his money in
loose living. (By asking for his inheritance, he was really saying
to his father "I wish you were dead so I could get what is coming
to me.") When a famine occurred in that far off country, the
destitute prodigal took a job feeding pigs, a task which no self-
respecting Jew would do. Half starved and desperate, he decided
to return to his father's house, expecting to be hired as a day
laborer, a position more precarious than that of a slave. But he
did not know that his father had watched the horizon every day
looking for him.

On his return, to his great surprise, his father welcomed him with
honor, joy, and love. His father received him with open heart and

arms and threw a big party for him with dancing and merriment. The older brother was angry and jealous and refused to come to the celebration. He was deeply offended by what he saw as his father's weakness in accepting back his prodigal son. He was so incensed that he refused to call him brother. He could not find it in his heart to forgive - and yet he also had received his share of the inheritance which, according to Jewish law, was twice as much as the sum received by the younger son so why was he so angry? The father kindly explained to his oldest son that he had to rejoice because what was lost and presumed dead had now been found alive. The father had no condemnation for either son. Neither does our heavenly Father condemn us. And he calls us to be like him.

4

"Do not be afraid, little flock, for your Father was pleased to give you the Kingdom." (Luke 12:32) This is incredible good news! It is amazingly good news to a world afraid of almost everything. We fear terrorism, weapons of mass destruction, cancer and other afflictions, contaminated food and water, unemployment, cataclysms, global warming, floods, earthquakes, God's wrath, and a whole army of little fears which affect our daily lives.

I think it was Billy Graham who pointed out that there are 365 occurrences in the Bible of "Do not be afraid." Another preacher pointed out there are actually 366 entries, even one for leap year. Yet we continue to live in fear which seems to grow without abatement. One observer noted that the only time people are free from fear is just after they leave their place of worship- but even there some sermons instill fear rather than peace and love. So how can we escape that sense of unease and push away the fear lurking in our lives?

How can we achieve peace and calm, and even recapture the joy which Jesus left us as our inheritance?

The first step is to take time every day for prayer and meditation, which is a recipe for true happiness outlined by the first psalm. The psalm clearly states that the one who prays and meditates on God's word will experience a blessedness that even spiritual drought cannot overcome. The one who prays is like a tree planted near running water - in prayer the running water is the river of life, the Holy Spirit - which bears much fruit. A person who prays on a regular basis will discover the power to overcome all fear and will even find time and energy to accomplish more than he had previously thought possible. So rather than view prayer as a time waster, those who pray know that the time spent with God is not only time well spent, but is indispensable for creativity and peace of mind.

After a while, the one who prays discovers a deep joy which is God's gift to all his children. It is a joy independent of what is going on in the world; a joy profound and impervious to fear. Some will say, if this is true why are so few people dedicated to prayer? Perhaps because they cannot believe that it is true. Perhaps they have never recognized a deep need for God which is part of our human condition, but which is often corrupted into longing for security or possessions or other worldly aims. Perhaps they have tried to pray but failed, burdened by the cares of the world. The answer is Jesus' invitation: "Come to me all you who labor and are heavily burdened and I will refresh you." (Matthew 11:28)

The refreshing presence of Jesus in prayer comes as we learn to seek him with all our heart. He promised that he will never leave us nor forsake us and that as one of his names, Emmanuel, affirms he will be with us always. In prayer he teaches us to trust deeply and to place our lives safely in his hands. As trust grows, so does our prayer life. As prayer grows, so does our love and service for the world. The ultimate outcome of all this is that we become disciples and can follow Jesus even to the cross, if required.

5

There is an old Irish prayer which goes something like this: "Give us today for bread the word of God from heaven" This prayer reflects the deep longing of the human heart for a relationship with God which is both substantial and life giving, with the warmth and savor of freshly baked bread. What the author was really asking for was to receive the scriptures in a new way each day, because he believed that God's word like his mercy is new every morning.

The word of God is new every day. St. John Chrysostom described the scriptures as a "deep well without a bottom," a source of wisdom and inspiration which can never be fully exhausted. Yet too many Christians let their Bibles gather dust on the bookshelves and live half-starved and impoverished lives. They deprive themselves of the greatest source of life and power. They behave as if the word of God is a dead letter, merely black letters on a white page, rather than what it truly is, a source of grace, peace, joy, truth and life-giving wisdom.

This reluctance to read the Bible is growing even among those who love and believe it to be the source of truth. There are several reasons for this, not the least of which is the decline of reading among all peoples. The television and computer, the busyness and consumerism of Western living, the decline of great literature, and the all-pervasive growth of the entertainment industry have all contributed to a serious decline in the reading of Scripture. But the main reason, perhaps, is the failure of many Christians to pray with the serious intent of encountering the living God - the one who breathed life into his word and into all living beings. They just have not been told that the Lord waits for them every day with his hands and heart full of the riches of heaven. They do not realize that heaven begins when they enter into his presence with expectation.

Jesus said, "Heaven and earth will pass away, but my words will never pass away." (Luke 21:33) The words of Jesus are packed with life and grace: words which lead us prayerfully into his presence because he told us that he is the light of the world and that when we follow him we will never walk in darkness. He promised that when we obey his call on our lives he will reveal himself to us. The word reveal, *emphanizo*, can also mean become visible. For two thousand years Christians have experienced the truth of that promise.

A most wonderful promise of Jesus in Scripture is, "If you remain in me and my words remain in you, ask whatever you wish, and it will be given you." (John 15:7 NIV) This is true because as we spend time reading Scripture our hearts become attuned to the desires of Jesus and we only ask for those things he wishes to give us. And they are many and beautiful. Scripture teaches us that when we accept Jesus he empowers us to become children of God. (John 1:12) And God gives his children priceless gifts. What more could we want! So as St. Augustine was told, *tolle lege*, pick up [your Bible] and read.

6

The parables of Jesus teach us about the Kingdom of Heaven in a revolutionary and startling way. Someone has written that the parables are subversive. We have heard these parables all our lives and have some idea of what they mean. But do we really understand them? Are we clear about what Jesus meant when he said, for example, "The Kingdom of heaven is like treasure hidden in a field. When a man found it, he hid it again. And then in his joy went and sold all he had and bought the field." (Matthew 13:44. NIV) Who hasn't day dreamed about finding a hidden hoard of gold? Or falling over a treasure chest, or finding a satchel stuffed with money which no one claims? Once someone actually found a huge sum of money in a brown paper parcel. (My four-year-old grandson found a treasure map on the back of a menu. He took me to my garden shed, found two spades and set me to work digging for buried treasure. After we had found nothing, he said, "It's OK granddad, we were only pretending anyway" - or were we?) So Jesus touches the dreams of almost everyone in this parable.

But the man in the parable seems to act in a dishonest way by keeping his discovery a secret from the owner of the field. The way I see it is that the man was a tenant farmer who worked, perhaps, for an absentee landlord which Jesus' listeners would have despised and would have approved of the man's actions. I also think that the man may have hit his plough on a rock every time he worked the field. So one day in desperation he worked and sweated to dig up the rock to get rid of this aggravating hindrance to his work. But imagine his joy when the rock finally moved and he found a buried treasure underneath it. What he thought was a burden, turned out to be a blessing.

He had no scruples about re-burying the treasure and selling all he had to buy the field. (Actually, the rabbis in his day were split on the issue of legality: some said "finders keepers" others taught he should return it to the owner of the field.) But Jesus was not telling the parable as a question of legality. He was teaching that one can find the Kingdom of Heaven in daily living, even in serendipitous ways, that the Kingdom of Heaven is waiting to be found and will bring joy to those who stumble over it.

Jesus was so sure that the Kingdom was easily accessible that he said it was like a woman who put leaven in three measures of flour and the whole batch rose. Rabbis did not use women as heroes in stories. So in a counter cultural way Jesus made a woman capable of ushering in the kingdom of Heaven to her family and friends, (The bread from three measures of flour could feed many families.) Three measures was also the amount used by Sarah when she and Abraham encountered a theophany by the terebinth of Mamre. There is much food for thought here.

Again, Jesus said "The Kingdom of Heaven is like a merchant looking for fine pearls. When he found one of great value, he went away and sold everything he had and bought it." (Matthew 13:45-46 NIV) Many Church fathers taught that Jesus is the pearl of great price. What have we "sold" to follow him?

7

"Take delight in the Lord, and he will grant you your heart's requests." (Ps.37:4) This promise seems too good to be true. Common sense and our experience tell us that no one gets all the desires of the heart. In fact, many people never achieve even their modest dreams and they see life through eyes dulled by disappointments. They have lost faith in their dreams and in themselves.

So what does that verse mean? Is there a way in which it can mean what it says? I believe there is. The first thing to consider is the imperative," Take delight in the Lord." Do we really delight in God above all things and seek him with an undivided heart? Do we seek the God of consolation, or the consolations of God? Are we looking to him to supply our needs or do we seek him for who he is. When we love God without conditions, regardless of our circumstances, we begin to experience a new life within. We no longer want what we previously thought important; our desires change and we want only those things which God desires for us to have.

The first of his gifts is a new inner life, a life radiant with the joy of his presence. He said "I am the light of the world," and he meant it. The darkness of disappointments and failure to obtain what we want turns into the light of a new realization - we see our previous desires for what they are, mere illusions and desire to pamper the ego. What matters now is to love God and to serve him with a passionate heart. Our desires are now enlivened by the gift of his Spirit, the Spirit of fire and of love.

Of course, this does not happen overnight. Usually, it is a gradual process whereby our inner lives are renewed by the Spirit day by day. However, for some the change can come quickly in the burning fire of repentance accompanied with deep a regret for a wasted life. Tears wash away the years of self-seeking and cleanse the penitent with the salt of sincerity. The sinner is sincere for possibly the first time in his adult life and the weight of wasted years is replaced by hope and possibilities. God is now real and the object of love and intense devotion. The prodigal has come home.

Whether our conversion was quick or gradual, we arrive at the realization that God has changed our heart. We have the new heart which Scripture promised over twenty-five hundred years ago. (Ezekiel 36:26) A heart responsive and ready to serve God and neighbor. A heart renewed by God's love; a heart blest by a pure gift. Jesus said "Blessed are the pure in heart, for they shall see God." (Matth. 5:8) This means that those who seek God with an undivided heart will find what they are looking for. To find God is the greatest goal in life, and the only one with an eternal guarantee.

So why do we spend so much effort seeking things which only have a passing value?

8

"Jesus Christ is the same yesterday, today, and forever." (Heb.13:8) That is a comforting thought, because while on earth Jesus went about doing good, healing, forgiving, and teaching crowds of people. He spoke fearlessly to all and his words had power, truth, and were an invitation to enter his Kingdom. The letter to the Hebrews teaches that Jesus, the one who speaks God's message, "shines with the brightness of God's glory; he is the exact likeness of God's own being, and sustains the universe with his powerful word." And his word gives life which penetrates to the very depth of the human heart.

Hebrews says that his word is sharper than a double-edged sword. The word translated as "double- edged is *distomon,* which means having two mouths. I have always understood that to mean that scripture spoken by the person reading it actually brings the word to life since the two mouths have spoken it - that of God and of the disciple. I believe this because Jesus said, "He who hears you, hears me." (Luke 10:16) What a tragedy that we so often fail to speak his word which would give life and comfort to the suffering, or bring hope to the hopeless, or give direction to the aimless. We can do that because he said he has given us the same glory that the Father had given him. (John 17:22) Unfortunately, we live for the most part as if that were not true.

In an utterly amazing statement Jesus said, "I tell you most solemnly, whoever believes in me will perform the same works as I do myself, he will perform even greater works, because I am going to the Father." (John 14:12 JB) We can understand what the words mean, but can we believe them? I suspect that we render that word unfulfilled by our unbelief. But I challenge us to ponder that word and to open our minds and hearts to its explosive power. We believe that we are unworthy of such a thing happening to us, and with false humility ignore the thing altogether. But John 1:12 says that when we believe in Jesus we are given the power to be children of God. The word here for power is, *exousia,* which means also, ability, capability, might, authority. I wonder if we have really understood the implications of that promise.

The New Testament is replete with wonderful promises, which the Apostle Peter calls "great and precious." One such promise is the gift of the Holy Spirit, the Spirit of Truth, which the Father sends to be with us forever. We will know him, Jesus said, because he lives with us and will be within us. (John 14:16-17) He is the one who will teach us the truth of Scripture and help us to understand our inheritance as children of God. Then, rather than fill us with pride, such a truth causes us to fall on our knees and ask for the grace to comprehend and to live such a sublime mystery.

Lord, how can we fulfill in our lives the promises of your word? Help us to believe it so completely that we will be instruments of your love in a world losing its center and moving further away from the truth. May we be light in the darkness, love in the loveless places, truth where there is falsehood, faith where there is unbelief. May we bring healing, peace, joy, forgiveness, and deep faith. In a word, may we bring you.

9

"The poor you will always have with you and you can be generous to them whenever you wish..." (Mark 14:7) Not only are the poor still with us, but they are with us in ever increasing numbers. And the generosity that Jesus said we could show the poor is not forthcoming. As a percentage of GDP and as a percentage of our individual earnings we give very little of our blessings to the needy. One statistic alone will suffice to prove this: every day almost 40,000 children die of malnutrition, lack of clean water, and lack of inexpensive medications.

The problem is that the well- fed think less and less about the world's hungry. Some of those who do think about the problem of poverty are sorry about it but have no idea how they can help. Others comfort themselves by believing they would help if they knew a poor family or if there were a relief organization that they could trust to give money to, but they believe charities spend too much money on administration and too little on the poor. This may be true in some cases, but many charities do wonderful work, giving 80 to 93 percent of funds to helping the poor. With all the information available it is not difficult to find out which charities do the best job.

Yet, ultimately the real reason the developed world as a whole gives so little to the poor is that there is no profit in it. The god mammon has replaced the God of love. Money is the "divine" motivator and is indeed the golden calf so many worship. Jesus said, "No one can be the slave of two masters: he will either hate the first and love the second, or treat the first with respect and the second with scorn. You cannot be the slave of both God and money." (Matt.6:24 JB) That saying of Jesus has, it seems, fallen out of favor.

However, those who are disciples of Jesus must care for those in need, because he said that when we feed and cloth the poor we are feeding and clothing him. When we visit the sick or the imprisoned, we are visiting him. Whatever we do for the least, he said, we do for him. He even went so far as to say that the poor are blessed because the Kingdom of God is theirs. St. Paul in his letters recognized that his listeners were poor and few were well born, yet he also said to them, ["The Lord] rescued us from the power of darkness and brought us into the kingdom of his beloved son." (Col. 1:13) To live in that kingdom means we care for one another and want for the poor what we have ourselves. After all, that is what love is, and Jesus commanded us to love one another as he loves us. That is another commandment of Jesus that seems to be forgotten, for even churches fail to do that. They even ask for tithes without tithing to the poor themselves.

To be mindful of the poor was so important to the first Christians that the Council of Jerusalem stipulated concern for the poor to be of paramount importance, which Paul said "was the one thing I was making every effort to do." (Gal:2:10) Can we say the same?

10

"Your word I have hidden in my heart, O Lord, that I might not sin against you." (Ps. 119:11 NKJV) In Hebrew the word hidden is *tsaphan* which can mean hidden treasure, a secret, or to esteem. How fitting! For when we hold God's word in our hearts it becomes for us a treasure of inestimable value. As the prophet Jeremiah said, "When I found your words I devoured them: they became my joy and the happiness of my heart." Jer.15:16) Psalm 119, which Jewish tradition ascribes to Ezra, contains 198 references to the word of God. It is an alphabetic prayer of simple beauty, with each verse of the first strophe beginning with the first letter of the alphabet, in the second strophe each verse begins with the second letter and so on through the whole psalm. Like Jeremiah, the author of psalm 119 finds joy and delight in the reading of God's word.

The psalmist prays for eyes open to the wonders in God's message. He asks for wisdom to understand the message and perseverance to continue meditating on the meaning of the Torah. He knows that the word of God gives freedom, hope, trust, comfort, and peace. So he asks for discernment to follow the wisdom that is revealed in the word. He says that the word of God is a lamp and a light which guides him on the path of life. In this light he recognizes that God is his refuge and his shield as he was to Abraham.

With humility he realizes that the revelation of God's word gives understanding to the simple and he gasps with open mouth in his sincerity to understand the Torah. He prays early in the morning for salvation and prays seven times during the day praising God for his justice, and at night he meditates on the promises of God. I am moved by his love for the Torah and by his desire to live a life pleasing to God. But some scholars have dismissed psalm

119 as a repetitive poorly thought out attempt to praise Scripture. They think it is naïve and lacking sophistication.

The opponents of Jesus also thought that his followers lacked the education to ponder the things of God. But Jesus said, "Father, Lord of Heaven and earth, to you I offer praise, for what you have hidden from the learned and the clever, you have revealed to the merest children, Father, it is true. You have graciously willed it so." (Matt 11:25) He also said that those who do not accept the reign of God like a little child shall not take part in it. (Mk 10:15) It is worth pondering that the very experts in the Tanaic (the Hebrew Bible) the ones who should have known who the Messiah was, were the very ones who rejected Jesus as an imposter. Sometimes we are blinded by our own brilliance.

So it is today. Jesus is grouped with Buddha, Mohammed, Confucius, Laotze etc., as a wise teacher who had some valuable teachings and who, like Socrates, was put to death for his criticisms of the system. But as C.S. Lewis pointed out, Jesus claimed to be God, so he was either God, a charlatan, a lunatic, or the "Devil of hell." A careful reading of the New Testament will disabuse any one from thinking that Jesus is merely a wise teacher.

11

"Who do you say that I am," Jesus asked his disciples. Peter answered, "You are the Messiah." (Mark 8:29.) But Peter did not yet understand what it meant to be the Messiah. Nor did the other disciples. Their minds were set on earthly power and prestige.

Jesus had to explain that his destiny lay in death. But even after he saw Jesus transfigured on the mountain, Peter's idea of the Kingdom of God was still a secular one. And sadly, many believers have the same view even today.

Jesus' question, "who do you say that I am?" came at the very center of Mark's gospel, thus stressing the importance of the question. Like a pearl in an oyster, the words hide a grain of sand that can become an irritant to the reader. Because we have to ask ourselves who do we really say Jesus is? Everything depends on our answer. If we answer like Peter, we have to abandon all our false dreams and follow Jesus, even to death. If he is our Messiah and King we have to surrender our own kingdom and accept the one he offers us If we accept him as Lord we must give up the lordship of our own lives and become his servants. This means that we have to be converted from self-seeking to seeking his will and his rule in our lives. In a word we must become his disciples. That is easier said than done.

Yet Jesus asked no less. He said that if we want to be his disciples we must take up our cross and follow him. I believe that the cross is denying our own desires and self-seeking and adopting the life of Jesus as our own. When we do this something quite remarkable happens. We experience a peace that is wonderfully energizing. We have a new sense of purpose and our goals are determined by asking "how can I serve?" rather than "how can I be served." We seek to provide the needs of others in preference to our wants. The grace of God enables us to love rather than seeking to be loved. We are able to remove the plank from our eyes and see clearly how we can help others do the same.

To understand the central question of who Jesus is sets us free from all the entanglements which ensnare us. Jesus becomes a real person, not just a historical figure who now resides in heaven, but someone who guides our daily lives and who is closer to us than we are to ourselves. He is the one in whom" we live and move and have our being." (Acts:17:28) He is the one who takes away our sins and who offers us every day his mercy and love. This love of Jesus is energized in us by the Holy Spirit who is given to us as proof that we are God's children. The Spirit empowers us to live vibrant and meaningful lives by following the pattern of service shown by Jesus. We are given gifts which enable us to benefit the lives of others. Such gifts are our inheritance and we should have joy in using them.

The more we use our gifts for the good of others, the more we are blessed with peace and joy - even under difficult circumstances. This is because the Lord is present to us at every moment, and scripture, which cannot lose its force, tells us that in God's presence there is fullness of Joy. So "rejoice in the Lord always! I say it again. Rejoice!" (Phil.:4:4)

12

"What is good has been explained to you, man; this is what Yaweh asks of you: only this, to act justly, to love tenderly, and to walk humbly with your God. (Micah 6:8 JB) This verse epitomizes the Good News. Jesus lived it, thus revealing the beauty and power of love. The Song of Songs reveals that God's banner over us is love. Jesus' banner over us is the cross, the greatest proof of love. What seemed to be a horrendous crime, the murder of Jesus, was transformed into the world's greatest good - the offer of salvation for everyone.

The death of Jesus is proof of a love which transcends normal human love. It is evidence of a love which refuses to condemn even its killers. From the cross Jesus asked for forgiveness for all of us, because we, like his executioners, hardly ever realize the enormity of sin. Today sin is considered to be a personal weakness or mistake, or perhaps human nature, something which is really not our fault. Some even wink at sin and dismiss it as irrelevant in the modern sophisticated world. But the current state of the world is such as it is because sin is endemic and ignored: the world has lost its sense of sin. Mankind is living in a way which denies the all-embracing love of God which can heal and renew the sinner. To see sin for what it is, rebellion against the good, is to recognize a need for healing. At such a moment, the love and tender mercy of God is available to change the sinner into a saint. That is something we all must pray for, both for ourselves and others.

The fire of God's love preached throughout the ages needs to be preached again with renewed enthusiasm. Sermons on the love of God like those of Francis of Assisi and Francis de Sales converted thousands to following Jesus with passionate hearts. We need such passion today. Our love is often lukewarm and self-serving, a weak love only kindled at brief moment. Those who really love God with passion and fervor are often dismissed as fanatics, or seen as a great rarity like a Mother Teresa, to be admired, but not imitated. God, however, creates such lovers so that we would see their goodness and desire to be like them. In the same way as St. Paul pointed out, urging us to imitate him as he imitated Jesus. That surely is one way of humbly walking with our God. We see the goodness and desire to be like it because we know we are light years away from the holiness of God.

The Song of Songs rather than being about human love, is really teaching us about God's love and his desire for us to be united with him. It is a love poem of mystical beauty calling us to realize that we are his beloved, but also reminding us that he is our beloved, too. He wants to be loved and known by us with the same love he has for his son. By sending his son to set us free from the law of sin and death he showed the depth of his love - for he gave us eternal life so that we would be his forever.

It is a love so deep that God desires to allure us into the desert to speak to our hearts; a love so profound that the Lord has espoused us to himself forever. (Hosea 2:16 & 21) He said he will heal our backsliding, and love us in such a way that he will give us the grace we need to turn back to him. Who can resist such love?

13

St. Paul's letter to the Ephesians is written to ordinary people telling them that God the Father has blessed them with every spiritual blessing in the heavens and has chosen them to be holy and blameless, in other words he will make them extraordinary people by his gifts. Furthermore, he is pleased to adopt them into his family and fill them with his Spirit and endow them with faith to realize the immeasurable scope of his power which every believer possesses. The believer is God's masterpiece "created in Christ Jesus to lead the life of good deeds which God prepared for us in advance." (Eph.1:10) What a sublime description of a Christian! How do we measure up? Do we believe that God will enable us to live such a life? Or do we shake our head and say it is impossible.

The life that God calls us to is his desire and plan for us, therefore he will make a way. He sent Jesus to redeem us from sin, weakness and mediocrity, and to endow us with the will to live lives made remarkable by love. He made each one of us capable of achieving the end for which we were created, union with him. Our abilities and strengths enable us to live up to his expectations, which are different for every individual. God does not make clones. He makes each individual a sacred part of his creation, giving them the freedom to grow and create their own future by the mystery of free will; we accept his will in love, but still keeping our own individuality and desires. There is no other life worth living; for once we understand the call of God on our lives we are at peace with ourselves and the world.

Of course, those who cannot accept the fact that God directs our lives while allowing us to keep our free will reject the Letter to the Ephesians as pious wishful thinking. But they have no philosophical reason for their unbelief, only their experience. Well, the Christian has his personal experience and he knows that God is real because he experiences his presence and guidance. As Ps. 32:8 states, "I will instruct you and show you the way you should walk." Isaiah wrote that the Lord will say to us "this is the way; walk in it." (Is. 30:21.) The Lord told Jeremiah, "I will place my law within them, and write it upon their hearts...All from least to greatest shall know me..." (Jer.31:33 & 34) Also, Jesus promised that the Holy Spirit would guide us into all truth. (John 16:15)

One name chosen for Jesus is Emmanuel, God is with us, signifying the promise to be with us always. Even some Christians wonder whether this is true, because their lives seem to be falling apart and they do not know what to do. When this happens it is almost certain that the individual has given up praying. The very thing that would extricate a person from his difficulties is abandoned. Prayer is no longer part of his life. He no longer seeks time with God, to talk with him and listen to him with all his heart. But God has not abandoned him. He is even closer to him than before, for he is like a sheep without a shepherd. Perhaps he will send you to bring aid and succor, to listen and to understand his plight. You will be a hand let down to help him up. Pray in your heart for your fellow man and watch what the Lord will do - he will not let you wait in vain.

14

In the parable of the unjust judge Jesus taught about the need to pray always and not to lose heart. (Luke 18:1-8) In it he chose a most unlikely hero, a widow who without a husband was powerless in the society of his day. Despite her situation, she came to him to ask for justice in a situation probably having to do with money. Perhaps her son or other relative refused to help her. As a woman she was powerless and needed a judge to obtain justice. But the judge refused. He was corrupt and had contempt for everyone, including God.

However, the widow did not give up. She pestered him every day until he could not stand it any longer. He said he was afraid that she would give him a black eye. (The Greek text can be translated that way.) Of course Jesus is being humorous, for what Judge would be afraid of a widow? His listeners would get the point that it was her persistence that got her justice, and not fear on the part of the Judge. Jesus said, "Listen to what the corrupt judge has to say. Will not God then do justice to his chosen who call out to him day and night? Will he delay long over them, do you suppose? I tell you, he will give them swift justice." Then Jesus made a startling statement, he said "But when the son of man comes. Will he find any faith on earth?" The message here is that the church must continue in prayer so as not to lose faith.

In both Matthew's Gospel and in the Gospel of Luke, Jesus tells his disciples that prayer gets results. He said, if we who are sinners know how to give good things to our children then "*how much more* will your heavenly Father give good things to anyone who asks him." (Emphasis mine. Matt. 6:11) God is willing and ready to hear us. In Luke's gospel Jesus tells the parable of the neighbor who has an unexpected guest and needs some bread because he has nothing to offer the visitor. It is midnight and all his friends are asleep, but rather than be disgraced for poor hospitality he goes next door and clamors for bread for his guest. He shouts aloud so that others will hear, thus putting them under the obligation to prevent the disgrace to the village for lacking in hospitality. His ploy works and he gets the bread. Jesus' comment is that the man's shameless persistence obtained the bread.

Jesus told this parable after the disciples had asked him to teach them how to pray. He is saying that if a human friend gets up at midnight to help his neighbor, surely God will do infinitely more when we persist in prayer. The message then is clear: keep on praying and you will keep on being heard. Jesus expressed it this way: "So I say to you, Ask and you shall receive; seek and you shall find; knock and the door will be opened to you." (Luke 11:9) He could not have said it any plainer than that. But when we pray and seem to have no answer we give up and think God has not heard or that he has said no. But I know a man who prayed persistently for some twenty-six years until his prayer was answered in a most wonderful way. His answer came one day like a bolt from the blue as he was just beginning his prayer. The rest of us would have given up long ago.

The Lord wants us to persevere in prayer because he desires to fill us with his very fullness - a prospect which I find totally captivating. (Eph.3: 19)

15

When Abraham interceded for Sodom and Gomorrah, he knew that God was merciful and would hear his prayer. Yet when he reached the number ten, the *minyan*, he ended his intercession. Was he sure that there were ten righteous inhabitants in Sodom, Gomorrah, Zeboim and Admah? Or did he fear to go any further? Would God have spared the plains of Sodom if Abraham had continued to plead with him? Of course there is no way of knowing. Yet Abraham was a friend of God and spoke to him face to face, surely he could have continued his entreaty on their behalf. Possibly he sensed that the matter was settled and it was too late for more entreaties.

Abraham knew that nothing was impossible with God for the Lord had told him so. (Gen.18: 14) He prayed for Abimelech and his family and all were healed. He had prayed for a son so often that it probably was his daily request of the Lord. Even if seemingly futile, he would go on interceding. When he saw three heavenly messengers approaching his tent near the terebinth of Mamre Abraham ran towards them and bowed low to the ground to greet them. Of course at that moment he did not know that the leader was Yahweh nor could he have suspected that his plea for a son would soon receive an answer.

Abraham invited the visitors to sit under a shady tree and rest whilst Sarah made bread and prepared a meal for them. After the meal, Yahweh told Abraham that he would return in a year to see Sarah's son. When Sarah heard this she laughed, and Genesis explains why. (Genesis 18:12). There is no record of what Abraham thought, but he soon realized who his three visitors were and he believed that Sarah would give him a son.

Jesus, in one of his parables, compared the reign of God to the leaven which a woman combined with three measures of flour to make dough. I think he had Sarah in mind when he told the parable, for she also took three measures of flour to make bread for the heavenly visitors. In a way, Sarah was just as powerful an intercessor as her husband. She is a matriarch and like Abraham she is the forebear of innumerable people - as Yahweh promised. And like Abraham, Sarah would also be a blessing to all the communities of the earth. (Exodus 12:3)

Sarah made bread for the Lord of all creation, and she probably prayed as she kneaded the dough. The Bible is silent about Sarah's prayer life, recording only Abraham's words of intercession. But the Bible does record that as with Abraham God changed her name thus indicating that she, too, received great favor. The Lord listened to the cries of her heart, and her laughter. The Lord listens to us in the same way, for we are her children in faith as well as Abraham's.

16

"How beautiful upon the mountains are the feet of him who brings good news, who proclaims peace, who brings glad tidings of good things, who proclaims salvation…" (Isaiah 52:7 NKJV) This applies to Jesus. He came as the Good News of God, as the salvation of God, as the Peace of God, and the fullness of God.

His message is alive with hope, joy, forgiveness, renewal, and grace. He spoke out fearlessly the truth of the Kingdom and invited everyone to join him in proclaiming the Good news. His offer lives on in every generation and empowers those who accept it to reveal the love of God to a world in dire need for something real and lasting.

Jesus claimed that he was the only way to the Father in heaven. He did not mince his words. He claimed to be God's anointed son and proved it by what he did. Even when the religious leaders of his day sought to trap him into making incriminating statements he infuriated them by his clever replies. When they accused him of being possessed by a demon he pointed out that their father was the devil- the father of lies. When they said that it is by Beelzebub that he casts out demons he silenced them by saying "How can Satan expel Satan. If a kingdom is torn by civil strife, that kingdom cannot last." (Mark 3:22-27) They even tried to trap him into making seditious statements. When they asked him if it was lawful to pay taxes to Caesar he asked for a coin and asked whose head was stamped on it. They said Caesar's. Then give to Caesar what is Caesar's, Jesus answered, but give to God what is God's. (Matt.22: 21) They were amazed at his reply.

In his Beatitudes, Jesus showed a wisdom completely at odds with the beliefs of the leaders in the Temple, the Chief Priests and the Sadducees. He said that those who suffer or who are poor, and single hearted are blessed by God. He taught that a hunger and thirst for holiness guaranteed God's response in filling the supplicant with his own holiness. He said peacemakers are especially blessed and will be called children of God.

He claimed that his followers would be the light of the world by spreading goodness and praise of God. He taught his followers not to worry, because God is their Father and will take care of them when they seek him above all things. His words possessed power and truth and encouraged the fainthearted to trust in God. His listeners admitted that they had never heard anyone speak like him. His words were authentic and bore the stamp of someone who had been with God. Even some of the Sanhedrin were swayed by what they heard, but were afraid to openly follow Jesus. It was mostly those who had nothing to lose who followed him.

His word is still true and full of wisdom, hope, and salvation. His promises in the Bible still speak to our hearts and proclaim that God is our Father. His message is an invitation to embark on the greatest journey we can ever make. It is a journey to the heart of God where we find fulfillment for our lives and the grace to live in the shadow of the cross.

17

"Look!" the boy shouted to his friend," Jesus is coming down the road." His friend peered down the dusty road into the distance and saw no one. "There's no one there, the second boy said, "you must be seeing things." His friend replied, "He should be coming because the pastor said he is almost here, and we sang 'soon and very soon we are going to see the king.'" They both stood staring as far as they could and seeing nothing were very disappointed.

The boys knew that Jesus would come one day, and they were told to be always ready to meet him when he came. They were right. He will come and all of us do need to be ready. But he comes to us every day in the distressing guise of the poor as Mother Teresa put it. He comes every time we pray and every time we attend church. So if we meet him daily in this way, surely we will be prepared to meet him at the Parousia. We will realize, too, that the day we die will also be the parousia for us. A day of joy, not the day of wrath and gloom envisioned by the prophet Joel.

During Advent we hear the readings telling us to watch and be ready, for he will come when we least expect him. That seems puzzling, for if we are prepared, how can he catch us unawares? Unfortunately, people soon tire of waiting for someone to arrive who seems to delay his coming. So we are told to walk in the light and shun the deeds of darkness. When St. Augustine read these words he was converted. We, too, are exhorted to put on "the armor of Light" and "to clothe ourselves with the Lord Jesus Christ." (Romans 13:12 & 14) In this way we will live as people ready to depart on the most extraordinary journey imaginable, for eye has not seen...what God has prepared for those who love him. (1 Cor.2: 9) And yet we spend more time in Advent preparing for the feast of Christmas than seeking the one whose coming we celebrate.

Other Advent scriptures call us to a deeper relationship with the Lord of the season. Mary reminds us that he can fill the hungry with good things and will send away empty those who are only satisfied with earthy riches. Zechariah rejoices because the Messaih has visited and ransomed his people. Simeon saw Jesus as the fulfillment of God's promise that as the Word of God he would be a revealing light to the Gentiles. Even the aged prophetess Anna gave thanks to God for the Advent of Jesus and preached the good news of his birth to all who would listen.

The coming of Jesus that has perhaps the most importance for each of us is the moment we welcome him into our hearts and surrender our lives to him. Such an Advent puzzled the learned Nocodemus who misunderstood Jesus' words regarding new birth. The Lord was talking about being born of the Spirit from above, a theophany granted to all who earnestly seek it. Nicodemus may have suddenly seen the light and rejoiced in what Jesus told him. Like Micah, perhaps he realized that he had been sitting in darkness while being in the presence of the Lord of light. As we meditate on the meaning of Christmas let us open our hearts to the light of God's word. His word has the power to save us, as it did St. Augustine, and the power to shake us to the very center of our being as it did to Herod.

18

In a great vision of the future Isaiah saw a time of peace when swords would be beaten into plowshares and spears would be turned into pruning hooks. (We are as far from that idyllic life as they were in Isaiah's day) It would be a time when all nations would come together to worship YHWH. A time when the weapons of destruction would be turned into useful implements. Isaiah called on the house of Jacob to "walk in the light of the Lord." (Isaiah 2:1-5) His way of light leads to peace - the way of darkness leads to war and destruction. But people did not listen. However, a Zionist organization in Russia in the 19th century took the words "walk in the light of the Lord" to heart and planned to return to Jerusalem to fulfill the prophecy. They believed that two witnesses in scripture were a guarantee of truth, so since Micah also predicted a similar outcome to Isaiah they were sure of the future of the new Zion. Such is the power of belief that it convinced them to emigrate to the Holy Land.

When the prophet Joel some three hundred years or so later said, "Beat your plowshares into swords, and your pruning hooks into spears." This encouraged those who wanted to immigrate to Palestine and convinced them that they and their descendants would live forever in Jerusalem. Even though Isaiah, Micah and Joel were writing about a different future their words became a source of inspiration to 19th and 20th century Jews.

The experiences of people in the Bible have helped believers in all ages to live vibrant lives and overcome serious difficulties. Many believers facing the most awful odds clung to God's word and became overcomers. They experienced the truth that the word of God is a living word which gives hope and empowers them to keep on going in the face of great obstacles. They emulated the great men and women of the Bible who understood that "Faith is the substance of things hoped for, the evidence of things not seen" (Hebrews 11:I NKJV) They trusted in the word of the Lord even when their friends and family called them foolish. By faith they lived and they died in faith. They believed the promises of God because they were confident that one who made them was trustworthy.

We are all called to have the same kind of faith. As children of God we are not only called to have a deep faith but also to live by it. Jesus spoke very clearly about the life of a disciple. It is a life of faith, service, and love, all based on a deep relationship with God in prayer. Anyone who chooses to pray seriously and regularly will find the grace and strength to live by faith. St Paul wrote that faith which expresses itself through love is the "only thing that counts." (Galatians 5: 6 NIV) He pointed out that faith enlivened by the Spirit, brings a wonderful freedom so that "All of us gazing on the Lord's glory with unveiled faces, are being transformed from glory to glory into his very image by the Lord who is the Spirit." (2 Cor, 3: 18) In other words, prayer changes everyone.

19

Job was not patient, but he was persistent. He insisted that he had done nothing worthy of the terrible calamities which befell him. His friends assured him that God was punishing him for some wicked deed, because God did not allow the just to suffer. Not only were they poor friends, they understood nothing about the causes of suffering. Nor did they know God. They were afraid of God and did not want him to punish them like Job. They spoke platitudes in their effort to show God that they were not like Job, who was angry with them as well as with God.

But Job did not understand the Lord, either. He thought that the terrors of God were arrayed against him. (Job 6:4) He complains bitterly to God expressing his innocence and tells God that he does not understand what is happening to him. (Millions after Job will make the same complaint.) But one of his friends says Job's words are useless and based on pride (This is typical projection). The three friends tell Job that he deserves his afflictions because he is a sinner. Job tells them that they are religious phonies and windbags. They were supposed to be his friends, but Job points out that they have no compassion and offer no real help. Job feels alienated from them and from God. Yet, in a flash of inspiration, Job believes in forgiveness and redemption because he says, "I know that my redeemer lives, and He shall stand at last on the earth...Whom I shall see for myself. How my heart yearns within me." (Job 19:25-27 NKJV) He knew there would be vindication. And he would see God.

In the midst of this encounter between Job and his three friends, a young man interjects and says he's angry with Job and his friends. He is in fact very angry, and yet he does not say anything different from the three friends, although he does see some meaning in suffering. He is conceited and full of self-righteousness as he presumes to speak for God. At the very moment when he is telling Job that no one can see God, the Lord speaks to Job out of the whirlwind. He does not answer any of Job's questions, but asks his own questions such as, "Where were you when I founded the earth? (Job 38:4) On and on he playfully asks Job question after question which Job cannot answer. His only reply, "Behold, I am of little account: what can I answer you? I put my hand over my mouth. Though I have spoken once, I will not do so again. (Job 40: 4)

Job admits that he had spoken about things he did not understand. But the wonderful outcome of all his suffering, humiliation, and seeking is powerfully affirmed in his greatest confession: "I had heard of you by word of mouth, but now my eye has seen you." (Job 42:4) The book of Job's greatest message is to seek God in earnest even in despair, and he will be found, which Jesus confirms. (Matt 7:7)

In times of great hardship we often forget what the book of Job can teach us: to persevere, cry out to God, but preeminently to

listen and meditate on his word. It was when Job was listening
that his answer came. So many of us have lost the art of listening
to God. The Bible tells us hundreds of times to listen. Are we
spiritually deaf?

20

"Rejoice always, never cease praying, render constant thanks:
such is God's will for you in Christ Jesus." (1 Thess.5: 16-18)
How can we do that? Who among us can pray all the time,
rejoice all the time, and be constantly thankful? We must not be
too literal in our understanding. The message means that we
should dedicate our lives our lives in joy, praise and
thanksgiving to God. Like love, joyful praise of God is a
decision of the mind, but inspired and graced by the Holy Spirit.
Joy is a fruit of the Spirit's presence and a fulfillment of the
Biblical promise that there is fullness of Joy when the Lord is
present.

Brother Lawrence understood this in a simple yet prefect way.
He realized that if we practice the presence of God, if we recall
that he is always with us, then our lives will be a constant, joyful
prayer. If we lift our hearts to God often during the day silently
saying "Jesus I love you," or "Blessed be God," or any other
brief word of love our hearts will overflow with thanksgiving.
We will see the beauty and wonder of Creation and grow in love
for its Creator. Brother Lawrence, an ex-soldier who spent thirty
years as a humble kitchen worker in a religious community in
France is beloved by Catholics and Protestants alike. He spent
his days meditating on the love of God while washing pots and
pans for he resolved to live a life ruled by the love of God. In
this humble task he discovered that those who live with God are
never miserable.

He always asked God for help, even in his daily decisions in the kitchen, or on his trips to buy provisions. In that way he seemed to do everything well, and he knew that it was the Lord who blessed him because he had asked for help and he was joyful in thanksgiving. In his pains and sicknesses he found speedy help because he was always talking to God and found strength in his presence. He believed that we need to know before we can love, and we know God by thinking about him and talking to him. Love soon grows from this habit of being with the Lord.

Like Francis of Assisi, Lawrence was aware of the need to daily renew his commitment to God. He wanted to make up for missed opportunities. Yet in his extended prayer time he liked to sit before the Lord like a dumb beggar at a rich man's gate, looking in silence at the master of the house. He did not recite elaborate prayers...perhaps he recalled the words of Jesus about those who did so.

Brother Lawrence's life was hidden in God, yet all of Paris knew of him. From the greatest cleric to the lowest peasant, Brother Lawrence's reputation for holiness was established and honored. Today, his wisdom can guide us through the perplexing difficulties of the 21st Century. His method of recalling to mind the presence and the goodness of God can help heal many of the mental sufferings our age is heir to. There is no one who cannot benefit from Lawrence's simple, yet sublime way of prayer. To think about God as being present can overcome fear, loneliness, insecurity, and rejection. It can energize us to live lives of service to others. It will renew our lives and give meaning to whatever we do. We will have found the pearl of Great Price and the buried treasure of the Kingdom of God.

21

The first psalm in the book of psalms sets the tone for the other 149 songs that follow. It opens in Hebrew with a plural word which can be translated "O the happinesses" of the one who avoids sin and delights in God's word and ponders its wonders. The usual translation is "Blessed the man..." which the Septuagint also translates as blessed or happy.

Psalm one teaches us that reading scripture puts us close to the river of life-giving water which sustains and nurtures us like a tree planted on the banks of a stream. Jeremiah wrote the same thing, adding that such a tree will have leaves that are always green, which means that faith will remain fresh and vibrant to one who hopes in the Lord. (Jeremiah 17:7-8) Isaiah promised such believers will be "like a watered garden, like a spring which never fails." (Isaiah 58:11) "The water I give," Jesus said, shall become a fountain within [[you] leaping up to provide eternal life." (John 4:14) Psalm one points the way to turning the desert of our hearts into an oasis.

The second psalm promises the same blessings to all who take refuge in the Messiah. Psalm three has a beautiful blessing for those who trust the Lord; verse four gives the image of God holding David's face in his hands and sustaining him. In the next psalm David illustrates the joy which comes to those who trust the Lord to answer prayer. His home is protected by the Lord so he sleeps secure in peace. When he wakes up, he tells us that the Lord is waiting to hear from him. The whole Psalter is full of assurances of God's loving faithfulness to all who seek him.

Many psalms are beautifully lyrical prayers speaking to God from a heart full of trust and praise. Others are songs of thanksgiving for healing. Forgiveness and deliverance from harm and death. David exulted in the Lord saying, "You changed my mourning into dancing...forever will I give you thanks." Psalm 30: 12) All of us have times of mourning and sorrow. If we imitate David we, too, can experience a new found joy. We may dance, or if we are too old for that, we can dance with the Spirit in our hearts. Either way, we will give praise to God.

The psalms of repentance, or the penitential psalms, are among the most moving. Psalm 32, St Augustine's favorite psalm speaks of what unrepentance feels like. It is a wasting away of the bones and a loss of strength and peace. But forgiveness washes away guilt and brings relief. Psalm 51 is the greatest of the penitential psalms. The sinner cries out for mercy and compassion, acknowledging his sins and asking God to create in him clean heart. The verb create can only have God as the subject, it means to create out of nothing - the sinner knows that only God can make a heart new and pure. He begs God not to take the Holy Spirit away from him, and he asks for a spirit of fervor and the joy of salvation. He is confident that God will not reject a contrite heart. Sorrow for sin stirs the heart of the Lord.

22

The Western man is afraid of silence. Noise surrounds him everywhere. Televisions and radios blare out day and night keeping us from silent meditation and preventing us from finding the center of our lives. Our hearts are encrusted with things, what some have called the "affluenza" of our age. This is a great tragedy. For the heart is the place where God chooses to speak to his children. As Pascal said, "The heart has its reasons of which reason knows nothing."

But if our hearts are full of self and constantly seek comfort, entertainment, and pleasure how can we hear the "still small voice," the whisper of God which Elijah heard after all the noise around him had ceased? (1 Kings 20:11-13) How can we find meaning and purpose when we are spiritually numbed by the endless activity of our acquisitive society. We have plenty, yet we want more, but nothing satisfies for long. Augustine had it right, "O greedy man, what will satisfy you if God himself will not?" Yet so many of us never even give God the time of day. To be silent before the immensity of a distant God seems a fearsome task and is left to fanatics or professional clergy. Thus we deprive ourselves of that which will make us whole.

It is in the silence of our hearts that direction and purpose for living will come. If we can trust the many witnesses who came before us, we can find the way to peace and well-being. We can find God. Many men and women of the past have left us their wisdom to guide us on the way. They are signposts to the place of true life. St. Ignatius of Antioch said "Man fully alive is the glory of God." To be fully alive necessitates sharing in the life of the Spirit. It was St. Teresa of Avila who counseled us to remember that the one who has God, has everything.

Dostoyevski wrote that we are all in paradise, but we are unable to see it. I am sure he was familiar with the phrase, "heaven and earth are full of God's glory" and perhaps he lamented our lack of vision. But in quiet meditation we can catch a glimpse of the glory the Bible speaks about. We can also see it, in part, on a starry night when we look at the heavens and contemplate the Milky Way in silent wonder. At such a moment noise would be a distraction and impede our vision of celestial beauty. And the constant noise of modern living prevents us from seeing God's heavenly beauty. After all, the word says. "Be still, and know that I am God." (Psalm 46:10 NKJV)

23

"This is my beloved son. Listen to him." (Mark 9:7b) Those words were heard by three disciples who accompanied Jesus to the top of the Mount of Transfiguration. Matthew tells us that they were overcome by the power of God and fell to the ground terrified. But Jesus laid his hands on them and told them not to be afraid. Later, Peter would write that since he was an eyewitness to the Transfiguration of Jesus his own preaching bore the authentic stamp of prophecy. He had heard and had kept the word in his heart. He urged us to keep our eyes fixed on the Word which is like a lamp shining in the darkness.

Jesus said those who listen to his words and put them into practice are established on unshakeable rock and nothing will sweep them away. He said "The heavens and earth will pass away but my words will not pass." (Matthew 24:35) His words are alive and thus give life. He said his words were spirit and life. When he spoke, he spoke with authority and even his enemies recognized it. His words had the power to heal, to raise the dead, to bring peace and forgiveness and they still do.

Just look how he spoke to those who came to him in need. He asked Bartimaeus what he wanted and then granted his request for sight. The woman caught in adultery was dragged shamelessly to Jesus for judgment, but he did not condemn her. He sent her away and she believed that she was forgiven. The woman at the well, who had been married five times and was living with a man who was not her husband, was astounded that Jesus asked her for a drink of water. When he told her that he was the Messiah, she ran off in haste to spread the news about Jesus. She became an apostle, sent by the Lord to proclaim his arrival.

Two small words sufficed for Peter James and John to leave their nets and follow him. He said: follow me" to Matthew the tax collector and he left his lucrative post and became his disciple. To Nathaniel he said, "I saw you under the fig tree," and Nathaniel replied, "Rabbi, you are the Son of God; you are the King of Israel." (John 1:49) What was it about Jesus that his words had such an impact on his listeners? It was the power of truth.

He speaks to us with the same authority and power. He assures us most solemnly that if we listen to his word (message) and have faith in God who sent him, then we possess eternal life and will not be condemned. (John 5: 24) [The word translated as "eternal" means God's life.] How incredible that listening to Jesus will give us God's life within us! How important, therefore, it is to read his words and take them to heart.

What is so important that we have no time to listen to the Lord of life?

24

In the years that my wife and I have been traveling to third world countries to help the poor we have seen many people who have great faith and love for God even in the most wretched conditions. In Albania we met Christians who had undergone unspeakable suffering but who were almost radiant with the love of God. One priest we met had been imprisoned for over twenty years and was treated abominably, but he had a joy and peaceful presence that we had only rarely witnessed.

In Ecuador, in the terrible slum called Guasmo Sur we met children playing in open ditches infested with mosquitoes who thanked God with touching fervor for whatever little they received. Near Salvador, Brazil, there is an unspeakable slum which despite government promises of help has been getting steadily worse. Yet the children were surprisingly happy and their parents had an unshakeable faith in God. In the midst of appalling poverty we saw a faith deeper and stronger than in the wealthy countries. It was the same in Africa, among Christians in China, and among the poor everywhere we went. It appears that the materialism of the developed countries has choked the spiritual life of millions and left them dissatisfied and yearning for more.

Jesus warned us of the danger of amassing money and possessions. He knew that possessions could enslave us and destroy our spiritual life. When we have all we need we tend to ignore the very thing we need the most - a relationship with God based on the truth that everything we have is a blessing meant to be shared. The poor can teach us how to appreciate the things we have. Their gratitude to God for the little they have is humbling to see. The have received the Kingdom of God like children, trusting in Divine Providence for their daily bread. Their trust, their ability to share what they have, their hope even in crushing need, are evidence that the mystery of the Kingdom is present among them.

Perhaps many of us in the rich nations have lost our way and no longer seek the Kingdom of God which Jesus taught us to seek above all things. He preached on the Kingdom more than on any other subject. For Jesus, it was the hidden leaven in our midst which can only be experienced by tasting it in the bread of his word. He gave us God's word from heaven to be our daily bread. But we are sated with a different food; our appetites are surfeited with self-indulgence. As Oscar Romero said, "Without poverty of spirit there can be no abundance of God."

"The poor you will always have with you," Jesus said, "and you can give to them whenever you wish." As a percentage of our wealth we give very little to the poor who increase daily. Over Three billion people live on less than two dollars a day! And yet, many of them are grateful for what they have...

25

"The Lord is the Spirit and where the Spirit of the Lord is, there is freedom." (2 Cor. 3:17) But what kind of freedom is that? It is the freedom of the new Covenant which sets us free from the law of sin and death. (Romans 8:2) It is not license, rather it is the freedom to express the truth with courage and humility which brings liberty to those whose minds are darkened by ignorance. This ignorance is a new paganism which sweeps through the modern world and declares that whatever we want to believe is the truth for us. It claims that there is no such thing as objective truth; truth is what you make it. However, this postmodernist thinking is not true freedom, it is a form of bondage to a lie, the lie which says all beliefs are the same and just as true as any other.

Yet there is an appearance of freedom in this thinking as it allows the individual to choose his own way in whatever circumstances he finds himself. Freedom to choose is the basic right of all of us and is God given. However, in order to choose the truth we must first understand what true freedom is. When the Creator breathed life into our fist parents, he put his life within them and gave them the ability to choose between good and evil, between truth and a lie. Only the truth sets us free, and as Jesus said, when his truth sets us free, we are free indeed. (John 8:36)

Jesus told Pilate that he had come into the world to testify to the truth, and anyone committed to the truth would hear his voice. "Truth!" said Pilate. "What does that mean?" (John 8:38) He didn't wait for an answer and went out to speak to Jesus' accusers, who like Pilate, seemed to have little respect for what truth Jesus was talking about. The central issue here is will those who really seek truth find Jesus to be the truth as he proclaimed. (John 14:6) Or will they be like Pilate and lose interest when they encounter the huge number of Christian denominations. But yet, they all believe in Jesus…and he did say that he is the truth.

Concerning the many religions and their beliefs, Aleksandr Solzhenitsyn wrote, "I have come to understand the truth of all religions in the world: they struggle with the evil inside a human being (inside every human being), it is impossible to expel evil from the world in its entirety, but it is possible to constrict it within each person." For Solzhenitsyn, the multitude of religions played an important role for each person, and therefore each person should be respected.

Jesus taught us to seek him, to listen to him and take his words to heart, and then, as Proverbs puts it, wisdom shall enter your heart. (Proverbs 2:10)

26

Jonah was angry with God. The Lord told him to go to Nineveh to preach impending doom. Jonah ran the other way and took a ship headed for distant Spain. But on the way the sailors, panicked by a storm and by Jonah's confession that he was fleeing from his God, agreed to throw Jonah overboard. Jonah was swallowed by a large fish and spewed up on the shore from where he finally obeyed God and went to Nineveh. Amazingly, the populace repented and Nineveh was spared. Jonah was again angry because he knew God would be merciful and he would look like a false prophet of doom and gloom. Besides, he did not want Nineveh, the traditional enemy of Israel, to be spared.

In Chapter eleven of Luke's Gospel Jesus said that he was a sign to his generation just as Jonah was in his time. When Jonah preached to foreigners in Nineveh the inhabitants repented, while Jesus was saddened by the refusal of his own people to reform their lives. Jesus is also a sign to our generation and his words are as often ignored today as they were then. Jerusalem became a ruin as Jesus regretted that it would. At another time the prophet Nahum gloated over the destruction of Nineveh and Zephaniah boasted that the Lord would make it a desert. The perils of ignoring the prophetic word are evident.

Today Jerusalem flourishes, though encircled by hatred and bloodthirsty enemies. While Nineveh, called Mosul today, is scarred by strife in Iraq. On one of the mounds where the ruins of ancient Nineveh lie there is a mosque called "Nebi Yunus" which means Prophet Jonah. Hanging in that mosque suspended from the ceiling is the bone of a whale How odd that Jonah is remembered in the city of his enemy and memorialized in a shrine of Islam. I wonder if the message to repent would be heard today if a modern Jonah were sent to Iraq. Perhaps someone has been called, but has refused to do it.

Although the Book of Jonah is a didactic tale based in the distant past it has a timely message for us today. It teaches that God is merciful and wants all people to hear his message of repentance and mercy. His message is one of peace and reconciliation. He calls us to live in harmony with one another and with the world that he has given us. After all, he said to Jonah, "Should I not be concerned" with all the inhabitants ... "and many cattle besides."

If God is concerned with cattle, how much more is he concerned about you!

27

"Because you are God's chosen ones, holy and beloved, clothe yourselves with heartfelt mercy, with kindness, humility, meekness, and patience. Bear with one another; forgive whatever grievances you have against one another. Forgive as the Lord has forgiven you." (Colossians 3:12-13) What a remarkable recipe for a peaceful life! Just to know that God has chosen us is enough to empower us to live grace-filled lives. To know as scripture teaches that we were chosen in love even before the world began is enough to transform our lives. Knowing that we are forgiven obliges us to forgive others, and understanding that we are loved, encourages us to love even as we are loved.

In fact we are commanded to forgive one another and to love one another. Jesus said that if we do not forgive others we can expect no forgiveness from our Father in Heaven. Until we comprehend the liberating truth that we have been forgiven it is almost impossible to forgive. The feelings of hurt and rejection are powerful emotions which not only linger, but which are felt every time we recall the incident which caused them in the first place. Given our fallen nature, it is more appealing to hold onto anger and hurt than it is to extinguish our desire to get even.

Even when we receive an apology, we hold on to the resentment and replay the offenses in our memories from time to time to keep them alive. Taking offense is a very strong emotion, which has a negative effect on our lives.

Fortunately, God does not remember our offences. The Bible plainly states that when God forgives, he chooses to forget. Psalm 103:12 has a wonderful word of forgiveness: "As far as the east is from the west, so far has he put our transgressions from us." Through Isaiah he said. "It is I. I wipe out, for my own sake, your offenses; your sins I remember no more." (Isaiah 43:25) In another scripture verse the Lord says that he wipes away our sins like mist and again says he puts our sins behind his back. (Isaiah 38:17) It is clear that with God forgiveness means forgetting as well.

The Apostle Peter asked Jesus if he had to forgive his brother seven times- a perfect number. Jesus told him to forgive seventy times seven, in other words unlimited forgiveness Then Jesus told the parable of the Unforgiving servant. In this story a servant owed his master 10,000 talents, a staggering amount which he could never afford to repay. Yet the master, with great mercy, forgave him the entire amount. The servant went off and met a fellow servant who owned him a pittance, yet he refused to allow time for repayment and had his debtor thrown in jail.

When the servants' master found out what had happened, he had the unforgiving servant punished, saying "You worthless wretch! I cancelled your entire debt...should you not have dealt mercifully with your fellow servant, as I dealt with you?" The point of the parable is that we are to forgive others because God has forgiven us so much that he redeemed us with the incomparable price of his son.

28

"You will receive power when the Holy Spirit comes down on you; then you are to be my witnesses in Jerusalem, throughout Judea and Samaria, yes, even to the ends of the earth." (Acts 1:8) The word for power, *dunamis,* means might, strength, ability, even capability. Such access to the Spirit's power is intended for all believers, since all those who follow Jesus are apostles. The title of Acts in Greek is literally "Acts of apostles," which can mean all apostles. As somebody said, the Church is Acts chapter twenty-nine, so modern day apostles continue the mission inspired and empowered by the Holy Spirit.

Each believer is called to a special task in the Kingdom of God. Like Jeremiah, before we were formed in the womb God dedicated us to speak words of life-giving promise. It was Jeremiah who said to the Lord, "When I found your words, I devoured them; they became my joy and the happiness of my heart." This expression indicates that when he first read the Torah he was consumed by wonder and gratitude to God. Even though he later spoke harsh words, such as telling the people of Judah that sin is "Engraved with a diamond point upon the tablets of their hearts," words which were impelled by his love for God.

Our task is much simpler and less caustic. We are called to proclaim the love of God made manifest in Jesus, the Messiah. We are led by the Holy Spirit to be signposts pointing to the forgiving heart of Jesus. The Spirit enables us to live lives which witness to God's love. The greatest message we can preach is to show love for everyone. We are called to speak words of peace and reconciliation; as St. Paul wrote, we are to say only the things which will really help people in whatever situation they are in. We are commissioned by the Spirit to use our spiritual gifts for the benefit of the common good. Therefore it is important that we are aware of our gifts lest they lie buried like the talent in one of Jesus' parables.

The Letter to the Ephesians includes this marvelous prayer:" May the God of our Lord Jesus Christ, the Father of glory, grant you a spirit of wisdom and insight to know him clearly...that you might know the immeasurable scope of his power in us who believe..." Ephesians 1:17-19) In a similar vein Jesus had promised that we would be able to recognize the Holy Spirit because "he remains with you and will be within you." He said the Spirit will instruct us in everything, and that if we have faith in him, we will be able to do the works that he did. (John 14) Can we ever live up to that promise?

St. Paul experienced the power of the Holy Spirit and he knew that truth, humility, and that preparedness to live the gospel even in suffering and doubt, would triumph. "This treasure," he wrote, "we possess in earthen vessels, to make it clear that its surpassing power comes from God and not from us." (2 Cor. 4: 7) The Christian power to proclaim Jesus as Lord and to live as witnesses to that power is our inheritance. Do you believe it?

29

Hosea is sometimes called the prophet of God's love. He was the first prophet to describe the relationship between God and the people as a marriage. One wonders if he inspired the poet who wrote the Song of Songs, since he spoke of God "alluring Israel" into the desert where he could speak to her heart. He said," I will espouse you to me forever, I will espouse you in right and in justice, in love and mercy." (Hosea 2:16) Through Hosea the Lord said he desired love and not sacrifice and he wanted his people to know him. In Biblical language to know is a very intimate word. God wanted to be close; but the people wanted him at arms length. Isn't that still true today. Intimacy with God is not the goal of most people, yet it is what God wants.

Further in his prophecy Hosea records these poignant words: "When Israel was a child I loved him...the more I called them, the farther they went from me...Yet it was I who taught Ephraim to walk, who took them in my arms. I drew them with human cords, with bands of love...yet though I stooped to feed my child, they did not know that I was their healer." (Hosea 11:1-4) Despite the tenderness of such love, the people did not listen. But God had the last word, for at the end of the Book of Hosea there is a remarkable word of the Lord which in Hebrew is amazingly good news: "I will heal their defection." In other words, God will heal our inability to return to him. He will give us the grace to overcome disloyalty and backsliding. That is what forgiveness (given in advance) means. It is God's prevenient grace and the proof of his eternal love in the person of Christ Jesus.

There are other prophets who, like Hosea, see the advantage of the desert as the place where God can speak to our hearts. Isaiah said the desert of our lives will bloom and exult because it is there that God will save us. He said the deserts will also flourish, because rivers there will flow with copious waters. (Jesus promised that those rivers of water would flow out of the barrenness of our hearts when he gives us to drink.) In those desert areas there will be a way called the highway of holiness which leads to the Lord and everlasting joy. (Isaiah 35:1-8) John the Baptist was a voice crying out in the desert "Make ready the way of the Lord, clear him a straight path." (Luke 3:4) And the greatest prophet, Jesus, entered the desert in preparation for his ministry. When confronted by the Devil, Jesus told him that man lives on the bread of God's word, the true food of everlasting life. It seems that this heavenly bread mainly comes to us when we are in the silent desert of our hearts listening for the presence of the Lord.

The desert is not a place to be afraid of, rather it is to be welcomed when barren times afflict our souls. For it is there that

God speaks to our hearts in the silence of our listening. As has been said so often, God is closer to us than we are to ourselves. In those quiet moments when we truly listen, we dwell with God in a realm of delight. Then our desert blooms with abundant joy and indescribable peace - a peace which is infused into our spirit and is impregnable to the world.

30

In all his letters Paul sent the greeting, "Grace and peace from God our Father and the Lord Jesus Christ." He knew that without those two gifts of God the tribulations of life would crush the ones he was writing to. They are two wonderful words. Peace, the Hebrew shalom, refers to completeness of life. It is a prayer asking for everything we need for our spiritual, emotional, physical, and financial well-being. With such peace we can live fulfilled and vibrant lives. The second word grace, in Greek is *charis,* a beautiful word rich in meaning, such as favor, gratitude, graciousness, and care of God, and ever since Paul's time it has the primary meaning of divine help. With peace and grace the Christian life is a blessed one.

In his letter to the Philippians Paul gives us a key to receiving the peace and grace of God: "Do not be anxious about anything, but in everything, by prayer and petition, with thanksgiving, present your requests to God. And the peace of God, which transcends all understanding, will guard your hearts and your minds in Christ Jesus." (Philippians 4: 6-7 NIV) In his book, Gratefulness, the Heart of Prayer, Brother David Steindl-Rast reminds us that everything is a gift to be thankful for. He wrote, "Even the predictable turns into surprise the moment we stop taking it for granted." How often do we take God and his gifts for granted! If we prayed with heartfelt thanksgiving our lives would be renewed and wisdom would enter our souls.

Jesus prayed with a thankful heart. When he raised Lazarus from the dead he thanked his Father for always hearing him. At the Last Supper he gave thanks to his heavenly Father for the bread and wine and declared them to be his body and his blood of the new covenant. What Jesus did at that Passover meal has been called Eucharist ever since, a word which means thanksgiving. Broken down, Eucharist is made up from the prefix eu which means good. So giving thanks is full of good grace, full of gratitude and graciousness. That explains why it is so important to live thankful lives.

Psalm 136 speaks of God's mercy twenty-six times, "Give thanks to the Lord, for he is good, for his mercy endures forever." I think Paul had this psalm in mind when he wrote to Timothy. His greeting was his usual one wishing peace and grace, but in both letters to Timothy he added mercy. When we experience the mercy, grace, peace, and love of God we are made whole and holy. Timothy was equipped to proclaim the marvelous good news and Paul reminded him to stir into flame the gifts of the Spirit he had received when Paul laid hands on him. But his letters are also written to us and we are gifted by God and called upon to stir up love, joy, peace, and goodness, and to use the unique gift we have received as children of God.

So let us give thanks and rejoice in the goodness of God who has called us into his Kingdom of light where his love and mercy are everlasting.

31

"See what love the Father has bestowed on us in letting us be called children of God. Yet that is what we are." (1 John 3: 1.) It is axiomatic to say that God is love, yet what does it mean to say he *is* love? The Bible affirms that he is love and says that the evidence of that love is the gift of his son who suffered a terrible crucifixion and redeemed us from the law of sin and death. The love of God freely invites us into his Kingdom and lavishes his Spirit upon us. The gift of the Spirit is further proof of his love which enables us to cry out Abba, father, by revealing to us that we really are God's children. (Romans 8:15-16)

It is difficult to understand and live the truth that we really are members of "the household of God" (Ephesians 2:19) I believe we have to accept it as true and pray for the grace to live it. I had great difficulty living that truth and as a boy I always believed that priests, religious, ministers and church leaders were members, but I was not. I felt like a poor boy looking into an expensive confectionary, with my nose pressed to the glass admiring the delectable cakes that I would never taste. The church was a wonderful place, with its mysterious liturgy and mystical saints and angels who, as I was told, filled the church whenever the celebrant presided. It was a place where others had the right of membership, but I would always be an onlooker with no right of full membership. No one ever told me that I was a child of God.

Of course, in my young mind I knew that Jesus was the Savior, but I never realized that he had saved me. Salvation was for others. Even when I grew to adulthood I still had the uneasy sense that I was the outsider looking in. I do not recall ever having heard a sermon which invited me into the family. Then one day, I was surprised by what I can only call an invasion: I was overwhelmed with love, forgiveness, and a delicious sense of inclusion into the things of God. I was an exile no longer. I had arrived at my promised land.

I wondered how I could have missed what was now obvious to me, how could I have been so blind and deaf to the insistent call of the Gospel? But I realized that the fault was only partly mine. For when I was young the laity were not expected to do anything, at least in my denomination. We were onlookers in the great scheme of things and never challenged to go into the whole world to proclaim Jesus as Lord. Professional religious did everything and we were left to stack the chairs and collect the hymnbooks.

Fortunately, things have really changed and lay folk are all over the world as missionaries, spreading the Good News and exulting in the call of the Gospel on their lives. All of us now realize, or should, that Jesus calls us to follow him and to spread the fragrance of God's love by the way we live. If you have never been told that Jesus wants you, I am telling you that he does. He says today what he said two thousand years ago, "Come away and proclaim the Kingdom of God is at hand."

32

"In the silence of prayer, encounter with God is actuated." (John Paul II) An ancient Celtic spirituality put it this way: find the thin side of your soul where Jesus can break into your hearts. The "thin side" is the place where we find God waiting to empower us with his presence. He pours his love from within, a love which enables us to serve our neighbor, it is a "marvelous love for the faithful ones who dwell in the land" (Psalm 16, The Grail, 1963) Such a grace comes to those who seek God in the silence of prayer. Psalm forty-six urges us to "Be still and know that I am God."

The prophet Isaiah understood the need to be still and listen to God speaking to our hearts for he said "By waiting and by calm you shall be saved, in quiet and in trust your strength lies." (Isaiah 30:15) Being quiet and waiting for the Lord is not palatable to twenty first century believers. It seems to be a waste of time sitting and waiting for something that may or may not happen. We want instant action. We live in the world of fast food, electronic banking, and same-day-service. The prospect of sitting in silence actually terrifies us. Silence is the place where all our fears and failures well up from our subconscious. In silence we feel alone and vulnerable...it is not a good place for our age. And yet, it is the safest and most beneficial place we can find. It is in profound silence that God speaks to our heart, because in silence we can empty ourselves of self-seeking and be open to the healing presence of God.

Perhaps the main reason why our age is reluctant to seek God in silence is our indifference. Elie Wiesel wrote, "The greatest evil in the world is not anger or hatred, but indifference." One fact alone suffices to show our indifference: every day many thousands of children die of starvation and related illnesses." If we listened to the Lord we would see the world's poverty as our own and we would do something about it. I have no doubt that the rich nations could save those children...

Listening to God is vital for a life lived well. Judaism's great confession of faith, the *shema,* prayed daily by the faithful, begins with the verb "hear" or "listen." Listening to God is essential for those who love him. Lovers communicate. It is unthinkable that God would listen to us day after day and not reply. The greatest sign of God's response is the change which goes on in a praying heart. No one can pray for long without being moved by the grace of God to make changes in his life. Profound changes take place in silence as we listen for God. Day by day we may not see what is happening, but after some time of waiting for God in prayer our inner landscape is transformed.

"Those who wait on the Lord shall renew their strength they shall mount up on wings like eagles." (Isaiah 40:15 NKJV) The image of an eagle soaring is an apt simile for prayer. The courage and energy required to witness to the love of God is given in prayer, and the one praying finds the direction and wisdom to live fully for the Lord. Listening and meditating on God's word is the path to fulfillment and joy. What are we waiting for?

33

"Behold, the virgin shall conceive and bear a son, and they shall name him Emmanuel, which means God is with us." (Matthew 1:23) What an incredible statement! We have heard and read it so many times that we overlook the truly extraordinary miracles it contains. That Mary, the mother of Jesus, was a virgin and bore a son through the Holy Spirit is an unequalled event in all of history. God intervened in the normal course of time and impregnated a young virgin with her consent. She said, "Let it be done to me as you say." (Luke 1:38) Her "yes" to God opened the door to all the graces which come to us in Jesus her son. The miracle of the Incarnation began the saving advent of God.

The other miraculous gift is his name. Emmanuel, God with us, which is the promise that we will never be alone. The name declares that God will always be with us and there is no need to be afraid, for those who have God, have everything. (Teresa of Avila) Jesus said that he would be with us always, thus living up to the name prophesied by Isaiah. When we live in the truth that he is with us, our lives have extraordinary meaning. When we ignore him and live by our own strength and will, we end up in a mess. Yet even then, the Lord is ready to rescue us because he was there waiting all along for us to call upon him for help.

The Good News of the New Testament is that God loves us so much that he sent his son to save us and heal us of our self-centered pride. He sent Jesus to enable us to see what God is like, so that we could love him without fear. Jesus said that he and the Father are one; when we see him we see the Father. So the Father is revealed in the works of Jesus, who healed, forgave, rescued the poor and the outcasts, and who included everyone in his mission. He has enabled us to be friends of God. No one seeing Jesus can be afraid of the Father. So the idea of a distant

God who needed to be placated, who kept a record of our transgressions, and who was waiting to strike us down, such a vision of God was no longer tenable in the light of the message of Jesus. The love of God became tangible and believable in the person of Jesus.

So the names Jesus and Emmanuel rank highly among the many names and titles of our Heavenly Father. The plural names *Elohim* and *Adonai* which point to the Trinity, the name YHWH which speaks of eternal existence, and other names which signify that he is the healer, the provider and the one who sees our needs. The power of a name, especially in Hebrew, lies in its meaning. A name signifies what characteristics a person will have. For example Abraham means father of a multitude, Judah means praise, Peter is a rock, and John is a sign that God is gracious, So the Biblical names of God reveal some aspects of his nature. He has revealed part of himself to us so that we will seek to know him more. As James says, "Draw close to God and he will draw close to you." (James 4:8)

Drawing close to Jesus is life's greatest adventure. He invites us to come to him and shelter in the light of his truth. He calls us to follow him because he is the way. He bids us come to him for he is the King in the Kingdom of God, and the "Kingdom of God does not consist in talk, but in power." (1 Corinthians 4:20)

34

I remember being amazed when I first read the prayer by Jeremiah. "Why is my pain continuous, my wound incurable, refusing to be healed? You have indeed become for me a treacherous brook, whose waters do not abide." (Jeremiah 15:18) He is complaining that God is not trustworthy, he is like a brook which promises water to drink but runs dry when he is thirsty. It is tantamount to calling God a liar! I was shocked. But later, after suffering myself, I could understand the pain of Jeremiah's cry. To see real suffering in a loved one and get no answer to the question "why" is a deep sorrow. But in our darkest moments our struggles become noble as we, Job-like, seek an answer from God.

In the Bible we get a real look at sincere prayer from the heart. Abraham interceded for Sodom and Gomorrah and only gave up when he thought that there would surely be found ten righteous people to save Sodom from destruction. Jacob, certainly no saint, fought for his blessing from the Angel of the Lord to undo the pain he had caused by cheating his brother out of his father's blessing. He may have been a cheater, but he became truthful in his struggle with God. Job's answer was to find himself in conversation with God and realize that he was God's friend.

Psalm seventy-four opens with the prayer, "Why, O God, have you cast us off forever?" And psalm twenty-two, prayed by Jesus on the cross, "My God, my God, why have you forsaken me?" They are real prayers to a real God. Isaiah trembled when he prayed and cried out, "Woe is me, I am doomed! For I am a man of unclean lips, living among a people of unclean lips..." Isaiah knew that he, too, bore some responsibility for the sin of the world. But God touched his lips and he was healed of his sin. Then he cried out, "Here I am," God, "send me" to speak for you. How many of us try to speak for God but have not understood that we also share in the evil of the times. The humility of Job, Abraham, and Isaiah should teach us something profound. Even the petulant prayer of Jonah, asking for the Lord to take his life, was spoken in truth.

When Daniel prayed to the Lord asking for wisdom to understand the scriptures he said thirty-two times "We have sinned," thus associating himself with the sins of the people. He did not take the attitude so often seen among the self-righteous who recognize sin in others but not in themselves. In his letter to the Romans Paul wrote "For all have sinned and fall short of the glory of God." (Romans 3:23 NIV) Even the Lord Jesus took upon himself the sin of the world: "For our sakes God made him who did not know sin to be sin, so that in him we might become the very holiness of God." (2 Cor. 5:21) So we who are sinners must bear our share of the transgressions of mankind. As has so often been said, if we are not part of the solution, we are part of the problem. But prayer is an effective solution.

When we pray, opening our hearts to the light of truth in Jesus, we receive the grace to help remedy the hurts in the places we live and work. We become peacemakers and reconcilers and learn to see God in others. But if we are blind to our own shortcomings and only see them in others, we cannot proclaim the Kingdom of God in any effective way. Only in humility. Can we be of service to those God puts in our path.

35

In the Gospel of Mark Jesus seems to be always on the move. He goes from place to place healing the sick, preaching that the Kingdom of God is at hand, and calling on sinners to repent. Everything happens at a rapid pace in Mark's gospel, as if there was a very limited time for Jesus to accomplish his mission of inaugurating God's rule in people's lives. He said the opportune time had arrived and would brook no delay. His call is urgent and he expects his followers to go with him at once, which they do. On their journey they will learn what it means to be a disciple.

He calls some of them as he walks along the lakeshore (The Greek word used here for walking means as a god passes by, thus showing the divinity of Jesus. Mark 1:15) He heals Peter's mother-in-law, casts out demons from many, and heals all those in the neighborhood who came to him. His power amazed them. But already his opponents were plotting against him, particularly when he healed a man with a withered hand on the Sabbath. He looked in the eyes of his accusers and they were silenced. They left the synagogue and those who had formerly been opponents of one another, the Herodians and the Pharisees, began to plot against Jesus.

Jesus continued his mission and very soon the scribes, the theologians of his day, began to attack him. They accused him of blasphemy and of being possessed by Beelzebub. It seems that the experts and religious leaders, those who should have been able to recognize the Messiah when he came, saw Jesus as someone who was a threat to their position and they conspired to get rid of him.

Not long after this, Jesus taught the crowds from a boat on the lake while the multitude sat and listened to his first parable, which is included in all three synoptic Gospels. He spoke about the seed and the conditions of the soil on which the seed was sown. In Jesus' day the farmer sowed the seed first and then ploughed it under. So the seed was visible, and thus vulnerable. Jesus' words were evident for all to "see" and could be lost like some of the seeds. The seeds on the good soil produced more than was usual in Palestine at that time, thus indicating that despite some losses, the harvest would be great. Since the seed stands for God's word, and Jesus is the farmer, the parable is very encouraging. It teaches us to share God's word without worrying about results because the word, like the seed sown on good soil will get results.

Isaiah has written that the Lord said his word "shall not return to me void, but shall do my will, achieving the end for which I sent it." (Isaiah 55: 11) Such is the faith he has in the word of God. He also has faith in those who receive his word with sincere hearts for they shall bear abundant fruit. The urgency of the message in Mark's day is just as vital today. Let those who have ears to hear, listen.

36

One day a friend of mine overheard a street preacher interrupted by a heckler in the small crowd that was listening to the message. The heckler shouted out, "Why do I need to be saved? "What am I supposed to be saved from?" the preacher said, "You must saved from your sins." The man responded by saying "I don't need a savior, I have everything I need."

In a materialistic society more and more salvation has been usurped by the goal of obtaining consumer goods. Our lives revolve around things, and are dedicated to work in order to buy more things. Our possessions define us. Sin seems old fashioned and out of place in this new acquisitive age. But the preacher could have answered the heckler by saying he is not only saved <u>from</u> something, but he is being saved <u>for</u> something. Perhaps then the man in the crowd would have had his interest piqued to ask, "Well <u>for what </u>am I saved?" It is a good question. Jesus did call his followers to something, he called them to a life enriched by the presence of God. He offered them the rule of God to bring order and divine favor to their lives. He called it a jubilee from God, a promise to release us from all that imprisons us. He also said there would be hardships and persecutions...but they afflict us all, believer and non-believer alike.

The essence of Jesus' message is that he came to give us eternal life, God's life, which we would receive from a gracious and loving heavenly Father. He challenged his listeners to repent and turn away from self-centered living, to serve others in the joy of the good news from God. He told them that a person's value does not consist in the goods he owns. He taught that there is a higher value in human life, a transcendent and imperishable destiny which can be refused but not taken from them. He believed that people could be transformed by the power of his message, and he commissioned his followers to preach the same good news. Unfortunately, sometimes the message is obscured by an undue stress on rules and modes of behavior which become ends in themselves. That was the big problem with his opponents, the Scribes and Pharisees. Jesus said of them, "Their words are bold, but their deeds are few. They bind up heavy loads, hard to carry to lay on men's shoulders, while they themselves will not lift a finger to budge them." (Matthew 23:4)

Perhaps that was what the street preacher was doing, placing burdens on his listeners rather than proclaiming the good news that Jesus had come to set us free to live vibrant and fulfilled lives. To take our burdens and replace them with his yoke, which he said is easy and light. Actually it could be translated that his yoke is beneficial, even benevolent. Who would not want to replace the heavy burdens we often place on our own shoulders and exchange them for the gentle and benevolent yoke of life with Jesus? Only those who have not heard the really Good News. Have you heard it?

37

"Each one of us has received God's favor in the measure in which Christ bestows it." (Ephesians 4:7) The Lord, we are told, does not ration his gift of the Spirit. He gives generously and constantly to those who seek him with a sincere heart. Unfortunately, so many of us are satisfied to have God on our own terms and do not enter into the relationship he has in mind for us. We do not really "strive to acquire a fresh, spiritual way of thinking." (Ephesians 4:23) Paul said it even stronger in his letter to the Romans: "Do not conform yourselves to this age but be transformed by the renewal of your mind, so that you may judge what is God's will, what is good, pleasing and perfect." The translation "be transformed" can also be rendered "be transfigured," letting the light of our Heavenly Father shine into the darkness of our minds and changing them in love.

The great gift of God is his Spirit which will transform us into the image of Jesus when we lay aside our former selves and seek to be one with him. The great wonder of the Gospel of Jesus is that it leads those who follow it into the place of peace and reconciliation. We are reconciled with God and with one another. The one touched by the fire of God's love has no longer any hatred, anger, rancor or arrogance towards his neighbor. He is aware of the great mercy and forgiveness the Lord has given him and he longs to share with everyone the message that the Gospel is "the power of God leading everyone who believes in it to salvation" (Romans 1:16)

A great problem today hindering full acceptance of the Gospel is the scandal of division among Christian denominations. The conservatives, the liberals, the fundamentalists, the independents, and a host of mega churches, each with its own agenda and beliefs. Each group jealously guards its own bailiwick and uses litmus tests to ascertain orthodoxy. Once when the Apostle John came to Jesus and said, "Master we saw a man using your name to expel demons and we tried to stop him because he is not of our company." Jesus told him in reply, "Do not stop him, for any man who is not against you is on your side." How long it has taken us to adopt that truth!

Jesus accepted everyone who came to him. He called an amazingly disparate group of followers and in his presence they got along. So what is stopping us today? We all believe that he is Emmanuel, God with us, but we do not live it. I think if we asked for that transfiguration of our minds; if we asked for wisdom in our innermost being; and if we asked to know love and serve Jesus with all our hearts, we would all get along and cooperate in spreading the good news. But we poach one another's churches for members and openly call other denominations misguided or plain heretics. I have even heard on more than one occasion ancient churches, who preserved the Bible through many dark centuries, called idolatrous and non- Christian.

This is the time to stop condemning one another and to love each other and to join Jesus' prayer that we all may be one as he and the Father are one.

38

Jesus had been across the lake in the Gerasene territory. Back in Capernaum a synagogue leader called Jairus (his name means "he enlightens") was looking for Jesus. As soon as Jesus crossed back and landed near Capernaum Jairus saw him and fell at his feet pleading for his little girl who was critically ill. Jairus was not proud, he publicly knelt before Jesus saying, "Please come and lay your hands on her so that she may get well and live." (Mark 5:23) They went off together followed by a large crowd.

While on their way a women who had suffered with a hemorrhage for a dozen years pressed through the crowd and touched the hem of Jesus' outer garment. "If I just touch his clothing," she said to herself, "I will be healed." She reached out for the tassel on Jesus' prayer shawl. For her, the blue of the tassel signified healing. Immediately she felt healing power run through her whole being. Jesus, sensing that power had had gone out from him turned around to see who had touched him. The woman was afraid because according to the law she was unclean and her touch rendered Jesus ritually unclean as well. But Jesus told her not to be afraid and he praised her for her faith which he said had healed her.

Why did she touch the hem of his garment? On the hem of every prayer shawl there is a fringe or tassel (*tsitsit* in Hebrew). According to the Book of Deuteronomy the tassel had a blue cord and was a reminder of God's law. So the woman placed her trust in God's word and touched the tassel. The remarkable thing is that *tsitsit* has a numerical equivalent of 600, (Hebrew letters also function as numbers) the tassel had a combination of 13 knots and cords, so 13 and 600 equals 613 the total number of individual commandments in the Torah! Her example inspired others because later on in Mark's Gospel we read that many people came to Jesus for healing, begging him "to let them touch the tassel of his cloak. All who touched him got well." (Mark 6: 56)

Jairus must have been very anxious when he saw Jesus stop to see who touched him. When his friends came and said his daughter was dead he must have been besides himself. But Jesus said to him, "Don't be afraid; just believe." (Mark 5: 36 NIV) Jairus trusted in Jesus and his daughter was brought back to life. She was twelve years old, the age of betrothal. If Jesus had not raised her up they would have had a betrothal ceremony at her funeral, according to local custom. Thus he spared them a terrible grief.

It is worth noting that although Jesus was on his way to save a dying child he took the time to stop and find out who had touched him. He did not overlook the immediate need in order to hurry and take care of the urgent situation. The woman was in need and Jesus took the time to acknowledge her faith, even though his disciples wanted Jesus to ignore her. If he had not stopped we would never have known the depth of her faith nor heard of the miracle which has given such consolation to countless believers. We can be assured that Jesus will stop for us too when we reach out in faith trusting in his love and power.

39

In the older translations of Luke's Gospel the angels at the birth of Jesus sing "Glory to God in the highest and peace on earth and goodwill toward men." More recent translations say "Glory to God in the highest, and on earth peace to men on whom his favor rests." (e.g. NAB, NIV, etc.) The older translations tell us that God's blessing is for all mankind, while the newer translations point out that God's peace is only for the select few, or for those men "of His Good Will" I think it is clear that the older translations are better when we remember what the angels proclaimed to the shepherds, they said that they had good news for "all people." (See Brad H, Young, Jesus the Jewish Theologian, p.7)

The good news of Jesus is for everyone. Too often we have made it the exclusive purview of our particular denomination, or for Christians at the exclusion of Jews, or as something opposed to a secular state. But Jesus said "Go into the whole world and proclaim the good news to all creation. (Mark 16 15) That seems to make it quite clear that the good news is for everyone. And the good news is the person of Jesus.

Often Christians are bent on evangelizing non-believers by use of programs or different types of teachings. But I see how Philip led the Ethiopian eunuch to an understanding of Isaiah 53 by telling him "the good news about Jesus." (Acts 8: 32-35) The Eunuch asked for baptism without undergoing a long period of catechesis. The Holy Spirit prepared both Philip and the Ethiopian. Perhaps we need to trust the Holy Spirit more and ask for heavenly guidance to spread the Gospel. We also need to reflect the presence of Jesus among us. As Charles H. Spurgeon observed, "I would not give much for your religion unless it can be seen. Lamps do not talk, but they do shine."

That is what Jesus meant when he said our light must shine for all to see. The true light will attract hungry hearts as a lamp attracts moths. He said we are to be as a city on a hill which is visible to all. Our "light must shine before men so that they may see goodness in your acts and give praise to your heavenly Father." (Matthew 5:14-16) When Jesus taught this he was acknowledging that actions often speak louder than words. The greatest witness of the power of the gospel is the generous way true Christians live. Their lives reflect the love of God because they spend time with him in prayer. In the Acts of the Apostles when Peter and John were brought before the Sanhedrin it is recorded that the chief priests and elders recognized them "as having been with Jesus." (Acts 4:13) Would that all of us could be recognized in the same way!

In our age the gospel is seen as just another belief system in which we can pick and choose what is acceptable and what we do not want to believe. But if Christians live the truth that Jesus is really Emmanuel, God with us, even non-believers will recognize that there is something wholesome and good to be desired. If we are in love with Jesus and follow his teachings we will be the lamp which attracts others to his light.

40

"We are not the sum of our weaknesses and failures, we are the sum of the love of God and of his son our Lord Jesus Christ." (John Paul II) How many of us need to write that thought on our hearts until it becomes a reality for us! Too often we live in condemnation and guilt. We replay the record of our failures and seem incapable to erase the past and get on with the present. (Someone said it is called the present because it is a gift.) Self-condemnation and guilt cripple us and prevent us from living in the joy of the present moment. A good saying I like is the following: "When the devil reminds you of your past, remind him of his future."

One way to live in the present is to remember verse nine of Psalm 116: "I believe that I shall walk in the presence of the Lord in the land of the living." If we keep in mind that we are actually in the presence of God we will live richer lives. God does not berate us about our past sins and mistakes; he sees us as created in his likeness with the ability to become the saints he wants us to be. We are God's beloved, called to live in grace and peace. We are his children and inherit all the blessings he promised. The door to that life is opened by prayer. But we are impoverished by our feeble attempts at regular, meaningful time with the Lord. We read about prayer, talk about it, hear sermons on it, but fail to put what we know into practice.

We say we are too busy to pray, but never too busy to eat, or sleep, or watch our favorite show. But we can pray anywhere at anytime. How long does it take to say, "Lord I love you?" Our hearts can be a shrine where we carry the Lord with us and speak to him in fleeting moments all through the day. It does not take long to get the habit of lifting our hearts to God. It can become as natural as breathing. All it takes is the desire and the persistence in asking the Lord for the gift of prayer. If we make it a point to pray for wisdom before we undertake a task, or if we remember to be thankful for the gift of life, we will draw close to God "and he will draw close to us." (James 4:8)

King David said to his son, Solomon, "If you seek him he will let himself be found by you." (1 Chron. 28:9b) That is just as true today. God wants a personal relationship with all his children and waits expectantly for us to speak to him. The God of the Bible is a Father who reveals himself in many different ways to many different people. When the time was right, he sent Jesus to reveal in the flesh the depth of his love. The unseen God, the God "up there" became the visible God, the God "down here." The "God in whom we live and move and have our being." Yet many of us still have not heard that good news deep in our being.

Mother Teresa of Calcutta said many times, "God does not call us to be successful; he calls us to be faithful." So do not worry if you are dissatisfied with your prayers, just keep trying and you will eventually be given the grace to pray with joy and thanksgiving.

41

"Blest is she who trusted that the Lord's words to her would be fulfilled." (Luke 1:45) This often overlooked verse sums up the faith, trust and courage of Mary the mother of Jesus. The angel Gabriel told her that she would bear a child by the Holy Spirit. Her acceptance would open Mary to the sentence of death by stoning because she would be accused of infidelity to her betrothed husband. Even though she and Joseph were not married yet, the betrothal in their day was as binding as marriage. Mary was afraid, but she agreed to the angel's message. Gabriel told her that "nothing is impossible with God." Mary said "I am the servant of the Lord. Let it be done to me as you say." (Luke 1: 37-38) Her faith was like Abraham's - she said "yes" without knowing where it would lead.

Mathew's gospel tells of Mary's pregnancy from Joseph's perspective. He must have been deeply perplexed by what appeared to be her infidelity. He struggled within himself. He wondered if he should hand Mary over to the Law, or should he have compassion on her and divorce her quietly. He also had his relatives to contend with. Marriage in Israel was a family affair, both families made the contract for the benefit of the larger family unit. How would he deal with that? What should he do? During all this Mary said nothing. How incredible that she did not tell Joseph, but let the matter be resolved how it may. However, God intervened at the critical moment and sent his angel to Joseph in a dream with the message that the child was conceived by the Holy Spirit.

The angel gave Joseph the task of naming the baby, which meant that by adoption the baby was his. (Thus Matthew's genealogy is the ancestry of Joseph.) Call him Jesus, the angel said, because he will save his people from their sins. Like Mary, Joseph had faith, trust and courage. He opened himself to ridicule and the whispers of the village. It was obvious to others that Mary was with child so Joseph was either the father and guilty of sin, or Mary had betrayed him with another. But Joseph did as the angel said and took Mary into his home.

Thus the birth of the Messiah came in extraordinary circumstances and in difficult times. The Romans ruled Jews with an iron hand and the Jews had not been free for many decades. As Mary's time to deliver the baby drew close the Emperor Augustus called for an Empire wide census. Joseph took his pregnant wife to Bethlehem to register. However, Mary's time to deliver the baby had come, but there was no room for them even in a caravansary. Joseph found a cave where animals were stabled and Jesus was born and laid in a manger where animals eat. Indicating that he would be food for all. Thus he was born in Bethlehem, the house of bread.

The Lord of Glory, the living God, became man and was born in the most humble circumstances to proclaim to the poor, long suppressed, that they would have a divine champion who experienced their circumstances. He would tell us that we must also be poor in spirit to be blest by God and inherit the Kingdom. An honest evaluation of our lives would reveal that we, too, are poor, weak, sinners incapable of saving ourselves, but have a champion in Jesus who will save us from our sins.

42

"Call to me and I will answer you and tell you great and unreachable things you do not know." (Jeremiah 33:3 NIV) That word is still true today. When we meet God in prayer he impresses on our hearts "the unfathomable riches of Christ." (Ephesians 3:8) By divine grace he infuses into our hearts Christ's love" which surpasses all knowledge, so that [we] may attain to the fullness of God himself." (Ephesians 3:18-19) I can never read that verse without having profound love and gratitude to God for his mercy to us who are sinners. We, his creatures, are so loved that God desires to be with us totally. Yet, we withdraw from him and seek earthly things in preference to his love. It has ever been so. That's why God sent the prophets to call us back to him. But we killed the prophets and finally executed his son who came among us to restore our relationship with his Father.

Where are the prophets among us today? Where are the voices crying out in our wildernesses "prepare the way of the Lord." The way seems lost to so many. Even churches seek him among the moneychangers and in the palaces of the rich. Jesus said we do not go into the wilderness to see prophets living in opulence. John the Baptist was not a reed shaken in the wind. He was a mighty voice heard by multitudes. Jesus said of him that he was the greatest man born of woman up to that time, "but the least born into the kingdom of God is greater than he." (Matthew 11:11) Now that tells us where our prophets should be. Do we recognize them and listen to them?

Prophets are not born they are made; forged in the difficulties and paradoxes of life. They are gifted with vision and truthfulness by the Spirit and they may not be in our church or denomination. They make us uncomfortable by saying such things as "Nothing is resolved by war. On the contrary, everything is placed in jeopardy by war" Or again, "We must see another's poverty as our own and be convinced that the poor can wait no longer." (John Paul II) Or single mothers confronting our society head on and crying out for their children's well being. But like Rachel they get no comfort, because they are insignificant. There are other voices demanding that we recognize that the course we are on will only lead to the destruction of society and the end of freedom. Unfortunately, they are ignored and considered stupid to think that our society could actually fall apart.

We need God now more than ever. We need believers who trust God and love him so much that they willingly face ridicule and rejection for the sake of truth. People who will point out the fallacies of our system, its hypocrisies and callous treatment of the least among us. Men and women who though afraid, will refuse to be silent in the face of injustice and exploitation. In a word, people who obey the Gospel, who live the Beatitudes, and who want to imitate the Rabbi from Nazareth.

But it all begins with prayer. If we have the courage to pray "Lord make us prophets to cry out the way" and have a hunger for justice in our hearts, we will inspire those around us to change, and we will change with them. "To have lived well, means to have changed often" someone wrote. Yet we are afraid of change, it makes us very uncomfortable. But change we must if we wish to enter the Kingdom of God.

43

"He could work no miracle there, apart from curing a few who were sick by laying hands on them, so much did their lack of faith distress him." (Mark 6:5-6) At first when Jesus returned to Nazareth his neighbors found his words appealing (Luke 4:22), but soon they chased him out of the town and wanted to kill him. Their fury was evoked when Jesus praised a foreigner, a widow in Zarephath, to whom God sent the prophet Elijah to miraculously feed her during a famine. Zarephath was in Phoenicia and was hated because many invading armies passed through it on their way to Israel. But their real anger was stirred by Jesus' criticism of their refusal to welcome him as a prophet and healer. Their faith was lacking because they knew him, or so they thought.

This situation in Nazareth speaks volumes to us today for it took place in a house of worship. How many churches today are lacking in real faith in Jesus? How many members in the pews do not really know Jesus and have only an immature faith in the Gospel? Do his words make many of us uncomfortable or do we only hear the message in our heads, but not with our hearts? (Mark Twain noted that it was not the words of Jesus he did not understand that disturbed him, but the ones he did understand.) Or, are we like millions of people who never go inside a church because they do not see Jesus in us? Gandhi once remarked that the reason why he was not a Christian was because he had never met one who lived the Gospel! It is the same today when churches in some European countries are empty and sold to Muslims to be used as mosques. There are churches sold and used as garages, art galleries, workshops, even trendy homes.

It is up to those who really believe in Jesus to live the Gospel in their daily lives. Christians are meant to be the salt of the earth - the savor, the preservative, the cleansing element in society. (Or in the Greek idiomatic use of salt, to have a lively wit and intelligence in our dealings with one another.) This does not mean they have to go around just talking about Jesus; they have to live like him and let him shine through them. By caring for one another we can turn the tide of unbelief and lukewarm faith. By caring for the least among us we can effect changes in our neighbors. "Actions speak louder than words," is particularly true of love of neighbor. Jesus told us who are neighbor is - the one who needs help. As long as the needy in our midst are ignored, the Gospel is mute and ineffective.

The Gospel is so important that it cannot be left to the scholar or historian to tell us what it says. The Holy Spirit, alive in hearts hungry for God, empowers the Good News within the community to be the witness Jesus intended. Every believer, in effect an apostle, must be "tuned in" (to use John Paul II's phrase) by prayer to what the Spirit is saying to the churches. Jesus has not left us as orphans, he is Emmanuel, God with us, who will save us from ourselves and set fire to our cold hearts and lukewarm faith. After all, he did say "I have come to light a fire on earth." (Luke 12:49)

44

Anyone with a knowledge of the past will know the terrible things religion has meted out to those who hold different opinions. The Crusaders killed more Christians than the Muslims they were supposed to be fighting in order to free the Holy Land for Christians. The internecine wars between Christians over icons or the word *filioque* in the *Credo*. The mass slaughter of Cathars, the executions of Hussites, Lollards, the brutal struggle between the Catholics and the Lutherans and on and on. Much of the struggles arose over fundamentalist interpretations of the Bible. Literal meanings were used as an excuse to crush those who had the temerity to see a different way of understanding the scriptures. Admittedly, those doing the punishing often believed that they were trying to save from Hell those they deemed guilty.

Furthermore, we cannot ignore the ungodly and terrible treatment of Jews throughout most of the past two thousand years, culminating in the horrors of *Auschwich* and *Buchenwald.* In Jerusalem at the memorial of the Holocaust, *Yad Vashem*, there is a deeply moving shrine to the one and a half million children who were murdered by the Nazis. The building is dark except for over a million pinpoints of light, each one representing a child who died in the death camps. It is impossible to linger in the windowless building because the emotions and sorrow are too acute and intense. I might add, so is the repentance for having lived in a culture which made such evil possible. Sadly, at *Yad Vashem* there are only a few thousand names of the righteous gentiles who helped the Jews; would that there were millions of entries.

And yet, we are not changed. There is still a fundamentalist self-righteous attitude which is creating new hatreds and fears. There is religious bigotry and arrogant pride which considers its own beliefs true and every other understanding wrong, or even wicked. Christians are called to be reconcilers, peacemakers, ambassadors for Jesus, and leaven in the complex dough of world opinion. Yet too often we are divisive, wrong headed (and "wrong hearted"), ignorant of the religion we are condemning, and intolerant of different ways of thinking. Believers should be the first to respect others, but sadly we are often the last to do so. Mother Teresa said something I have never forgotten: she said she loved all religions, but had fallen in love with her own. To her, everyone was her neighbor, even those who vilified her.

Christianity is called to a radical living out of the Gospel. We are to show that the supreme gift of the Messiah is the gift of forgiveness. The parables of Jesus teach forgiveness as seen in the parables of the Prodigal Son, the two debtors, the lost sheep, the laborers in the vineyard, the Pharisee and the tax collector, and others. Jesus taught that to refuse to forgive can exclude us from his company. He told his parables so that we who follow him can see ourselves in them and seek forgiveness for ourselves and for the world at large. As an old adage says, "to err is human, but to forgive is divine," Lord, help us to be forgivers...

45

"God has granted the man [or woman] who is in covenant with him power over his heart." (Hans urs von Balthasar) As incredible as it sounds, those who really love God do have power over God's heart. As a lover, God is unequalled so it is perhaps natural that he responds to love and is moved both by the weakness and fervor of his children. The history of Christianity reveals many instances of believers who had such a relationship with the Lord that their prayers had incredible success. Great miracles of healing and conversion have taken place when faithful believers asked with compassion and love.

Even today, the prayer of faith in God's love moves the heart of God. But so many of us pray with a kind of doubt: we pray for something but even as we are praying we are thinking how we can work out the problem ourselves. We ask for something but do not really believe that God will answer. It is a kind of negative prayer, said because we think we are supposed to ask, but said without conviction. Sometimes we feel so unworthy that we do not even ask. Now that is a mistake, because our very unworthiness and failings touch the tenderness of our Father and he reaches down to comfort us with his love. God knows our sins but the moment we humbly acknowledge them and reach out to him we find he is already with us, and has been all along!

Our greatest way to God's heart, prayer, is the thing we do the least in the present time. Prayer is the least favorite activity and most of us put it off in any way we can. We occupy ourselves with a hundred tasks rather than sit quietly before the Lord. We are depriving ourselves of access to the power we need to live meaningful and vibrant lives. Our hearts do not long for God and we forget that he inhabits the praises of his people. We have too many idols, too many masters, and not enough spiritual discipline to live lives of prayer. Thus we deprive ourselves of life's greatest blessing, the presence of God.

We can see this most clearly at Christmas time. The preparation for the birthday of Jesus, which should be spent preparing our hearts to understand the mystery of "God with us," is spent in hectic shopping, urged on by blaring advertisements from the high priests of our materialistic society. Christmas means money, we are told, because many merchants make most of their annual profits in December. The red in Noel ribbons must not show up in the bottom line of our emporia. As if this were not enough, it seems that more layoffs occur just before Christmas than in any other season.

Every year we see renewed efforts to make Christmas into a generic holiday with no religious significance. The tree is called a "holiday tree". The time is called the "holidays," and "happy holidays," is the favored greeting, in the hope that the word

Christmas will fall into disuse. Once it is realized that holiday means "holy day" it is probable that it will be dropped for "happy winter fest." But since Emmanuel means "God with us" we can never be deprived of his presence nor can his love be erased from our lives. Since he will never leave us or forsake us, the season of Emmanuel will always remain, even if it is only in the hearts of the believers.

46

"And this hope will not leave us disappointed, because the love of God has been poured out in our hearts through the Holy Spirit who has been given to us." (Romans 5:5) Our hope in Jesus Christ is not an illusion, rather it is confirmed by God's love which is poured copiously into our hearts by the Holy Spirit. We are meant to experience that love in this life. Paul said as much to the Ephesians (Ephesians 3:19) if we are not experiencing the abundant love of God, we need to ask why, because without it we are only half alive.

God's love is made manifest when we seek him with open hands and hearts. His love is further evidenced when we allow his gifts to fall into our empty hearts and hands and share them with others. The more we seek the love of God the more we find it, as long as we give it away. Love held onto and hoarded is mere lust; love given away is enriched and doubly returned to the giver. Jesus told Paul that it is more blessed to give than to receive. (Acts 20:35b NIV) This is a beatitude which was revealed privately to Paul. It was obviously a powerful truth in his life; perhaps the key to his extraordinary self sacrifice in sharing the good news. He understood that sharing the Holy Spirit's love with others was of paramount importance.

The blessedness of giving can only be experienced in practice. As we learn to share our goods and our lives with others we begin to feel the joy and the peace of Jesus which the Spirit pours into generous hearts. The story of Scrooge wonderfully illustrates how giving can renew a life hardened with avarice and greed. The joy he experienced when he began to give away his surplus wealth is deeply moving. As he began to live the Gospel, a new life flooded his whole being and he was changed. He became synonymous with the feast he had despised; what he called picking a man's pockets every year became for him the time to empty his pockets to care for the poor. Dickens understood the power of love and the wondrous effect of generosity on the hearts of giver and recipient alike. Dickens knew that "God loves a cheerful giver." (2 Corinthians 9:7)

When we begin to give without grudging or without self-interest, we also begin to be changed. Giving is a powerfully liberating act which frees us from cupidity and selfishness. We grow in the love and the knowledge of God. Since his nature is one which gives, we take on his nature when we become giving people. His grace and love empower our actions and ennoble what we do. As a Father, God entrusts his poorer children to the generosity of those who love him the most. To love God means that we not only love our neighbor, but we share with them when we see them in need. This makes God's love visible to a doubting world.

Love seen is greater than love preached about.

47

"Go into the whole world and proclaim the good news to all creation." (Mark 16:15) Clearly the message of Jesus is for all peoples. But if the message is muted, how will it be heard? If it is not lived, how will it be believed? To spread the gospel requires a deep and abiding commitment on the part of its adherents. Lukewarm messages and tepid faith touch no one - they are even counterproductive in that they discourage believer and unbeliever alike. Jesus came to baptize his followers with the Holy Spirit and with fire: the fire of God's loving presence. Like the burning bush we are called to be on fire, but not burned out.

God's love is a fire of renewal and of life-giving ardor. His love is hidden in his message and is unfolded when it is read or preached with the convincing power of the Spirit. The Holy Spirit fell on the disciples at Pentecost as tongues of fire, indicating the kind of believers they were called to be. This let them know that when they proclaimed the message, the Spirit of God would light a fire in the hearts of the listeners. It is the Spirit's task to anoint their words or they would end up with weak, not life-giving messages. Such messages smother the fire within. Smoldering embers must be fanned into flame by the breath of the Spirit; to use Paul's words, we need "to stir into flame" the gifts of the Spirit. (2 Timothy 1: 6) Religion is not meant to be a once a week mediocre visit to a service. Religion, from the Latin word *re-ligare* to bind together, is meant to be a union with God and fellow believers seven days a week. Anything less is not genuine Christianity.

We do our children a great disservice when we insist on Sunday observance but do not also live as daily reminders of God's love. One of the problems of our age is that we are too busy, too occupied with things that do not last. Whatever occupies our time and is given our allegiance is our religion, binding us to the things of this world at the expense of eternal ones. This attitude is supported by such sayings as, too much religion is dangerous, or we can be too heavenly minded to be of any earthly good. But I believe the opposite is true. We must be heavenly minded in order to be of any earthly good, for true religion is the bond which binds people together in the Lord.

The message of Jesus is simple and profound at the same time. When we love God and one another we bring heaven to earth and raise earth to heaven. When we make room in our hearts for the Son of God who came as a baby to live among us, we become agents for change, agents of God's compassion and love.

We no longer "obscure divine plans with words of ignorance," (Job 38:2), but have the words of Jesus, which are the words of eternal life. We bring light to the darkness, and sight to the spiritually blind, and hope to the hopeless. Most of all, we bring life where there is death and heaven where there was only hell. What a prospect!

To such a challenge we have all been called.

48

The understanding of "word" in biblical Hebrew is much different from modern usage. In the Hebrew way of thinking when a word was spoken it had a life of its own. The word *dabar*, also means a thing as well as word. We see that in the Letter to the Hebrews where the word is called a living word, a word imbued with power, is a thing which can penetrate into the very center of our being. Job said that he treasured the word of God more than his necessary food. Such was his belief in the power of the word. (Job 23: 12 NKJV)

In John's Gospel Jesus is called the *logos,* the word, the message, the reason of God. He is the Word from the beginning, through whom all things were made, and this "Word became flesh and made his dwelling among us." (John 1:14) Jesus is the message; he is *the* Word who brings God's message to a waiting world. The world is not to be afraid, not to lose hope. He is the word of joy, peace and love. His spoken words are full of power and majesty.

The Centurion who came to Jesus knew the authority of the spoken word. He knew that Jesus had only to "say the word" and his servant would be healed. (Matthew 8:8 NIV) The Scriptures tell us that Jesus was amazed that a non-Jew understood the power of the word more than his own people. Jesus said that he had not found such faith in Israel. Does it make us wonder if there is the Centurion kind of faith in our country? After all, we have been told more than once that nothing is impossible with God.

Our faith must rest on our relationship with the Lord. When we know him, we can trust his word. When we trust his word we can live a life empowered by his message. His message is a living one, a life-giving one, an eternal word from heaven to teach us how to live. Yet we spend very little time reading the Bible, if at all. God's word has become enshrined in bookcases to be looked at, spoken about, pointed to, but seldom read. It is a treasure map, showing the way to Jesus, the pearl of great price, the treasure beyond all treasure. It contains the covenant with the Lord of Lords and the King of Kings. It is where God speaks to us words of majestic truth...but we have let those gilded words drop to the floor of our money temples to be lost in our rush for perishable gold.

However, the poor can teach us to value something greater than wealth. We need them more than they need us. They are the poor of Yahweh of whom the Scriptures say,"when the poor cry out" the Lord hears them. He hears them because they have only God to rely on, and their reliance on him is far greater than our trust in gold. The poor show us how to believe, how to trust in what is unseen. Whereas we show them to believe in what is tangible and visible. If we blame them for being poor, we are ignorant and uncaring. Their poverty is not of their own making. As Jesus said we can give to them as often as we like, if we are genuinely concerned about their plight.

Poor or rich, we can all conform our hearts to God's word and live in God's abundant blessing. In him and through him we have everything we need.

49

"Because he dispensed justice to the weak and the poor, it went well with him. Is this not the true knowledge of me? Says the Lord." (Jeremiah 22:16) Those words were spoken about Josiah, perhaps Judah's greatest king who ruled for 31 years. The Book of Sirach written over five hundred years after Josiah's reign said of him," Precious is his memory, like honey to the taste, like music at a banquet." (Sirach 49:1) Josiah cared about the poor and Yahweh said that meant he had true knowledge of God. Perhaps James had Jeremiah's words in mind when he wrote that looking after orphans and widows in their distress is "Pure and undefiled religion before God...." (James 1:27 NKJV) we see in the Acts of the Apostles a similar concern for widows, orphans, and the poor. (Acts 6:1) The Council of Jerusalem gave Paul the mandate to go to the Gentiles with the stipulation that he should be mindful of the poor, "the one thing," wrote Paul, "that I was making every effort to do." (Galatians 2:10)

Those few examples clearly indicate the Biblical injunction to care for the poor. In Scripture God is called the Father of the fatherless and protector of widows - the most vulnerable in the ancient world. Today we have huge numbers of people who live on the margins of our affluent society. Hundreds of millions live on the perilous edge of starvation with no access to health care. Countless children have no hope, no education, no way out of poverty. Millions of children have no father in their family unit and watch their mothers prematurely age under the burden of caring for their offspring. And the tragedy is that they could all be helped if the will was there to serve them. John Paul II said, "We must see another's poverty as our own and be convinced that the poor can wait no longer." Sadly, we do not see it that way.

James said we must be "doers of the word, and not hearers only, deceiving yourselves." (James 1:22 NKJV) The message is clear, we must share our bread with the hungry, clothe the naked, help the sick, and be neighbors to those who need help. This means our efforts should be regular and generous, not just at Christmas. If we could make an effort to learn what Mother Teresa of Clacutta taught, "to see Jesus in the distressing guise of the poor," we would respond with generous hearts. For He is truly with them: "On high I dwell in holiness, and with the crushed and dejected in spirit. To revive the spirits of the dejected, to revive the hearts of the crushed." (Isaiah 57:15) He revives them through our hands and hearts and treasure, which he has given us. We take from his hands what we give to the needy.

Our secular age is moving farther and farther away from positive help for the hungry, except in catastrophic natural disasters which quickly get forgotten. Whether we realize it or not, too many of us believe the poor deserve what they get. If we do not believe that, why are so few of us helping them? Are we indifferent or callous? Either way, we have turned our backs on the word of God which urges us to be good Samaritans. "Today, if you should hear his voice, harden not your hearts..." (Hebrews 3:7-8)

50

"Then God said, Let there be light, and there was light." (Genesis 1:3) For many centuries Rabbis, philosophers, mystics, saints and scientists have been pondering about the nature of light. According to Genesis the sun and moon were created on the fourth day, so the intriguing question arose as to what actually was that light created on the first day according to the Hebrew story if creation.

Perhaps it is related to the "Theory of Everything" which states that everything in the Universe is made from minute bits of vibrating energy called strings. This so-called String Theory cannot be observed nor tested by experiment, and hence it can never be proved. So rather than science per se, it is perhaps a philosophical theory and maybe much closer to theology than to physics. But thinking about this String Theory intrigued me and I thought about Jesus coming as the light of the world in the midst of darkness - just like the flash of light at the Big Bang. Which no human eye saw. Jesus came unseen by those who were watching for him, and entered life in a cave unheralded and unknown. Only his star was visible to the watching Gentiles. (A star will come out of Jacob…Numbers 24:17) Heavenly light for a heavenly child.

John's Gospel begins like Genesis with a burst of poetic language: "In the beginning was the word…Through him all things came to be…Whatever came to be in him, found life, life for the light of men. The light shines on in darkness, a darkness that did not overcome it." (John 1:1-5) This light of men became flesh and came into the world through the door of Mary his mother, an unknown virgin whose light had been given by God at her conception. Joseph was given light in a dream and the shepherds saw angels of light singing the good news. There was light a-plenty, so the darkness of Herod and his minions could not overcome the child of light.

Darkness cannot hide in the light. We can pierce the darkness with a beam of light, but we cannot pierce the light with a "beam" of darkness. The light, which God pronounced "good," is God's own way of showing us that when we live in the light we can never be extinguished. And even if we are walking in darkness the light can find us and lead us home. Perhaps the greatest discoveries in science came because artificial light enabled researchers to work even at night; light bringing more light to enlighten our humanity.

But the brightest and purest light is the wisdom of God in the Holy Spirit. The Spirit breathed light and life into the Word of God which can penetrate our darkest thoughts and dispel our deepest fears. The Bible is light, and the darkness of evil stands revealed by that light. As the psalmist wrote, "For with you is the fountain of life, and in your light we see light." (Psalm 36:10)

51

It is a truism to say that the family is under attack. One might say that the traditional family in the United States is in danger of collapse. As the extended family fell apart so too is the nuclear family crumbling under the stress of modern life. There are many reasons for the decline of the family, not the least of which is the pressure to succeed financially which separates families. The high divorce rate with the consequent large numbers of single parents is further proof that the family is in rapid decline. There seems to be no solution to the problem, at least no human solution. But there is a spiritual solution if people are willing to accept it.

I suggest that the Holy Family of Jesus, Mary, and Joseph can help struggling families stay together. Devotion to the family of Nazareth is neglected by most Christians. In Protestant churches there are more sermons on Abraham. Job, David, and almost any other biblical figure than there are on the Holy Family as a unit. Even in the Catholic Church where traditional devotion to the Holy family has a long History, there is a decline in examining the virtues of Joseph's nuclear family.

Joseph married Mary under very difficult conditions. But he persevered and followed instruction of divine intervention. Under attack from Herod who was a bloodthirsty tyrant of the worst kind, Joseph and Mary took Jesus to Egypt, becoming refugees and political exiles. Two years later, after Herod's death, they returned home, but had to settle in Galilee for fear of Herod's son, Archelaus, who unlike three of his brothers was not murdered by his father. In addition to the ever present threat of robbers, Joseph settled in Nazareth where the Roman rule was brutal and all pervasive. In the midst of all these difficulties,

Joseph and Mary raised Jesus with love and great devotion to God.

Mary taught Jesus to speak and to pray and to trust God. Joseph taught him a trade and how to be a man. Even though Jesus bore the divine nature, he lived a fully human life. As Paul wrote, "Who being in the very nature of God, did not consider equality with God something to be grasped, but made himself nothing, taking the very nature of a servant." (Philippians 2:6 NIV) He saw his parents serve and he naturally became a servant like them. We know that Joseph died and left Mary to raise Jesus alone. Jesus stayed with her and supported her until he began his public ministry at the age of about thirty. Such family love and loyalty ought to encourage and evoke in us the same devotion to those we love.

The Holy Family of Nazareth is the model of a perfect family, who despite seemingly insurmountable odds, faced their difficulties together and trusted that God would deliver them. Each family member was able to make the other members their prime concern above self. That is the key to saving our families. If we learn to see others as more important than ourselves we will not only be happy, but whole and holy ourselves. After all, the only real happiness is finding how we can serve others and then do it for the glory of God. And the place we must learn that is in the family.

52

"He will keep in perfect peace all those who trust in him, whose thoughts turn often to the Lord." (Isaiah 26:3 LB) This paraphrase in the Living Bible aptly describes the path to peace. Trusting in God and regular prayer are the solution to stress and the lack of peace of mind. It is amazing to consider the vast sums of money spent in looking for peace of mind, when the solution for most of us is as simple as the verse from Isaiah suggests. Sadly it is often the last solution people look for, and even some ministers of religion tell suffering members of their congregation to see a therapist rather than counsel prayer as a first resort.

Repentance is also a path to peace. Unforgiven sins are like barnacles on a boat. Hidden beneath the water line they do their work efficiently and unseen. But bring the sins to the light of a forgiving God and in an instant they fall away like dead barnacles. Sometimes, however, we do not believe we have been foregiven, or we wallow in guilt and keep revisiting our sins of the past. The antidote for guilt is trust. Believe that we are forgiven and forget our sins because scripture tells us that God remembers them no more. As Corrie Ten Boom said, God drops our sins into the sea of forgetfulness and puts a sign there saying, "Do not fish!" We are forgiven, so do not keep on dragging up the sins of the past.

Forgiveness changes things. "I cried out to you and you healed me...you changed my mourning into dancing" (Psalm 30:1 & 12) Now that's what repentance does! Augustine of Hippo knew the blessed relief of God's forgiveness. His favorite psalm began, "Happy is he whose fault is taken away, whose sin is covered." (Psalm 32:1) As brilliant as Augustine was, he knew that without forgiveness he could never be at peace. But when he made that life changing step of repentance his whole being was flooded with relief. "I confessed my faults to the Lord, and you took away the guilt of my sins." (Psalm 32:5)

Then there is the need to forgive those who have injured or emotionally hurt us. This can be very difficult for many people who spend half a lifetime nurturing grudges and hate. Their self-image is wrapped up in a blanket of unforgiveness and injured self-righteousness. They refuse to forgive or forget and insist that their cause is just. Sometimes it can help them to realize how much they have been forgiven by God and in this way begin to forgive others. But for those who do not believe in God, the task is more difficult, but not beyond help. They can be made to realize that hate and unforgiveness damages them more than the ones they refuse to forgive. If they can see that hate and unforgiveness cripples them emotionally and causes physical damage they can learn to let go of the past and find peace.

The real peace, however, is found in Jesus. The prophet Isaiah called him "the Prince of Peace" whose reign in our hearts brings lasting contentment. He commanded us to love and to be at peace with everyone. He even said we are to love our enemies! Only a few have learned to do that. We have a long way to go to make peace on earth. But if we let it begin in our hearts we can then give it to others.

53

"I will give thanks to you, O Lord, with all my heart..." (Psalm 138: 1) This is called the "Hymn of a grateful heart" and it teaches us the power of being thankful and of realizing that God's kindness endures forever. We can be thankful every day for the gift of life and the gift of God's love in Jesus Christ. We are thankful for life because it will last forever, and what seem to be hardships or suffering can lead to real discoveries of God's eternal loving kindness.

When we are thankful people we are also joyful, because we have learned that everything is gift and we have opened our hearts to the one from whom all good things come. Being thankful puts us in God's presence and where God is, there is fullness of joy. (Psalm 16:11)

Gratitude for life's gifts is an antidote to greed, sadness, and despair. Thankfulness opens us up to praise God and leads us to live in peace and harmony with family and neighbors. When we realize how much we have to be grateful for we can no longer be unhappy and ungrateful.

Every year in the United States and Canada people celebrate Thanksgiving Day with feasting and family reunions. But once a year is inadequate time to thank God for all his many blessings. We need to learn to see the gifts that God has in store for those who love him. As Paul wrote to the Ephesians, "I pray also that the eyes of your heart may be enlightened in order that you may know the hope to which he has called you...and his incomparably great power for us who believe." (Ephesians 1:18 NIV) That is something to be thankful for: to have an inner wisdom which enables us to understand and receive the grace that God gives us.

If we spent as much time thanking God as we do complaining we would soon learn to look beyond the daily inconveniences and see the things which really matter. I have seen children in third world countries show amazing gratitude to God for the littlest thing. In Romania we met a little girl of about eight who was astonished that someone would give her a small bag of oranges. She kept repeating in seeming disbelief, "Are they really for me? Are they really for me?" In Ecuador we met a woman whose face was so marred by burns that she had no nose and no real eyelids. She was horribly disfigured. When she received the small gift we gave her she fell on her knees and thanked God. I was deeply moved by her gratitude to the Lord who is the source of all goodness.

A child in Uganda praised God for the aid she received. In a desperately poor barrio in Mexico where my wife and I had delivered food for the children, a girl of about eight said the grace before the meal and movingly thanked her heavenly Father for the food he had sent them, and asked a blessing on all their benefactors. In so many places we saw how the very poor live lives filled with thanksgiving for what little they have. Here in the affluent countries we forget to be grateful most of the time. How many of us remember to thank God for our daily bread, or show gratitude for the warmth of the sun or for a downpour of rain. We often live in ingratitude and selfishness. No wonder we are so often downcast.

54

Somewhere near the middle of the Book of the Prophet Jeremiah we find four chapters startlingly different from the rest of the book. These chapters are frequently called the Book of Consolation because the message is filled with a joyful hope and the promises of a new, unconditional covenant, a covenant which the Lord will write on our hearts. In lyrically beautiful and poetic language Jeremiah envisions not only the return of the remnant of Israel from Babylon, but foresees the wonderful work of Jesus the Messiah in the distant future.

"Shout with joy the Lord has delivered his people, the remnant of Israel." (Jeremiah 31:7b) God spoke to them saying, "I have loved you with an everlasting love; I have drawn you with loving-kindness." (Verse 3) Loving-kindness is the translation of the Hebrew word *hesed*, which is how Miles Coverdale translated it in 1535. It is also translated as love, compassion, greatness, grace, even mercy. It signifies the generosity and benevolence of God. Only two other prophets, Isaiah and Hosea, used the word. Because of his *hesed* the Lord turned "their mourning into Joy" (verse 13) and lavished his blessings on priest and people alike. He said his heart was stirred with compassion and he had to have mercy on his people.

Then came that incredible message fulfilled in the coming of Jesus the Messiah: "The days are coming, says the Lord, when I will make a new covenant with the house of Israel and the house of Judah...I will place my law within them, and write it upon their hearts. I will be their God, and they shall be my people...All from the least to the greatest, shall know me, says the Lord, for I will forgive their evildoing and remember their sins no more." (Verses 31-34) It sounds impossible, and Jeremiah must have thought so, too, because the Lord said to him, "Is anything impossible to me?" (Jeremiah 32:27) Then the word of the Lord came to Jeremiah again saying, "Call to me, and I will answer you; I will tell to you things great beyond reach of your knowledge." (Jeremiah 33:3)

In Jesus, the word became flesh to live among us. The word *hesed,* the word *logos,* the living Word of God was born of the Virgin Mary and became man. Jesus came to show us that God is for us. That his Father loves us with an everlasting love and will never cast us off. He came to teach us how to live, to love, to be joyful in all things good. He revealed the tenderness of God who came as an innocent and vulnerable baby to prove his love for us. He came in peace to a world that knew no real peace; he came as the Lamb of God to take away the sins of the world. Of course, Jeremiah could not see that. But in his words we can see a deeper meaning, a sense of the greatness of the coming-one and the blessings of the Father on all his children.

God's covenant with his people is an everlasting one. Whether Jew or Christian, when we take his word to heart and live in the light of his promise we live as one family with one Father. God is infinitely greater than our division and he can heal the breach among us at any time. All he is waiting for is that we love one another as he loves us.

55

The first words spoken by Jesus in John's Gospel are, "What are you looking for?" A searching question to ask and one which we need to answer in order to know what we are called to do. Andrew and John who had been with John the Baptist were following Jesus and it was to them that he posed the question. They replied, "Rabbi (which means teacher) where do you stay?" Jesus said, "Come and see." (John 1:38-39) Jesus invites all of us to come and see, to find out for ourselves who Jesus is and where he stays.

I find the first words of Jesus in each gospel intriguing. In Mark Jesus says, "The time is fulfilled, and the kingdom of God is at hand. Repent, and believe in the gospel." (Mark 1:5 NKJV) They are succinct, direct, and require a response. In Mark's gospel the good news is so urgent that Jesus is constantly on the move, demonstrating in action that he himself is the good news from God. Mark's language is simple, he often writes in the historic present as an eyewitness and the story flows along at a rapid pace. In the very middle of Mark, Jesus asks the central question of Peter, and us, "Who do you say that I am?" (Mark 8:29) How we answer tells us who we are.

In Luke's Gospel Jesus is a boy of twelve whose first words were in answer to his mother who with Joseph had searched for three days in deep sorrow before finding him in the Temple. Mary said to Jesus, "Son, why have you done this to us? You see that your father and I have been searching for you in sorrow." Jesus replied, "Why did you search for me? Did you not know I had to be in my Father's house" (Luke 2:48-50) He wanted to know why they had looked in other places instead of coming first to the Temple where they should have known he would be. Luke says they did not understand what he meant.

Jesus' first words in Matthew were spoken to John the Baptist in the River Jordan. When John saw Jesus he said to him, "I need to be baptized by you, and do you come to me?" Jesus replied, "Let it be so now; it is proper for us to do this to fulfill all righteousness." (Matthew 3:15 NIV) With those words Jesus identified himself with sinners, even though he himself was sinless. He came on our side and stood with all of us to fulfill God's will, just as he would at death, being crucified between sinners as the sacrificial lamb of God to take away the sin of the world.

First words in the Scriptures can be wonderful starting points for meditating on God's word. Genesis commences, "In the beginning, God..." In Isaiah we read, "Hear...for the Lord speaks." The prophet Joel begins, "Hear this you elders..." In

Malachi the Lord says,"I have loved you..." Each introductory word opens us up to listening for God's word in our hearts. In these books of the Bible we meet our heavenly Father who speaks to us words of wisdom, love and compassion. Are they neglected words in your life?

56

The prologue of John's Gospel, often called the fourth gospel, begins before the beginning of the Universe. There is no nativity, no crib, no shepherds, no Magi. He is the eternal word made flesh who came to live with us and among us. He who was with God from the beginning is the word or *logos* of God. He is the logic, the reason, the message of the Father. He speaks for the Father and tells us what the father thinks. He is the exact representation of the Father's being. This Jesus, the Son of God, became a son of man so that the sons and daughters of men might become the children of God. He came as light to dispel the darkness of our minds and lives.

John the Baptist recognized him as the "Lamb of God who takes away the sin of the world." (John 1:29) At Cana Jesus changed 180 gallons of water into wine to save the embarrassment of the married couple, thus showing he was the creator and that he had come to bring God's joy to a sad world. (An ancient Jewish saying said there is no joy without wine.) To Nicodemus the teacher of Israel, Jesus said, "God so loved the world that he gave his only son, that whoever believes in him may not die, but may have eternal life." He assured Nicodemus that his father did not send him to condemn the world, but to save it. (John 3:16-17) And he revealed to the Samaritan woman at the well that he was the long awaited Messiah.

But it is in the "I am" sayings of Jesus where he clearly indicates his divinity. Over seventeen times Jesus uses the Greek expression, *ego eimi*, which means I am, but which is the title

YHWH gave to Moses when Moses asked his name. Jesus said, "I am the bread of life. (John 6:35) The very food that came down from heaven. (John 6:41) He, the living word of God, feeds his followers with word and sacrament. He said "I am the light of the world," (John 8:16) and his followers would never walk in darkness. He said, "I am not of this world," and immediately added, "If you do not believe that I am, you will die in your sins." (John 8: 23-24)

Perhaps his most startling statement to his listeners in the temple was "I solemnly declare it: before Abraham came to be, I AM." (John 8:58) The crowd then picked up rocks to stone him for blasphemy, but he slipped away. Probably the most well known and most loved of the "I am" sayings is in John's tenth chapter. He said "I am the good shepherd" and "my sheep hear my voice, I know them, and they follow me." (John 10:14 & 27) I once witnessed exactly what Jesus meant by that. I saw two shepherds lead their flocks to water and I saw the sheep mingle together and I wondered how the shepherds would be able to sort them out. After the sheep had drunk, one of the shepherds called out and walked away and his sheep, recognizing his voice, followed. The other flock followed its shepherd. So we follow Jesus because we recognize his voice. His authentic word spoken into our lives is recognizable and we follow it with our heart.

"I am the resurrection and the life (John 11:25) is the "I am" saying which comforts those who are afraid of death for it promises life eternal And his final "I am" saying, tells us that he is the vine and we are the branches so we will bear abundant fruit and glorify his father in Heaven. (John 15:5) The Song of Songs says beautifully, "I am my beloved's." Amen!

57

The King of Aram sent some of his troops to capture the prophet Elisha. The soldiers arrived by night and surrounded the city of Dothan where Elisha was staying. The next morning Elisha's attendant went outside and saw the forces arrayed against them and was terrified. "Alas! he said to Elisha, "what shall we do, my lord?" "Do not be afraid," Elisha answered. "Our side outnumbers theirs." Then he prayed that his servant's eyes would be opened and then he was able to see the army of angels surrounding Elisha.

In our darkest moments it would be good to remember that story. For we, too, have our angel to protect us. Jesus said that each of us has an angel which beholds his heavenly Father's face at all times. He was also ministered to by angels in the desert and in Gethsemane in his time of need. As psalm 34:8 reminds us, "The angel of the Lord encamps around those who fear him, and delivers them." The deliverance may be either physical or spiritual as countless believers can testify.

An angel came to Joseph in a dream and told him to go to Egypt to save Jesus from Herod's butchery. Later he was told in another dream to go to Galilee for safety. If Joseph had not believed in angels the consequences would have been unimaginable. But he must have been very familiar with Psalm 91, "For to his angels he has given command about you, that they guard you in all your ways." And he would have known the many occurrences of angels in the Jewish Bible. In the Christian Bible there are about 280 references to angels, many of them in the New Testament. Angels, it seems, are very much part of God's plan.

Hebrews 1:14 informs us that angels are ministering spirits which are sent to serve those who are to inherit salvation. The great archangels Michael, Gabriel and Raphael have the special tasks of protecting the people of God, delivering God's messages, and leading believers into their specific vocations. In our present age, Michael is called upon to defend us against the snares of the Evil One and to be our safeguard in times of great stress. An other archangel named Uriel, which means "God is my light," is according to Jewish Midrashim the one who enlightens Israel.

Seen or unseen, believed in or not, angels have a place in our daily lives. They are an invaluable help in times of distress and fear, and we are weakened when we ignore their role in our lives. They are God's great gift to us and how impoverished we become when we reject their help! Since our citizenship is in heaven, we already share heaven with them. And we would do well to imitate them in realizing that we are in the presence of God.

58

"Eye has not seen, ear has not heard, nor has it so much as dawned on man what God has prepared for those who love him." (1 Cor. 2:9) This is an amazingly incredible statement. But Paul did not stop there. He went on to write, "Yet God has revealed this wisdom to us through the Spirit." So what at first glance seemed to be a promise of our lives in heaven, clearly has to do with our life now as well. I find that almost too good to be true. It tells us that God has indescribable gifts to shower on those who really love him with all their heart.

In his letter to the Ephesians (which may have been a letter to all the churches in Asia) Paul said it another way: "[His] power now at work within us can do immeasurably more than we can ask or imagine." (Eph.3: 20) That, too, is an astonishing statement. These are words spoken by someone who is totally in love with the Lord and who understands that God is a generous and cheerful giver who would supply our every need fully, "in a way worthy of his magnificent riches in Christ Jesus." (Philippians 4:19) Yet often when we pray we think we have to beg for the crumbs falling from the master's table. We are his children, members of his family, heirs to the riches of his son Jesus. He has prepared more than a table for us.

He allows us to gaze on his loveliness and tells us that we can see his bounty now in the land of the living. (Psalm 27) God wants to have an intimate relationship with all his children and the Scriptures make that quite clear. But it only comes from habitual prayer. Personal revival and growth in love and grace can only come through a deep, intimate relationship with the Lord. His greatest gifts are given to the soul who longs for God and who sees his desperate need for God's saving power. The gift of his presence is so precious that he gives it to those who long for him with the fire of love.

But lest we despair of such love, it is God who grants it to all who ask with fervor. He sees our weaknesses and will quickly heal them when we approach him in love. God is a lover who delights in giving gifts. But how many of us want the fire and light of his presence? Too many people are afraid of the light. That seems to be why so few of his children long for spiritual beauty. Some people, mistakenly, are afraid of the word mystical and look askance at mystics as deluded. But Paul was a great mystic, who ascended to the third heaven and heard words that could not be repeated. His wisdom came from the Spirit whom he allowed to live mightily within him.

We are all called to come before the Lord to receive his loving comfort. "Come to me all you who are weary and find life burdensome, and I will refresh you." (Matthew 11:28)

This is a very clear message that the Lord wants all of us to come with expectant hearts to receive comfort and consolation in our prayers. Of course, there are times when we do not receive comfort, those are the times when we must pray all the more. But as a general rule, fervent prayer is often rewarded by his presence.

59

"O Lord, you have probed me and you know me; you know when I sit and when I stand; you understand my thoughts from afar.... Even before a word is on my tongue, behold. O Lord, you know the whole of it." (Psalm 139: 1-4) Often we behave as if that were not so. We pray as if to someone who doesn't know the facts. We say long, complex prayers informing God of the situation and telling him what to do. But after a while we end up praying as psalm 139 does. We ask God to probe our hearts deeply, to point out our hidden faults, and lead us to his heart.

To help us pray, to help us in our relationship with the Father we have been given the Holy Spirit. "The Spirit too helps us in our weakness, for we do not know how to pray as we ought, but the Spirit himself makes intercession for us...for the Spirit intercedes for the saints as God himself wills." (Romans 8:26-27) Paul said the Holy Spirit is the pledge or earnest deposit of our inheritance; the down payment by the Lord as proof of what he promised. (Ephesians 1:14) (The Greek word for down payment in Ephesians means engagement ring in Modern Greek. A lovely use of the word, since that, too, is a symbol of a pledge.)

Jesus said that he would not leave us orphans, that he would give us the Holy Spirit to be with us as an advocate or as someone who stands with us to help. He promised that the Spirit would teach and guide us since he is the Spirit of Truth and that the world would not receive the Holy Spirit because it does not recognize him. He assured us that we would recognize him because he will be within us. (John 14) The word translated as recognize, *ginosko*, means to have a relationship with someone, to know a person well. Jesus said we would know the Holy Spirit well. How well do we know him?

Paul wrote to the church in Corinth that his words had the convincing power of the Spirit, so their acceptance of his preaching rested not on the wisdom of men, but on the power of God. (1 Cor. 2:4-5) He told the Corinthians that they were the temple of God because the Holy Spirit dwelt in them. For temple he used the Greek word *naos* which is used for the sanctuary of the temple in Jerusalem where only the priests could enter. Later in the same letter he would remind his readers that they are the sanctuary of the Holy Spirit so they should glorify God in their body. Despite the sins and failings of the Corinthian Christians, they were endowed with all the gifts of the Spirit. (! Cor.1: 5-7) that can also be said of the church in the twenty-first century.

In every age the Holy Sprit leads the people of God to a deeper understanding of what it means to love and to serve the Body of Christ. In our age we are being called to seek unity in the Spirit and to respect and love one another. Let us all ask the Holy Spirit to teach us wisdom in our innermost being that we might know the great hope to which we have all been called.

60

"We are truly [God's] handiwork, created in Christ Jesus to lead the life of good deeds which God prepared for us in advance." (Ephesians 2:10) The word for handiwork is, *poiema*, from which we get the word poem. This led someone to translate it as, "We are truly his artistic masterpiece." Whilst that seems too grand a concept, it has merit, because it refers to our being God's workmanship in a new creation, that is of the redemption. We live in the life of God's son, and are therefore empowered to do good works which keep us close to the Lord.

God prepared in advance the good works he wishes us to accomplish. We are part of his plan for the world; he delights in us as his children and his plans for us are for our good and our joy. These good works are signposts on the road to eternal life and they lead us to God and keep us close to his son in whom we live and move and have our being. We are co-workers with him in the work of salvation for he has made known to us our share in the Gospel. (Which G.K. Chesterton called "almost a book of riddles"). It follows that we need faith to act on the proposition that God has a plan for our lives and desires us to share our life with him so he can order things aright.

"We cannot be children of God in the Lord without simultan-eously being assigned a task and a corresponding empowerment. Otherwise our status as children would not be active, it would not really belong to us; it would be a mere title, not a truth. Implicit in our state of grace is a mission." (Adrienne Von Speyr, The Letter to the Ephesians, Ignatius Press, p. 31) Each mission is as individual as we are, yet in Christ it is a work for the good of all and a work which makes us one with the church at large, the body of Christ. The grace which God gives to fulfill the tasks he has prepared, is a grace for others as well as a particular grace for the one receiving it. This, too, requires faith to put into practice.

When we accept this as true and seek to serve as the Lord directs, he empowers us to do what by our own strength we would be incapable of accomplishing. His grace enables us to go beyond ourselves and to reach out in directions we would previously have thought impossible. His power in the believer is a sign to the world that the mission is really God's. When a life is fully surrendered to God's will, wonderful things are done in his name. One only has to look at the life and work of Mother Teresa of Calcutta to see that what she was able to do is beyond human ability, it is a work of God. She was the first to admit that it was God's grace and not her abilities which spread her congregation around the world to help the poor.

The witness of such champions of the faith as Dietrich Bonhoeffer, Martin Luther King, Oscar Romero, and countless martyrs in the past 100 years, tell us that God is active in and among us. And others whose personal peccadilloes seem to detract from what is being done, would, no doubt, say that God is able "to draw a straight line with a crooked stick". After all, it is his grace which accomplishes all things, for even in weakness his power reaches perfection. So let us not allow our failings to stop us from seeking the will of God, for his grace is sufficient.

61

"How lovely is your dwelling place, O Lord of hosts. My soul yearns and pines for the courts of the Lord. My heart and my flesh cry out for the living God." (Psalm 84: 2-3. In some translations it is verses 1-2). This desire for God's Shekinah, his presence, is echoed many times in the Bible. Psalm 63 describes a fervent longing to be with God: "O God, you are my God whom I seek; for you my flesh pines and my soul thirsts like the earth, parched, lifeless without water." The psalmist clings fast to the Lord and shouts for joy in the banquet of God's presence. Other psalms echo the same sentiment. (See Psalms 42 and 143.)

"Take delight in the Lord, and he will grant you your heart's request." (Psalm 37:3) I think this means that when God is the love of our lives he plants in our hearts those things he wants to give us, so that what we ask for is according to his good pleasure. To delight in God, to desire him, means that we want to live the life for which we were created. Anyone who chooses to serve God and neighbor with a fervent heart will find peace and fulfillment. It is surprising that most people make New Year's resolutions to lose weight, to stop smoking, to get fit, and a whole host of other projects, but so few want to know the Lord as he is worthy of being known. Most resolutions are broken rather quickly, but a firm desire to seek God has the best chance of succeeding, because that is what God wants, too.

We can make and remake that resolution every day of our lives. If we slip, there are three verses of scripture which can refocus our lives. These three scriptures are what the Jewish scholar, C.G. Montefiore, called the kernel, or nucleus of the gospel. The first is Mark 10:4:"The Son of Man has not come to be served but to serve-to give his life in ransom for the many." The next two are taken from Luke's Gospel. "I have not come to invite the self-righteous to a change of heart, but sinners." (Luke 5:32) And perhaps the words most helpful in changing our lives, "The Son of Man has come to search out and save what is lost." So there is no need to give up and be discouraged, because the Lord is actively seeking to restore our lives.

Getting to know and love God more deeply is a great resolution. The Bible teaches us that when we draw close to God, he draws close to us. (James 4:8). Because of who Jesus is we can boldly" approach the throne of grace to receive mercy and favor and to find help in time of need." (Hebrews 4:16) We can grow in grace and love and joy and peace and in service to others. We need only to take the first step to begin.

To those who are well on the road to the heart of God there is a verse of the Bible which can cause you to make a resolution as if for the first time: "Give up everything that does not lead to God." (Titus 2:12.) Now that is a resolution to end all resolutions!

62

" I will give you a new heart and place a new spirit within you, taking from your bodies your stony hearts and giving you natural hearts." (Ezekiel 36:26) A spiritual heart transplant is greatly needed in this age of clogged spiritual arteries. Our hearts, as Augustine wrote, are restless until they find their home in the

Lord. Jesus told us not to let our hearts be troubled. He said that believing in him and his Father was the antidote to worry. (John 14:1) Worry and stress damage both the physical and the spiritual hearts.

The strange thing about worry is that most of the things we worry about never happen. Stress on the other hand is the result of the difficulties which do arise. In the midst of stress it can be helpful to commit the situation to Lord at once. Someone has written that God will take full responsibility for the life fully surrendered to him. That is a very wise saying, one which I have personally relied on in very trying times. To place all thing in his hands and allow his light to penetrate our hearts guarantees a peace which no one else can give. The peace he gives is beyond anything the world can give and it stands guard over our "hearts and minds." (Philippians 4:7) Such help in the midst of turmoil is priceless.

Of course it requires faith and courage to let go of our worries, but Jesus told us to be courageous because he has overcome the world. There is nothing the world can inflict on us that he is unable to cope with. He gave us something within us "that is greater than he that is in the world." (1 John 3:4) In other words, the presence of God in the believer is a bulwark against all troubles. It is a great witness to see Christians tranquil in the midst of chaos and uncertainty. The Christians' weapon is the sword of the Spirit, the word of God. The psalms in particular are powerful in moments of danger or stress. Psalm 91 is a perfect place to be in times of danger or stress. "Because he clings to me, I will deliver him." (Verse 14) Three times in that psalm it says God will deliver us when we seek shelter in him.

"You shall not fear the terror of the night..." psalm 91 says, which should be a great help to those millions who lie awake at night half paralyzed with fear and worry. The terror of the night and all other fears dissipate when we have the Lord for our refuge. The Devil knew the power of this psalm; that is why he quoted it to Jesus in the desert. And Jesus responded by saying, "it is written..." He, too, knew the power of God's word. After all, he is God's word made flesh!

Some may smile condescendingly at what I have written, but perhaps that's because they have never tried putting faith in God. Were they sincerely to try it, I believe they would get a pleasant surprise.

63

When we read the Gospel of John we are led to ask the question, "Is God really like Jesus?" Jesus said to Phillip, "Whoever has seen me has seen the Father." (John 14:9) Jesus said that he and the father are one and that he is equal to the Father. Quite plainly on several occasions in John's Gospel, Jesus made it clear that he was indeed, "the Word made flesh." Jesus made it known that his Father sent him, not to condemn, but to save. (John 3:16-17) Whoever believes in him, he said, has eternal life, and that he would prepare a place from them in his "Father's house." (John 14:2) These verses and many others show us that Jesus was telling us that God is just like himself.

If God is like Jesus, we have no reason to fear God. Jesus accepted all who came to him seeking help, so our heavenly father also accepts us just as we are and responds to our cries for help. Since Jesus is "the Word of God" his message reveals the heart and mind of God to us. Jesus' message is God speaking to us through human means. Jesus is, as it were, the Torah of God in the flesh. He said his words have eternal power and will never fall into oblivion. When God speaks a word it has the force of God and always finds its mark.

"For just as from the heavens the rain and the snow come down And do not return there till they have watered the earth, making it fertile and fruitful, giving seed to him who sows and bread to him who eats, So shall my word be that goes forth from my mouth; It shall not return to me void, but shall do my will, achieving the end for which I sent it." (Isaiah 55:10-11)

The message of Jesus is God speaking to us clearly and directly. His words are not complicated nor too obtuse to understand, although some scholars like to think some of Jesus' words are indeed difficult. Other scholars are convinced that Jesus did not say most of the things attributed to him by the gospels. How they arrive at their conclusions is complicated and unhelpful, and I might add, often the result of unbelief.

We believe that the Scriptures are God's revelation to us inspired by the Holy Spirit. We believe that since Jesus is the "Word made flesh" his message is a reliable representation of God's will for us. What he said can be trusted and acted upon. His words contain the power of heaven's promise. He is "God-with-us," always guaranteeing his promise never to leave us nor forsake us. To those who trust in his word he reveals himself in countless ways. (John 14:21) His light of truth will shine in the minds and hearts of all those who hold fast to his message, the *logos* of God.

I am the light of the world.
No follower of mine shall ever walk in darkness:
No, he shall posses the light of life. (John 8:12)

64

"I am not ashamed of the gospel." (Romans 1:16) Paul uses a strong word for ashamed, which could easily have been translated, "I am certainly not ashamed…" Obviously the early Christians were attacked by fellow Jews and Gentiles for believing in a crucified God. Paul wrote to the Corinthians "we preach Christ crucified, - a stumbling block to Jews, and an absurdity to Gentiles." (1 Cor.1: 23) It is a stumbling block today as well.

One wonders how Paul and the other Apostles were able to overcome the prejudice and aversion felt by their listeners hearing of the crucifixion. Of course, as Paul observed, it can only be accepted by faith which is a gift. (Romans 1:17)

Francis Xavier met with similar resistance when he began his missionary endeavor in China. Therefore he began by teaching the children who were not "blinded" by the critical minds of adulthood. He told the gospel simply and in a straightforward manner. Some adults were afraid of this new teaching and sent word to the emperor, who wanted to know what the Christians were teaching. He was informed that the message told of a god born of a virgin in a cave, who was crucified on a cross, and then rose from the dead. The emperor replied by saying do not worry, "no one would believe such a tale." How wrong he was!

Paul knew that preaching Christ crucified was in reality proclaiming "Christ, the power of God and the wisdom of God. For God's folly is wiser than men and his weakness more powerful than men." 1Cor.1: 24-25) The very idea that God would take human form and die a hideous death to show his love has been for many people a deeply moving proof of that love rather than a hindrance to faith. However, many of us today do not reflect deeply on the mystery of a God crucified. The stress is often on the cross itself, empty of the corpus, and hailed as the instrument of salvation, which it is. But it was the body of Christ which bled, not the cross. (Some churches today have expunged the word "blood" from all their hymns, and no longer talk about salvation by the blood of Christ.)

However, it was his blood that brought our salvation. Jesus at the last supper said, "All of you must drink from it [the cup], for this is my blood, the blood of the covenant, to be poured out in behalf of many for the forgiveness of sins." (Matthew 26:27-28) Paul wrote that Jesus said, "This cup is the new covenant in my blood". And as he pointed out, "This means that whoever eats the bread and drinks the cup of the Lord unworthily sins against the body and blood of the Lord." That was and should be the faith of the Christian church.

"Thus it is written that the Messiah must suffer and rise from the dead on the third day..." The suffering of the Messiah, movingly foretold in Isaiah 53, was God's plan from the start. "He was pierced for our offenses, crushed for our sins; upon him was the chastisement that makes us whole." (Isaiah 53: 5) The shed blood of Jesus guaranteed pardon for our transgressions. This message has been preached to the whole world since Pentecost. We, too, are called to live that Good News and to pass it on to the next generation.

65

The Baal Shem Tov, which means the "Master of the Good Name," was a famous rabbi whose teachings were the source of the Hasidic movement. His great belief was that God is omnipresent, and he taught that communion (*devekut*) with God was to be sought so that one could serve God with Joy. One Sabbath when he was on a visit he heard that a rabbi was vilifying his people and he became angry and then shed many tears because the rabbi had denigrated people who loved God. People over whom the angels of God rejoiced, said the Master of the Good Name. (Dan Ben-Amos & Jerome R. Mintz, In Praise of The Baal Sem Tov, p.183)

I find that incident very moving and remember times when I have been in Church and heard the preacher denigrate the congregation. Jesus told his listeners that his father has given angels charge over all his children and to scandalize them was a grave sin. If preachers, teachers, and parents would remember that, they would be very careful how they address their charges. The position of leader is a special calling and a solemn obligation. The Master of the Good Name knew that and prayed often for God's wisdom to guide him. Sadly, many of his Gentile contemporaries looked down on him as someone strange to be avoided.

Today we are more tolerant and more able to take what is good from others and leave alone what we cannot accept. The Lord has asked that we love all people and seek to do them good and not harm. The tragedy in South East Asia of the earthquake and Tsunami gave rise to a massive outpouring of aid and love such as had never been seen before. What a wonderful message it sent to the people of that devastated area. People in America, Europe, Japan, Australia and many other regions were grieving for the lost and the millions of homeless. It was concern on a massive scale, and millions of people showed their love in concrete ways, regardless of the beliefs of the suffering. That was a great sermon in action and it spoke loudly of the truth that we live in a global village and we are our brothers' keeper. Respect for the homeless was evident everywhere and grief for the lost and orphaned children was palpable.

For a time the world was united in a vast humanitarian effort and God was glorified. Surely the angels rejoiced over all who reached out to help. Let us hope that this generosity will continue and grow. The good that comes out of such tragedies reaffirms our belief in the basic goodness of most people. For a while everyone was united in the effort to help relieve the suffering and the needs of the victims. It was love on a vast scale.

Beloved, let us love one another, because love is of God; Everyone who loves is begotten by God and knows God. (1John 4:7)

To know God is the greatest gift of all - when we love, God reveals himself as the source of all love.

66

"A bruised reed he shall not break, and a smoldering wick he will not quench." (Isaiah 42:3) This image of the Messiah as someone who has great concern for those who are vulnerable is very encouraging. Jesus came to find what was lost and to rescue the marginalized in the world and bring them into the kingdom of his Father. Peter proclaimed Jesus as the one who "went about doing good and healing all those oppressed by the devil." (Acts 10: 38)

To emphasize that he had come to call all of us to newness of life he allowed John to baptize him in the Jordan, thus standing in unison with all who need forgiveness. He himself was sinless, but he identified himself with mankind to show that he would take away the sin of the world. Hence no one is beyond his reach; no one is beyond his desire to forgive. Every one is precious in God's eyes and is loved with an everlasting love. No matter where we are or what we have done, God stands ready in Jesus to heal, to forgive, to bless, and to bring us into the kingdom of his marvelous light.

Isaiah wrote that the Messiah was sent by God as a covenant, as a sign of God's providence, to "open the eyes of the blind, to bring out prisoners from confinement, and from the dungeon, those who live in darkness." (Isaiah 42:6-7) In some ways we are all blind, all confined by some habit we can't break, and too many of us live in prisons darkened by our own weaknesses. The Good News is that Jesus has come to set us free. His freedom is not burdensome; rather it lifts from us those self-imposed chains which entrammels us. As Dickens put it in <u>A Christmas Carol</u>, they are the chains we "forge in life." Jesus came to break those things which bind us and to release us to serve God and one another in love.

Since it is true that Jesus came to free us from sin, how is it that mankind is still imprisoned in sins of its own making? It is because the gospel has not really been heard, nor has it always been seen in action. Where it has been heard, many are too busy with seeking the things of the world rather than those of heaven. We often exchange the eternal gift of God for the passing glory of the world. Sometimes fear and the desperate need for security robs us of faith and hope, but, "Who indeed can harm you if you are committed deeply to doing what is right." (1 Peter 3:13) When we are united with Jesus and seek to do good, we can never be separated from him. He is the everlasting one who has redeemed us from the law of sin and death, and who will never leave us or forsake us.

Jesus promised that those who turn to him will never be rejected. (John 6:37) He came to bring us into the family of God and to let the light and love and grace of heaven be with us every day of our lives. Who could possibly refuse such blessedness?

67

Jesus said, "Let the children come to me. Do not hinder them. The Kingdom of God belongs to such as these. And he laid hands on their heads before he left that place." (Mathew 19:14-15) We are used to thinking about the love Jesus had for the children, but in his day it was unusual for children to be in the company of a rabbi. Children in those days were not given the pride of place they often have in our society. Possibly because many died in childbirth or as infants, children were not doted on as in our day. So the disciples who tried to get rid of the children and stop them from bothering Jesus were only doing what was acceptable. Jesus, however, saw in the children the perfect image of a disciple. He received them and told his disciples to be like them in their trust, openness and humility.

Of course it is quite difficult for adults to "become as little children." Most might say that it is impossible. We are the ones in control and do not want to give it up. Children on the other hand have no power and are controlled by adults. Adults fear the loss of power over their lives and recoil from any suggestion that they lay down their power and their selves in service to others. Yet, the greatest happiness is to be found in helping others. When we learn to place the center of our being outside ourselves and put others first, something wonderful happens. We suddenly seem freer than we ever were before and we seem to be the ones who are served. It sounds paradoxical, bur Jesus promised that those who lay down their lives would be the freest of all.

Mother Teresa understood this perfectly, and taught her sisters how to put it into practice. Once when my wife and I were with her she said, "Please pray that when I am gone, the sisters will remain true to this gift of service to the poor." She wanted her Order, The Missionaries of Charity, to cling fast to the way of service that she lived. In the many contacts we have had with her sisters in many countries we saw her wish carried out to the letter, especially in their care for the least, the children.

We must learn to see all children as belonging to us. They are our future and we are responsible for them to the extent that we can provide for their well being. Children need love and a safe place to live and learn. We can all understand that. They are precious in God's eyes and he will hold us accountable for the way we care for them. With all the resources available today, no child should go hungry or be deprived of medical attention or schooling. Many organizations exist to provide for them, and we can help by donating to them. It is surprising how little it takes to ensure that a child in the third world is being cared for.

If we do not help them, who will? They cannot wait any longer. The hungry children of the world die at the rate of over two thousand per hour. It is time we put a stop to it.

"Lord, give us generous hearts to love the children of your world. For everything we have comes from you." Amen.

68

"Strive for peace with men, and for that holiness without which no one can see the Lord. (Hebrews 12:14) It is no accident that the writer of Hebrews links peace and holiness together. The two are inseparable. Peace is essential for holiness; holiness is essential for peace. We cannot grow in one without affecting the other. Peace and holiness are like two hands joined in prayer.

In the Beatitudes, Jesus promises marvelous rewards for those who seek holiness and make peace: they will not only be called children of God, but they will be filled with God himself (Matthew 5: 6 & 9. See also Ephesians 3: 19) the peace and holiness that Jesus was teaching about begins in the heart. They take root in our lives and are nurtured by prayer. As we draw closer to God, there manifests within us the fruit of the Spirit and we begin to live empowered lives nourished by the Holy Spirit. This readily happens when we really hunger and thirst for holiness. However, it can only happen when we refuse to speak ill of others. As James points out so bluntly: "If a man does not control his tongue and imagines that he is devout, he is self-deceived: his worship is pointless." (James 1:26.)

That is a harsh word, telling us that our worship is useless if we cannot control our tongue. In fact, James is so insistent on this point that he wrote a whole section on the abuses of the tongue and how we can become polluted by its misuse. He said that if we use our tongues to praise God and then speak ill of others who are made in the likeness of God, then blessings and curses come from the same source. He added, this should not be. In order to have peace we must learn to control what we say, which, of course, begins in our hearts. We ought to say only those things which help people, as Paul reminds us to do. (Ephesians. 4: 29) When we do that, we will receive a great blessing, "for the fruit of righteousness is sown in peace by those who make peace." (James 3:18 NKJV)

Making peace is doing the work of God. It is bringing together those who were once apart, as Jesus did by uniting us in himself with the Father. He is the Prince of Peace and he came among us to give his gift of God's peace to mankind. When we receive the Prince of Peace in our lives he enables us to become peacemakers. He imparts to us the wisdom from above. This wisdom "is first pure, then peaceable, gentle, willing to yield, full of mercy and good fruits, without partiality and hypocrisy." (James 3:17 NKJV) Surely we all want to share in this blessing! And we can do that in prayer, and by desiring to say only the good things which will bring true peace.

Let us try for one week to say only the things which will edify and encourage. I suspect that many of us will find it very difficult to do.

69

One of the great truths of scripture which blesses me every time I think about it, is the fact that God has willingly obligated himself to us. In Genesis 15, God told Abraham that he would be his shield and his "exceedingly great reward." Abraham was not satisfied with that promise alone because he wanted an heir. So the Lord swore to Abraham that his descendants would be so numerous that he would be unable to count them. Abraham believed that promise because he knew the integrity of the Lord.

In Exodus 3, God again obligated himself to man, this time promising Moses to free the Israelites from Egyptian bondage. In a glorious way, "with outstretched arm," he fulfilled his promise and freed the people from the shackles of slavery. In the New Testament, we see the most perfect promise that God made to us. Jesus made a covenant with us by bearing in his body the wounds which redeemed us from the slavery of sin. With "outstretched arms" on the cross, Jesus rescued us from darkness and brought us into the kingdom of his marvelous light. He obligated himself to save all mankind and we have the freedom to accept it or reject it.

This is a sublime truth; a majestic act of surpassing love. That is why Paul said he preached Christ crucified everywhere he went. He proclaimed that the crucified one was the "power of God and the wisdom of God." (1 Cor. 1:24) This is indeed good news for a world crumbling under its burden of sin. It is the message which must go out to all the world. God has sworn in the person of Jesus that he will give us life when we open our hearts to him. So let us live this good news from God. Let us love one another, refusing to judge our neighbor, and seek instead to love them as the Lord has commanded. If we live an authentic Christian witness, we will surely bring others to the Lord. Unfortunately, our behavior is often unchristian and the following words of Henry Drummond ring true:

How many prodigals are kept out of the Kingdom of God by the unlovely character of those who profess to be inside.

If we keep in mind how deeply the Lord has obligated himself to us, we will grow like him and yearn to share in his great desire to save the world. The proof of his commitment was letting himself be nailed to the cross. Our part is certainly easier.

In the postmodern world commitment is almost a dead letter. Fewer and fewer people are willing to make lifetime contracts with each other. Prenuptial contracts are a clear indication of that. But God did not make a provisional covenant with us. He swore by himself that he would never leave us or forsake us. He promised that his love would last forever. That is incredibly good news for a weary world. Let us tell someone today!

70

"God has not given us a spirit of fear, but of power and of love and a sound mind." (1 Timothy 1:7 NKJV) There is great comfort in this verse. It lets us know that the love and wisdom of the Holy Spirit resides in us who believe. So there is no need to succumb to fear and unbelief. Yet sometimes we forget that the Lord is with us and that his spirit lives in us. We allow the darkness of this present age to cast its shadow over us, and we walk away from the light.

The Spirit of power which fell at Pentecost enabled the disciples to walk in the light of the gospel, thereby fulfilling Jesus' word that they were the light of the world. They bore witness to the truth and love and glory of Jesus. We are called to be like those early disciples, for we are equally empowered to be his witnesses. Just as the Apostles and prophets and saints of the early church stood against the evils of their age, so are we to stand against the present darkness. Paul's letter to the Ephesians proclaims, "Take up the whole armor of God, that you may be able to withstand in the evil day, and having done all, stand." (Ephesians 6:13 NKJV) The armor of God is, of course, the belt of truth, the breastplate of righteousness, the Gospel of peace, the shield of faith, the helmet of salvation, the sword of the Spirit, and (what is usually overlooked) prayer.

I believe that prayer is the most neglected piece of spiritual amour in the Christian defenses. We say we are too busy to pray. We ignore the example of Jesus who rose early or pray. Many of us cannot ever tear ourselves away from the TV early in the evening to pray.

We lament over the drug problem and over numerous other evils which beset our world, but do we try to do something about it? Do we intercede for those in bondage? Tragically, when we fail to intercede for the world, we are handing it over to evil.

Scripture clearly teaches that God made us to love and to do good. Even before the world began he had ordained good works for us to do with him; to be coworkers in the plan of salvation. Intercession is one of the good works he had in mind for us. If we fail to pray for our community and our country we are refusing to take part in the warfare which Paul described in Ephesians 6:12.

When we pray for others and seek God's help for them, we are entering into a close relationship with God by doing the work Jesus called us to do. God expects us to be intercessors. His willingness to hear Abraham's prayer for Sodom and Gomorrah indicates just how merciful he is- Abraham however, stopped interceding when he had reached the minimum (*minyan*) he thought God would accept. Later on, God said to Ezekiel, "The people of the land have used oppressions, committed robbery and mistreated the poor and the needy; and they wrongfully oppress the stranger. So I sought for a man among them who would make a wall, and stand in the gap before me on behalf of the land that I should not destroy it; but I found no one." (Ezekiel 22:29-30 NKJV)

Will we stand in the Gap?

71

"Who will separate us from the love of God?" (Romans 8:35) Obviously, the answer we expect is "no one." Yet there is someone who can separate us from the Lord - ourselves. Unfortunately, when we become lukewarm in our devotion to God we are actually drawing away from him. We make the choice. We are either moving towards him and being renewed in his love, or we are moving away from him and rejecting his love.

Jesus wants there to be no separation between us; he wants to be in our hearts. He taught us that our hearts will always be where our treasure is. If he is the Lord of our lives, we can be certain that he is the treasure in our hearts. Jesus showed us the mind and heart of God; when we hear him, we are also hearing the

Father. Jesus is like God; God is like Jesus. What a great consolation it is to know that the love and compassion of Jesus are the love and compassion of God. Jesus showed us the mind and the heart of God. He lived and walked and ate with sinners, he had compassion on the sick, the needy, the poor, the indigent, the outcasts. He turned no one away. As Luke records it, "He received them and spoke to them of the reign of God and he healed all who were in need of healing." Matthew quoting Isaiah wrote: "It was our infirmities he bore, our sufferings he endured." (Matthew 8:17)

Thus he demonstrated the loving nature of God. God welcomes everyone who turns to him in need. If we are truthful, we know that every one of us is needy. "For all have sinned and fall short of the glory of God." (Romans 3:23) Incredibly, our need is itself a blessing; it leads us to God. When we recognize how helpless we are without him, we begin to seek a deeper relationship with him. As we open up to his grace and have our hearts and minds renewed, we begin to see just how we need God and then we experience how powerfully he works within us. (Ephesians 1:19) Then we can begin to recognize his presence in our lives and surrender fully to him. We will then begin to grasp the depths hidden in the following verse: "Is it possible that he who did not spare his own son, but handed him over for the sake of us all, will not grant us all things besides." (Romans 8:32).

It is difficult not to be awestruck by the implications of that verse and by its authority. It means that no matter how desperate our situation may be, we have a loving, heavenly Father who is ready to help us in our need. Yet sadly, many of God's choicest blessings are ignored as if they were of no value. Countless people reject him and live their days heedless of his love while God wants to shower them with his grace. He is always waiting for us to come to him with open hearts so that he can fill them with great blessings. As scripture says: "My God will supply every need of yours according to his riches in glory in Christ Jesus." (Philippians 4:19RSV)

That is quite a promise!

72

"Cast all your cares on him because he cares for you." (I Peter 5: 7) In this marvelous advice is contained one of the great truths of scripture: God loves us so much that he is concerned about all our anxieties. In fact, he wants us to give them all to him and to place all our trust in him. Yet how tenaciously we hold on to our worries and cares, picking at them like sores, and refusing to allow God's healing balm to comfort us.

The Apostle Peter was quoting Psalm 55 when he wrote to believers urging them to give their anxieties and concerns to the Lord. I find it interesting that the word Peter used for "cast" actually means to throw articles of clothing across an animals back to make the rider comfortable - a comforting image. Perhaps the most important advice on cares and worries is found in chapter six of Matthew's Gospel: pointing out that worry is a denial of God's love, Jesus told his followers three times to "Be anxious for nothing." He assured us that when we "seek first" God's kingdom, everything we need will be given to us.

In Luke's Gospel, Jesus' advice against worry is beautifully illustrated in one of the loveliest verses in all of scripture: "Do not be afraid little flock, for your Father has been pleased to give you the kingdom." (Luke 12:32 NIV) If we would meditate on that word for a few weeks, we would realize the uselessness of worry. Perhaps that is where our problem lies. We do not meditate enough on the words of Jesus and so we ignore the power that God's word has to change us. In Hebrew, to meditate means to "murmur" or to say something over and over. That is the kind of meditation we need. If, for example, we would meditate on Matthew 6:25-34, slowly repeating the words and letting them penetrate our spirits, we would grow in trust and faith.

Furthermore, our minds would be renewed by the power inherent in God's word, and we would overcome the cares and worries of this world. I believe that daily meditation of scripture, for example Psalm 23, accompanied with heartfelt thanks to the Lord, can cure all our worries. But perhaps the greatest benefit we receive from meditating on the word is the promise of Jesus in John 14:23. He said that if we love him, and are true to his word, then he and the father will come and make their home in us. In such company, who could worry?

So, let us take to heart the word of the Lord and with Isaiah firmly believe that the Lord is willing to relieve us in times of distress: "You will keep him in perfect peace whose mind is stayed on you." (Isaiah 26:3 NKJV) Perfect peace is an incredible treasure...yet not unobtainable. Paul agrees: "Dismiss all anxiety from your minds. Present you needs to God in every form of prayer and in petitions full of gratitude. Then God's own peace, which is beyond all understanding, will stand guard over your hearts and minds, in Christ Jesus." (Philippians 4:6-7) Who can say more?

73

Prayer is power. Most people would probably agree with that statement. Yet how much praying do we really do? Most of us will readily carry on a conversation with a friend for an hour or so. With a special friend we might talk for hours. Why don't we do that with our greatest friend, Jesus? Believers are in danger of forgetting that prayer solves great problems, and today prayer is needed more than ever. Perhaps the problems facing us seem too great, and we have become weak in faith. Therefore, it will help us to consider some great men and women of prayer in the Bible and learn from them.

When the prophet Elijah prayed, the dead were raised, fire fell from heaven, the rains poured or ceased at his word, and the widow of Zarephath miraculously received flour and oil for a whole year to feed herself and her son during a drought. Elisha, Elijah's successor, prayed for a double portion of Elijah's spirit and worked twice as many miracles as his former master. Elisha prayed to open his servant's eyes, and the servant saw the mountains around them filled with fiery chariots of the Lord which were protecting Elisha from the Arameans. Elisha did not seek to destroy the Arameans, rather he asked God to blind them temporarily so they could be rendered harmless. Then Elisha had the king of Israel freed the Arameans and let them go. So touched were the Arameans by Elisha's kindness that scripture records, "no more Arameans raided the land of Israel." (II Kings 6: 14-32.) Elisha knew how to pray.

So did the prophetess Deborah. Her prayers were so effective that the Israelite general, Barak, would not go to war unless Deborah went with him. (I wonder if that is the origin of the saying, "to hide behind a woman's skirt?") Then there are the great people of prayer, Abraham, Moses, Joshua, Ruth, Esther, and a whole host of others who knew how to intercede for God's people.

The New Testament, too, is filled with men and women who believed that the Lord answers every prayer, and who worked signs and wonders in his name. Their actions are recorded for our example. We are called to imitate their faith in Jesus. In fact, we are told by the Lord himself to expect even the impossible when we pray. (Matthew 17:20) Jesus also said, "You will receive all that you pray for, provided you have faith. (Matthew 21:22) The more we pray, the stronger our faith will become.

The Lord said that the least born into the kingdom of God is greater than John the Baptist. He also said that John was like Elijah. (Jesus actually said, "If you are prepared to accept it, he is Elijah, the one who was certain to come." Matthew 11:14) That means our prayers ought to be at least as effective as Elijah's. Now that is something to think about!

74

"Though I sit in darkness, the Lord is my light." (Micah 7:8) That is a great confession, one we could readily make our own. For although the darkness of evil sometimes appears foreboding, we can rest secure in the power of his presence to enlighten the darkness around us.

Children who are afraid of the dark sleep with a light on which dispels the darkness and the fear. When one little girl was told not to be afraid because God was with her, she said, "I want someone with me who I can touch," But when she was given a light the darkness vanished away. So it is with God's light. As David wrote, "The Lord is my light and my salvation; whom shall I fear?" (Psalm 21:1) His light is impervious to fear because darkness cannot penetrate it. In St. John's words, "the light shines on in darkness, a darkness that did not overcome it." (John 1:5)

In the center of God's light, almost like the eye of the hurricane, there is a place of great peace and joy. David must have known that when he wrote, "In you is the fountain of life, and in your light we see light." (Psalm 36:10) To be able to see light in light requires contrast. For example, on an overcast day when the sun suddenly bursts through the clouds, we can see the rays of the sun standing out against the clouds. Thus in daylight, we can see, as it were, extra light from the sun, although in fact the sun's light has remained constant. Perhaps that simple analogy will help us understand a little more clearly what David meant by "in your light we see light."

We know that God is always present, always powerful and loving, always shedding his light on us, but suddenly, in a moment of need, or in a time of prayer, he reveals to us a little more of his light. Sometimes we are overwhelmed by the impact of it; the brightness seems blinding to spiritual eyes accustomed to the normal light. Yet God wants us to be bathed in his light. He created light even before he created the sun. He spoke light into existence, and he "saw that the light was good." (Genesis 1:3) Indeed, the real light of the world, Jesus, promised his followers that they would possess "the light of life." (John8: 12)

Often we are reluctant to believe that we possess the light of life. It seems that we are more willing to accept darkness than we are to embrace the light. But we must walk in the light, and love one another, if we are not to be overcome by darkness. (1 John 2:15) God has called us to walk in his light, and whenever we pray to him we are actually entering the center of his light where peace and joy abound. If this is so, why are we so reluctant to spend time alone with God? Why do we keep him at arms length? Is it because we have yet to distinguish the light within the light? Remember he has already said, "Let there be light..." And he waits for us to approach it.

75

St. Paul delighted in being the one called by God to preach to the Gentiles "the unsearchable riches of Christ." (Ephesians 3:8) That is a wonderful calling, and Paul wonderfully carried it out. I like the way in which the Living Bible renders Paul's statement in Ephesians 3:8: "I was the one chosen for this special joy of telling the Glad News of the endless treasures available to them in Christ." What a marvelous thought, and what an infinity of graces are ours in the endless treasure which is Jesus!

Paul loved to talk about the riches of Christ, for he was certain that the more we meditate on the limitless blessings given to us in Jesus, the more we will come to know the Lord. Yet he knew that knowledge alone was not sufficient. The greatest treasure of all is God's love, which "surpasses all knowledge." Paul taught that it is the love of Christ which enables us to "be filled with all the fullness of God." (Ephesians 3:19)

How is that possible? How can we be filled with the fullness of God? How can the creature contain the creator who himself is greater than the whole created universe? The simple answer is love. God loves us so much that he allows himself to be encompassed by those who respond to his love. I do not understand it, but I believe it. And St. Paul believed it, that is why he wrote about God's power in us being able to do "exceedingly abundantly above all we could ask or think." (Ephesians 3:20 NKJV) We cannot imagine all the endless treasures of Christ, nor can we understand the fullness of God, but that does not mean they are not available to us. In serving God, it is not important to think a great deal, but it is vital to love a great deal.

In order for us to love as he wants us to, he has given us the supreme gift of his Spirit. He has made us temples of the living God. Just as temples in the ancient world were depositories of great treasure, so are we, the Church, a rich deposit of God's blessing in the modern world. As Romans 5:5 puts it, the Father has lavished his love on his children through the Holy Spirit who is in us.

As if this were not enough, "each one of us has received God's favor in the measure which Christ bestows it." (Ephesians 4:7) And Jesus does not give sparingly from his endless treasures. Unfortunately though, we receive sparingly, for often we ignore the riches of heaven which Jesus has won for us. Therefore let us make an effort to open our hearts to the ever-flowing love from the sacred heart of Jesus. He wants us to come to him and share our daily lives with him in an intimate and vibrant manner. He wants our spirits to be united with his, so that in him, we can overcome the world.

He has given us "exceedingly great and precious promises…[so] that we might become sharers of the divine nature." (2 Peter 1:4 NKJV) Now that's a treasure we could never exhaust.

76

"Strive to come in through the narrow gate" (Luke 13:24 NKJV) what did Jesus mean by that? The verb "agonizomai" translated as "strive," originally meant to fight, or to struggle, or to engage in a contest. Our English word agony comes from it. One Greek scholar translates it this way: "strain every nerve to enter through the narrow door." Another translates it, "agonize to come through the narrow gate." They are strong statements, which means that Jesus did not attempt to sugarcoat his call on his disciples' lives. He asked for a total commitment to him in return for his total commitment to them.

Jesus promised that if we surrender our lives to him, he would see to it that we receive everything we need. Yet even here, accompanying that solemn promise to provide for all our temporal needs, he clearly indicated that persecution and hardships would accompany his blessings. (Mark 10:30) Today, bearing witness to that, many jails in the world house men and women imprisoned for the sake of his kingdom.

St. Paul also taught that persecution would follow those who were committed to the Lord. He said Christians should expect it. He did, and he gloried in the hardships he suffered for Christ. St. James, too, saw joy in tribulation - he even exhorts us to "count it all joy" when trials and tribulations beset us. (That is hardly Good News to our modern ears.) St. Peter also taught us to expect hardships and sufferings, and he urged us to face them with resolute courage. He saw the fight as a life-and-death struggle with the devil. However, when we vigilantly endure it, he said, God would perfect us and impart his strength to us. (1 Peter 5:8-10)

Peter had learnt his message from the Lord, for Jesus taught his disciples many times that they had to be vigilant. The Lord encouraged his followers to pray earnestly so that they would not be overcome by the trials and tribulations in the world. He also told them to take heart because he had overcome the world, and in him they would also be victorious.

Prayer is the key to victory. We must pray as Jesus prayed, expecting God to hear us and help us. Jesus prayed knowing that the Father heard him. He even struggled in prayer in Gethsemane, sweating blood in his effort to submit his suffering to the Father's will. That was agony.

One of Jesus' greatest prayers is the one he prayed for you and me. In the seventeenth chapter of John's gospel, he prayed that his disciples would be protected by the Father from the evil one. Then he prayed that we would be one as he and the Father are one, and that we would receive the same fatherly love that he had given Jesus. I believe the father answered that prayer and is waiting for us to live it.

The Father is also waiting for us to enter into serious fellowship with him. He wants us to meet him with love and fervor. Fervor like Jesus showed on the mount of Transfiguration when "his face changed in appearance..." (Luke 9:29) that was ecstasy. Whether in agony or ecstasy, we are called to be people of prayer.

77

"But I say to you, love your enemies, bless those who curse you, do good to those who hate you, and pray for those who spitefully use you." (Matthew 5:44) Let us ask honestly, do we obey this commandment of our Lord? The briefest acquaintance with history shows that we hate our enemies and frequently kill them in large numbers.

Jesus said that in order for us to become like our heavenly Father (and every good child wants to be like its parents) we must imitate him in loving everyone. This is one of Jesus' teachings that we are not too concerned about obeying. We prefer to love those who are loveable. Yet the very fact that we are children of God should stir us to love the unloved, the lost, the misfits, and the rejected. For it is Jesus in our hearts who urges us to reach out to help them. He wants us to help the lost in the way he helped them - by loving and serving them.

To do that we must be "rooted and grounded" in God's own love. He wants to fill us with his love which will empower us to love the unlovable. His love, which has been poured into us by the Holy Spirit, enables us to serve others with disinterested love, a love focused on the needs of others and not on self. But our hearts need to be prepared to accept his in pouring of love. Like a well prepared soil, dug deeply and tilled, the garden of our soul must be cultivated with prayer and the reading of his word. In this way we allow the Spirit to penetrate deeply into the very center of our being to help us grow and mature into vibrant members of God's household. Then we will be of great use to his kingdom, and be a blessing to others.

This kind of love, however, far exceeds any knowledge or understanding we may have of the Lord and his word. For it is a divine love that is imparted according to the riches of his glory. The Lord wants us to desire his love, to experience it, and the more we reach out to him, the more he will immerse us in the divine fire of his love. The more we seek him, the more we find him, and like a divine smelter, he burns away our impurities and refines us like precious metal. Yet how often we refuse to come close to him; how seldom we rejoice and linger in his presence.

Surely it is a great sadness to God that so many people have little time for him. That he laments our ignoring him is clearly seen in his words to Jeremiah, "my people have forgotten me." (Jeremiah 18:15) When we do that, we deprive ourselves of the greatest blessing in the world. We should ask ourselves honestly whether we are willing to love others as he asks. Let us also earnestly desire to experience more of his loving presence within us. He promised solemnly that if we seek him with all our heart we will find him in our heart, and we will be empowered by his love to love even our enemies.

Wouldn't that be something to write about?

78

"Rise up in splendor! Your light has come, the glory of the Lord shines upon you. (Isaiah 60:1) With such exultant language, Isaiah proclaimed the beauty of God's people. In majestic phrases, Isaiah prophesied that nations would walk in the light of Christ shining on the faces of his followers; a light which would last forever. Isaiah paints a lovely picture of the Church, yet how poorly we sometimes live up to its promise. Often it is as if we have no light, and that the Lord of glory does not live in our midst.

Isaiah also proclaimed that there was a time when the people of God were "forsaken, hated, and unvisited." But no longer. Now, he wrote, God would make his people "the pride of the ages, a joy to generation after generation. "Isaiah 60:15) That is the role of true Christianity, to be a joy to every generation. We must disseminate the good news that Jesus is the Lord and Savior of mankind, and that he is the only answer to our problems.

Sometimes we flounder around in search of answers which are already staring us in the face. Too many look for answers in the wrong place. I have read that over forty million Americans consult horoscopes, and that some famous actors pay large sums to have their palms read. Has no one told them about Jesus? Perhaps they do not see his answers in our lives...

Where is the light that Isaiah saw shining upon us so long ago? Have we put it under a bushel basket, or have we put it out? Whenever I read the Acts of the the Apostles I am moved by the faith, the power, the light, and the courage of the early Christians. With Jeremiah, I ask, "Lead us back to you, O Lord, that we may be restored: give us anew such days as we had of old." (Lamentations 5:21)

Jeremiah was pining for the "good old days" when Israel obeyed God and revered his covenant. Perhaps we, too, ought to yearn to have the faith of the early Church and to expect God to work as powerfully as they expected him. When they worshipped together, "the place where they were assembled shook as they prayed." (Acts 4:31) As one old wag noted, "there ain't a whole lot of shaking goin' on these days!"

I know that the "good old days" are often illusory, but in this case the Word tells us that those early days were indeed extraordinary. They were glorious, too, because the people of God were giving the world the astounding news that the God-man Jesus Christ is the answer, the way the truth and the life. We still have the same answer today. The intervening ages rather than dimming the message, have proved its enduring power. So isn't it time for us "to rise up in splendor" and spread the good news that Jesus is in our midst. Could we "turn the world upside down" as the early disciples of Jesus did?

As has been said so often, if we do not spread the good news, who will. If we don't do it now, when will we?

79

Sometimes the simplest things in scripture can have great meaning for us. For example, how often do we pay attention to the word stone? Yet we can learn a great deal from the many times that the Bible uses stones or rocks. One that comes readily to mind is the large, round stone which covered the entrance to the tomb of Jesus. As three women were on their way to finish embalming Jesus, they said to one another, "Who will roll back the son for us?" (Mark 16:3) When they arrived at the tomb they found that the stone had already been rolled away.

What is interesting about this incident is that the women went to the tomb in spite of the fact that they could not move the stone themselves. Apparently, they did not let difficulties prevent them from achieving their objective. Their determination and devotion can teach us a great deal. We can also allow the incident to speak to us on another level. For example, what heavy stones exist in our lives which prevent us from fulfilling our devotion to Jesus. Do we turn to him for help in rolling those stones away?

Many people have found that God's Word is the best source to help roll away the stones in their lives. After all, the Word does say, "Is not my word like fire...like a hammer shattering rocks." (Jeremiah 23:29) Even enormous rocks become manageable when they are smashed by the power of truth. When Satan confronted Jesus in the wilderness, he was put to flight by the word of truth. Satan proffered some flat stones to Jesus and said, "If you are the Son of God, command these stones to turn into bread." Jesus replied, "It is written, man does not live on bread alone." (Matthew 4:4) His word shattered the stones Satan wanted to use against him.

In John's Gospel the Scribes and Pharisees brought to Jesus a woman caught in the act of adultery. (No mention is made of the man.) Her accusers were ready, stones in hand, to batter her to death. The Lord spoke a word of truth which knocked the stones right out of their hands: "if any of you is without sin, let him be the first to throw a stone at her." (John 8:7 NIV)

Stones appear often in scripture. The Israelites set up stones at Gilgal amd the Jordan to commemorate God's love for his people. Jacob laid his head on a stone at Bethel where he dreamt about the angels ascending and descending the ladder form heaven. Elijah took twelve stones to build an altar at Carmel where he triumphed over the prophets of Baal. David had five smooth stones to use against Goliath - one sufficed. Ezekiel prophesied that the Lord would replace our hearts of stone with hearts of flesh and put a new spirit within us.

In the Book of Revelation there are numerous references to stones. The one I find most interesting is the white stone which the Lord promises to give to those who belong to him. On that white stone he will inscribe a new name, "to be known only by him who receives it." (Revelation 2:17) In other words, God will be so intimate with his beloved that he will use a special name of endearment to seal the relationship. That's one stone we won't mind receiving.

80

"Let the coming generation be told of the Lord." (Psalm 23:31) This verse should evoke in us a deep longing to tell the Good News to our youth. Many of our young people are so caught in the mesh of materialism, hedonism, and paganism, that they are lost to the Gospel. In the Book of Lamentations the prophet cries out for us to pray for our children even in the night. In one of the most moving verses in the Bible, he says:

Pour out your heart like water in the presence of the Lord!
Lift up your hands to him for the lives of your children,
who faint from hunger at the corner of every street.
(Lamentations 2:19)

That could have been written for our day. In every city, our children stand aimlessly at every street corner dying from hunger - hunger for love, for goodness, for truth, for beauty, and for something really real in their lives. Add to this the millions of children who are dying from hunger in the third world and we realize that countless millions are in great need.

In countries that have more Bibles than any other book, young people are lost because they have not been taught the Word of life. They are literally dying from spiritual malnutrition. They have not heard the majestic truth that anyone who loves Jesus, and is true to his word, will become the dwelling place, the sanctuary, the Holy of Holies, of the living God. (John 14:23)

Jesus warned us not to hinder the children from coming to him. He wants us to lead them to him, so that they might have life, and have it to the full. They will only seek him if they see his goodness in us. It is not what we say that really matters, it is what we do that has an impact on our children. If we tell them not to do the things that we are already doing, our words will fall to the ground. They will have no substance. If we tell them to go to church and to pray but they see no fervor in our lives, then they too will be lukewarm. Their love for God will reflect our love. If our love is shallow and self-serving, they will want nothing to do with the God we claim to serve.

The sure way our children will come to the Lord is if they see real love in our lives. No matter how they drift away in late teens or early adulthood, if they have experienced genuine, God-driven love, they will come back to it again. Their hearts have been touched by love, and like homing pigeons, they will always return to the place where they first encountered it. Therefore we ought to seek eagerly after love as scripture teaches. (1 Cor. 14:1) Love builds others up, it does not tear down. It is patient and kind: it is never rude. It does not brood over injuries. Love holds no grudges. When children see that kind of love, they will never forget it.

Furthermore, "There is no limit to love's forbearance, to its trust, its hope, its power to endure." (1 Cor. 14:7) If we allow God's love to flow through us so that our children will experience it, we will not need to lecture or to preach to them. As a well-known phrase puts it, "a picture is worth a thousand words."

81

One of the most fascinating incidents in the Old Testament is found in 1 Kings 19. The chapter begins with the prophet Elijah being harassed by Queen Jezebel. She had given him twenty-four hours to live. Elijah, fearful and deeply discouraged, ran away into the desert. After a day's journey into the wilderness he sat down under a broom tree, whose shade was meager at best. In deep disgust he cried out to the Lord: "Take my life, for I am no better than my fathers." (1 Kings 19:4)

Have you ever felt like Elijah? I am sure many of us have. There are times when we feel that we have had all we can take. We withdraw into our own private desert and die a little. Yet by God's grace we pull through, and we even get excited again about the Lord's work, just like Elijah did. As he sat under the broom tree he was told by an angel to take a forty-day journey to the mountain of God. That's not what Elijah had in mind. He was tired, discouraged, afraid, and he had already given up.

The angel ignored Elijah's depression and ordered him to eat some food which the angel provided. The meal gave Elijah new strength and courage. Now the prophet was ready for his journey. It was not Elijah's strength which enabled him to reach Horeb, rather it was the food which the angel had given him. That is how we are to journey to God's mountain, on the food from heaven which he provides. We go in his strength, not ours.

As Elijah traveled to Horeb I imagine him praying like this:

Send out your light and your truth,
let these by my guide to lead me
to your holy mountain and to
the place where you live. (Psalm 43:3-4 JB)

By the time he reached the mountain of God, Elijah was ready to talk to the Lord. He had it all worked out: he knew exactly what he was going to say. I can imagine his surprise when God asked him, "Why are you here, Elijah?" Elijah was obviously taken by surprise because he had gone to Horeb on God's orders. Surely the Lord knew why he was there! Obviously God did, but he wanted the prophet to look into his own heart, to examine his own reasons for coming. Elijah's answer to God reveals that he had indeed been looking into his own motives and rehearsing what he would say to God. He told the Lord that he was the only one left who obeyed him, and he believed that there was no one as righteous as himself. God was not convinced. And he revealed himself humbly as "a still small voice".

Elijah got over his discouragement and the Lord removed his pride. He once again served God with great fervor. That happens to all of us when we earnestly seek to serve the Lord. He gives us heavenly food, puts grace and courage into our hearts, and teaches us true humility.

82

"Do not be wise in your own estimation." (Roman 12:16) St. Paul knew how difficult that is. That is why in the same chapter he exhorted Christians to have the same attitude towards all and not to think too highly of themselves, but to look upon others as more important than themselves. Of course, that is easier said than done. The history of Christianity, with its thousands of denominations, is full of incidents which indicate that we do not consider others as more important. In fact the opposite is true: our history reveals quite clearly that the majority of denominations have at some time ended up considering themselves to be the sole purveyor of truth and better than the rest.

Many denominations have spent too much time running down other Christian groups. It seems that we are lacking in love, for as Paul noted, "Love never wrongs the neighbor." (Romans 13:10) Every time we criticize or condemn our neighbor we are actually saying that we are better than he is. We are also usurping the Lord's prerogative by setting ourselves up as judge in his place. Paul gave some wonderful advice when he wrote, "If possible, as much as depends on you, live peaceably with all men." (Romans 12:18 NKJV)

The key phrase is "as much as depends on you," for we are called to be peacemakers. Such is the nature of God's children. (Matthew 5:9)

Jesus promised his followers that his peace would enable them to undergo tribulation with courage and good cheer. (John 16:33) So his peace in our hearts can overcome our inclination to stand in judgment over others. And Paul's advice is very helpful in achieving that goal. We have to give up our habit of thinking that we are better than others if we believe God has given us more light on his word than our neighbor. We must remember that sobering word. "To whom much has been given, much will be required." (Luke 12:48) God does not give his children light so that they can lord it over their neighbors; he gives light to his children to dispel the darkness.

One powerful reminder to help us live peaceably with one another is found in the Book of Ezekiel (37:26) The Lord said he would make a covenant of peace with us which would last forever. Actually, the Hebrew text says "I will cut a covenant of peace." Isn't that what Jesus did on the cross. His battered body was the sign of God's covenant of love which he allowed to be cut for us.

Surely, when we contemplate the suffering God's son endured to give us peace, we cannot help but ask forgiveness for the many times we have broken that peace. When we break that peace, we are actually driving the nails into the Lord's hands all over again.

Scripture says, "He is our peace," so when we break peace with one another, we treat his sacrifice with disdain.

When we love one another, we exalt his sacrifice and peace reigns in our hearts.

83

In the Magna Carta of discipleship, the Beatitudes, Jesus gives us a perfect description of himself: the Beatitudes are a summary of everything Jesus was. In the fifth Beatitude, "Blessed are the pure in heart, for they shall see God," Jesus holds up to us a mirror in which we can see our own reflection: sometimes we are dismayed by what we see. The pure in heart are those who love God, not for what God can give them, but because he is worthy of their love and because he himself is infinite love.

When we compare ourselves to the way Jesus loves, we all fall short of the mark. However, Jesus holds the Beatitudes out to us as an achievable goal in this life, because empowered by the Spirit we can attain purity of heart if we truly desire it. The Greek word for pure, *katharos*," has many uses. It was used to describe clean linen, pure gold, clear crystal, pure water, an undefiled conscience, the best bread, and an army free from half-hearted and cowardly soldiers. It also means unmixed and unadulterated.

It is clear that when Jesus said the pure in heart are blessed, he was referring to those who have a single-minded devotion to God, and who are child-like enough not to be contaminated by greed and materialism. The wonderful promise of this verse is that the pure in heart will see God. As Rabbi Nachman of Breslov said, "For the true believer, believing is seeing." Not only are the pure in heart assured of a face-to-face meeting with God at death, but even during their lives on earth they will see

God in all that is good. They will encounter God in his Church, in his word, and in his people.

The pure in heart are the followers of Jesus who become the salt of the earth. Their very presence among us adds savor to our lives and preserves us from weak faith. They are the light of the world which is reflected from the Lord they serve, which enables others to see the love of Jesus working among us. Each of us is called to be pure in heart, to be single-hearted in our devotion and loyalty to the Lord. We cannot achieve purity of heart by our own efforts, it is given to those who draw close to God.

Hence, if we seek the Lord with all our heart, we will come to know his purity within us and he will change us "from glory to glory into his very image…" (II Cor. 3:18) What a magnificent promise that God will mold us into his image! But for this to happen we have to be supple and malleable like clay. We surrender ourselves to him and let him shape us as he wills. For he said to Israel through the prophet Jeremiah, "As clay is in the potter's hand, so are you in my hand…." (Jeremiah 18:18)

Hopefully, we will not fall apart on the potter's wheel.

84

Someone once remarked that we become what we most think about. There is much truth in that. I also believe that we become what we receive into our hearts: if we are open to God's blessings in out lives we will become a blessing to others. The wonderful thing about being a blessing to others is that we do not need to be extraordinary people. In fact, anyone can be a blessing if he wants to be. It makes no difference what kind of life a person has led, if he turns to God for help, he will become a blessing to others.

For example, let us consider the woman who met Jesus at the well. Not only was she a woman of ill repute (that's why she was getting water from the well in the noonday heat instead of in the morning to avoid the withering glances of the other women), but she was also a Samaritan. In Jewish eyes she was a total outcast. Yet Jesus blessed her with the knowledge that he was the Messiah.

Since Jesus came to save rather than condemn, he offered her the gift of eternal salvation. He said to her, "Whoever drinks of the water that I shall give him will never be thirsty; no, the water I give shall become a fountain within him, leaping up to provide eternal life." (John 4:14) Such is the blessing he offered her. She accepted his blessing and told the whole town about it. In other words, she became a source of life-giving water to others, and led them to Jesus.

Her example is worthy of imitation. She did not wait to share the good news, nor did she keep Jesus' blessing to herself. Rather, she went boldly and quickly to share her blessing with those who had previously condemned her for her way of life. Like the woman at the well, we, too, have been blessed by the Lord in order to bless others. If we hoard his gifts for ourselves they become useless. They may even be dangerous, because when love is hoarded it becomes greed, even lust, both of which are deadly to the spirit.

Another aspect worth noting about the Samaritan woman's witness is that she shared her blessing, in spite of her sinful condition. She looked at Jesus, not at her own failures, and so was able to evangelize her neighborhood. Too many of us are waiting to be "without spot and wrinkle" before we spread the good news. Hence we end up doing very little evangelizing.

Finally, her example is worth imitating because of its urgency. She left her water pot at the well and rushed back into town to tell the others the astounding news. She was so captivated by Jesus and his message that she forgot about herself and her reasons for being at the well in the heat. She was at that moment a perfect evangelist, pointing directly to Jesus.

After considering her example, what excuses do we have for not spreading the good news of Jesus Christ?

85

"It is enough for a disciple that he be like his teacher, and a servant like his master." (Matthew 10:25 NKJV) I am deeply challenged by this saying of Jesus, for how can we possibly be like him. Yet that is what he wants. Fortunately, we can take courage from what he said to his disciples: "The things which are impossible with men are possible with God." When we ask God to make us like Jesus, we can expect the Holy Spirit to work in us enabling us to bear fruit like him. What we need most is his love, and since God is love, he imparts it to us willingly and abundantly: "The love of God has been poured out in our hearts by the Holy Spirit who has been given to us." Romans 5:5)

In his first letter, St. John makes it clear that when we fail to love our neighbor, we are actually failing to love God. If we love God, he wrote, then we must love our brother and sisters. If we want to follow Jesus, we must first love as he loved: "This is my commandment, that you love one another as I have loved you." (John 15:12) When we let his love in us reach out to others, we begin to grow in joy. This joy, which is his very own joy that he bequeathed to us before he died, floods the souls of those who accept his message. (It was this fruit of joy which surprised C. S. Lewis by its pervading loveliness. Like many before him, he had not equated Christianity with joy.)

Along with joy comes the peace of Jesus, the peace which passes all understanding and which garrisons our hearts and minds and keeps us tranquil, even in the storm. The Holy Spirit imparts that peace into our hearts which enables us to follow the Lord even in difficult times. As the Holy Spirit continues to reveal Jesus to us, he strengthens our character and our resolve. He helps us to grow in patience, kindness, goodness, faithfulness and the other virtues which are the mark of mature disciples.

We see that Jesus bore abundant fruit in all these areas and his life manifested extraordinary power and perfection. He calls each of us to share in that perfection by letting the Spirit reveal Jesus to us more and more. When we know him, we will love him, and we will become like him, for scripture says, we become like the thing we love. (Hosea 9:10c NKJV)

Before Jesus ascended into heaven, he said to his disciples, "You will receive power when the Holy Spirit comes down on you; then you are to be my witnesses..." (Acts 1:8) To be effective witnesses we must love him and be led by the Holy Spirit.

The Bible says, "All who are led by the Spirit of God are sons [and daughters] of God." (Romans 8:14) Furthermore Romans then explains that since we are children of God, we are also heirs of God and joint heirs with Christ. It should be impossible to keep such good news to oneself.

86

Psalm 139:14 says that we are "fearfully and wonderfully made." In fact, we are so wonderfully made that we will live forever- at least our spirits will. When our nation is no longer in existence, C.S. Lewis reminds us, we will be alive with God eternally.

Unfortunately, we often behave as if it is our bodies which will live forever, and so we spend billions on diets, cosmetics, clothes, fitness programs, and in building increasingly larger and larger homes. In addition to all the money we spend, we spend hours and hours on self-pampering and self-exaltation. We really do live as if we'll be here forever.

But how much time and treasure do we spend on that part of our being that is really worth improving? How much time do we spend on our spiritual fitness? For example, do we spend as much time in prayer as we do eating? If we did, we probably wouldn't need to diet. We have become so preoccupied with self and so concerned with satisfying our desires that many of us have become our own idols. Affluent citizens of the West are so bent on consumerism, materialism and greed that they are in imminent danger of spiritual collapse.

Our Western world is so concerned with possessions, entertainment, and materialism that we are no longer a Christian culture. We are modern pagans. The truths which sustained and nurtured the faith of the past have been discarded or ignored by a large percent of the population. Jesus' warning has long been forgotten: "What profit would a man show if he were to gain the whole world and destroy himself in the process? (Matthew 16:26)

Our culture is in danger losing its soul and its moral compass, for morality is no longer upheld and our laws and ethical principles no longer reflect the principles of the Sermon on the Mount. One example will suffice to illustrate my point: the law protects an Eagle embryo in the egg, and severe penalties are inflicted on anyone who would tamper with the egg, yet we can abort millions upon millions of babies without penalties.

But there is hope. When I consider the price which Jesus paid to redeem us I know we can change our world. If God thinks so much of us that he gave his only begotten Son to save us, then he will surely help us now when we turn to him in prayer. If we value something and want it badly enough, we will pay the price. God wants us so much that he paid the greatest price possible - the life and death of Jesus. I am overawed by such a truth, that God so loved each one of us that he sent Jesus to buy us back from slavery to sin.

Since God paid such a price, he must believe that we are worth it, or he loves us so much that no price was too great to pay. But did he get what he paid for? Have we lived lives which reflect our gratitude for such an inestimable gift? If we really consider what Jesus has done, we are bound to be overwhelmed by God's generosity. Are we worth the price? Obviously the Father thinks so.

87

Jesus said that the greatest commandment is to love God. This commandment tells us we are to love him with our whole being, and by implication it also means that we must know him well - for we cannot love what we do not know. But how can we know God? To begin with, we come to know him by reading about him in his Word. It is not possible to really know God if we are ignorant of his Word.

In the psalms we learn that the Lord is our light and our salvation, (Psalm 27), and he is our strength and our shield. (Psalm 28) He is our refuge and "a very present help in time of need." (Psalm 46) Psalm 68 calls him, "a Father to the fatherless, a defender of widows" and a comforter of the lonely. When we are sad, "he turns our mourning into dancing. (Psalm 30) He rescues us when we are dejected in spirit, and he is especially close to the broken hearted." (Psalm 34)

In Hosea, the Lord says that his love for his people is so great that he holds them in his arms and feeds them like a mother. He even teaches us how to walk. (Hosea 11:1-4) Such an understanding of God is bound to lead us to love him. The prophet Zephaniah informs us that God loves us so much that not only does he "rejoice over us with gladness," but he will rejoice over us by singing to us!" (Zephaniah 3:17) Can you imagine just how amazing it will be to hear God sing a love song?"

As if that were not enough, the Lord promises us in Isaiah "as the bridegroom rejoices over the bride, so shall your God rejoice over you." (Isaiah 62:5) Through the same prophet, the Lord makes a poignant plea for us to return his love by letting us know that even if it were possible for a nursing mother to forget her child, he could never forget us. In another beautiful image, God says he loves us so much that he has carved our name on the palm of his hand. (Isaiah 49:16) That's more lasting than carving a name on a tree.

Obviously, I have only selected a few of the large number of verses which speak of God's love for us. But they are powerful enough to entice us into a deeper relationship with him. When we begin to hunger and thirst for God and seriously seek him, we begin to know him and to love him.

God wants our love. He is actively seeking it as the parable of the prodigal son illustrates. (Actually, as one commentator points out, it should be called the parable of the prodigal Father.) This parable shows God eagerly waiting for us to turn back to him. The least effort on our part meets with immediate response from the Lord; the more we seek him, the more we find him.

God's love for us is written in every book of the Bible, but no more powerfully than in the gospels. The greatest sermon on love in the gospels is Jesus dying on the cross. As St. John wrote:" Love then consists in this: not that we have loved God, but that he has loved us and sent his Son as an offering for our sins." (1 John 4:10) Amen!

88

"The cheerful heart has a continual feast." (Proverbs 15:15 NIV) Such is the power of joy! When our hearts are open to the Lord, he floods them with his divine presence, which is "joy inexpressible and full of glory." 1 Peter 1: 8 (NKJV)

The Bible has much to say about the heart, for example Proverbs 4:23: "With the closest custody guard your heart, for in it are the sources of life." Again in Proverbs 17:22(NKJV) we read, "A merry heart does good like medicine." How true that is! According to some medical researchers more than half of our ailments are psychosomatic, which would be alleviated by a happy outlook. We all know how relaxed we feel after a good laugh. Nor do we have to wonder how we can acquire a joyful heart, because it is God himself who puts "gladness" into our hearts. (Psalm 4:7)

Perhaps the surest way to receive the joy of the Lord is by repenting of our sins and our weak love, and by meditating on his gift of salvation. By recalling often that his death has purchased for us eternal life, will sure fill our hearts with joy, because in his presence there is "fullness of joy." (Psalm 16:11) Furthermore, when we remember that he is our strength and our protection we are not afraid and our hearts will rejoice. (Psalm 28:7) How could we not be glad when we realize we have the Living God for our shield.

Verse after verse in the scriptures teaches us about the joy our Father has available to those who turn to him in need; even if our heart is breaking, he is close by to heal it. (Psalm 34: 18) As soon as we commit ourselves totally to the Lord, we become alive with his love and joy. (Psalm 69:32; Jeremiah 33:3) Yet many people do not believe it and therefore do not seek him.

If we seek him diligently, our hearts and lives will be transformed by his presence. If we seek him as eagerly as we seek our own comfort and pleasure, we would be quickly changed by his grace. Jesus said, "Where your treasure is, there your heart will be also." (Luke 12:34) Whatever consumes all our time and energy is where our heart is. If we watch television for hours on end, and barely spend a few minutes in prayer, then television has supplanted God in our hearts. Consequently, if we do not have a living relationship with Jesus, our hearts become closed to his love.

The danger then is that we become insensitive to the needs of others, especially to the poor in our midst. The Rev. Jim Wallace has noted that over three thousand verses in the Bible mention the poor, but yet they are too often forgotten. But when Jesus becomes the center of our lives he warms our hearts with his love and we take delight in helping the unfortunate among us. That is because when he was on earth he did the same thing. So let us learn from him, for he is "gentle and humble of heart." (Matthew 11:29)

89

Jesus said that when we are insulted and persecuted because of our faith in him, we should rejoice and be exceedingly glad." (Matthew; 5:12 NKJV) I am sure that like me, you have wondered just what he meant. The word which Matthew used for "be exceedingly glad" is only found in the Bible - it has no profane or secular use. That is not surprising: no one in the world jumps for joy when things are going badly. It just isn't done.

Unfortunately, Christians seldom take Jesus' advice. What we do too often is grumble and complain, and look around for someone to blame for our misfortune, rather than praise God. The last thing we want to do is dance for joy. Yet, if we would remember to offer the Lord "a sacrifice of joy" then as David promised, our heads would be lifted above our difficulties. (Psalm 27:6) The problems may remain, but we will have the Lord's strength to withstand them.

It is vital for us to meditate on the joy and the goodness of God in order to counteract the pervasive pessimism which is characteristic of much of the world today. If we think often of

Jesus, we grow in love and he becomes our shield against negativity and depression. When we look to Jesus, we have found the path to inner peace. Thinking about the Lord renews us in mind and heart and spirit. St. Paul knew the wisdom of positive mental exercises, and he urged his readers in his letter to the Philippians to deliberately meditate on the beauty of God. In one of his most lyrical passages he wrote, "whatever is true, whatever is noble, whatever is right, whatever is pure, whatever is lovely, whatever is admirable - think about such things." (Philippians 4: 4:8 NIV)

St Paul understood that the Lord keeps in perfect peace minds that meditate on the Word of God. Furthermore, he wrote, if we learn to "Rejoice in the Lord always" and to be "anxious for nothing," then God's peace would surround our hearts and minds with its impenetrable defenses." (Philippians 4:4-8) This is not mind over matter, or some pie-in-the-sky idea to escape reality; it is reality. God is real, and he loves us and wants us to share our daily lives with him. When we do, we become channels of his love, and instruments of his peace.

Obviously, the battleground in our struggle for peace and joy is in the mind. Yet, we have control over what we think and over how we react to circumstances. Therefore, we are responsible for how we handle difficulties. Do we give in to them, or do we give them to the Lord?

The surest way to be an overcomer and to experience the joy of the Lord is to follow the advice of John the Baptist. He pointed to Jesus and said. "He must increase, but I must decrease." (John 3:30) If we consistently think more about Jesus and less about self, we will never be overcome by negative thoughts: we will keep our eyes on Jesus who "inspires and perfects our faith" (Hebrews 12:2). When we look to him, we are safe. (Isaiah 45:22)

90

"The Son of Man did not come to be served, but to serve." (Matthew 20:28) Jesus lived a life of total service to others. He said he is in our midst as one who serves, and he asked us to imitate his example. He stated quite clearly what service is expected of those who love him. We are commanded to feed the hungry, to welcome strangers, to clothe the naked, to visit the sick and the imprisoned. St. James, who added orphans and widows to the list of needy folks we should help, warned us that if we do not feed the hungry and clothe the naked, our faith is dead. (James 2:15-18)

The work we should be doing is all around us. Everywhere there are people suffering and in want. If we reach out to them in the love of Jesus, they will know that he is still in our midst as one who serves. For the Church is his body; we are his hands, so we must continue his work among the needy until he comes in glory.

When the Early Church cared for those in need and shared their goods with others something wonderful happened. The church grew in numbers and a great joy and fervor overcame them. They were so moved by God's presence among them that even their meals, which they shared with the hungry, were times of exultation. (Acts 2:46) Serving others brings such joy. When we take our eyes off ourselves and seek to help the needs of others something remarkable takes place in our hearts. We grow in God's love and we are motivated by the purest zeal to serve him without looking for reward.

There is always a great need for Christians to answer the Lord's call by seeking out the lonely, the lost, and the afflicted. For instance, there are many abused children, many who have been molested and neglected, and numerous "throw-away" children whom few seem to want. If we are unable to help them, we can support those who do.

As Christians we are instructed by the Lord to love those who are unloved and to help those who are unable to help themselves. Jesus told us that the whole law and the prophets are summed up in loving God with our whole being and in loving our neighbor as ourselves. If we keep that in mind, we will be a blessing to the poor and the outcasts and we will be true to the Sermon on the Mount.

Sometimes we give up on the needs of others even before we start to help; because we see that the problems are so many and the laborers so few. We are overwhelmed by the prospect before us and we leave it to others. In this case it may be helpful to remember the words of Jonathan; "It is no more difficult for the Lord to grant victory through a few than through many." (1 Samuel 14:6)

Are we ready to be one of the few?

91

In two of his letters written in captivity St Paul exhorts us to sing praises to God with all our hearts full of thanksgiving. (Ephesians 5:19 & Colossians 3:16) That is a perfect prescription for keeping joy in our lives.

Psalm 33 teaches us that when we turn to the Lord with a joyful song, we come to see and understand that "the earth is full of his unfailing love." (Psalm 33:5 NIV) It is a precious gift to be able to see that this world is full of his love and mercy. Just to understand John 3:16 floods the mind and heart with joyful thanksgiving. As psalm 34 illustrates, those who seek the Lord and exalt him for his love become radiant with joy. They experience and taste the goodness of God; they are overwhelmed by his presence. Paul and Silas knew that.

In jail in Philippi, at midnight, they were singing hymns to which, as it is written, "the prisoners listened." (Acts 16:25) Obviously those hymns were worth listening to! I suspect they were odes of joy to the Lord. I say this because within the hour the jailer and his family were converted and filled with rejoicing. Joy is contagious, especially after surviving an earthquake.

Joy is a sign of the Lord's presence among us and within us. Joy is a consequence of the encounter with Jesus. As psalm 43 has it, "send out your light and your truth, let them lead me...to God my exceeding joy." For where God is, there is fullness of joy (Psalm 16:11) Those who are not experiencing joy may say that what I have written is naïve, perhaps even simplistic. They may say finding joy is impossible when they are burdened with seemingly insurmountable problems. But they would be wrong, because at least five psalms and the prophet Isaiah tell us the Lord is close to those who are brokenhearted and to those who are crushed and dejected in spirit. Since he is close to them, so is his joy.

One of the gifts which Jesus promised to his followers was joy, his very own joy. A joy unsullied by the world; a joy which cannot be taken from us. A joy which is independent of circumstances. The kind of joy which Nehemiah said is our strength. (Neh. 8:10)

However, we can forfeit that joy when we turn away from God and seek our own way. As a result many negative things in our lives rob us of his joy. We are no longer in communion with the one who is the source of all good things. We stop reading his Word and we pray rarely. Sin enters our lives and our hearts grow unconcerned and our talents and gifts atrophy from lack of use.

Then a great tragedy occurs: our hearts robbed of joy become empty of love and harden. That is why joy is vital to a healthy

Christian life. If we lack joy we must seek him who is the source of all good things; thus renewed we are able to rejoice again. When we find him, we find everything, because the one who has God has everything, the one who has God, has a surplus to give away, even an abundance of joy.

92

"For here we have no lasting city." (Hebrews 13:14) I wonder how many live as if that verse were true. The older I get, the more I notice that we behave as if we will live on earth forever. I suspect that most of us spend more time fixing up and beautifying our earthly homes (and bodies) than we do our heavenly ones. We have heard the words of Jesus about laying up treasures in heaven, but the First Central Bank seems to be more appealing when it comes to our banking needs.

We know our present home is transitory, and we believe our heavenly home will be permanent, yet we insist on a lifestyle which indicates we really would prefer to stay here forever. The Apostle Paul clearly taught us to keep our eyes on heaven, our ultimate home: "So we fix our eyes not on what is seen, but on what is unseen. For what is seen is temporary, but what is unseen is eternal." (II Corinthians 4:18 NIV)

Jesus said our lives are eternal and destined for glory with him. In addition, he affirmed that when we know God, we are already sharing in the eternal glory which the Father has given us. (John 17:3 & 22) But what does it mean to know God? Do we know him in the way we know George Washington? In other words, do we know God by what we have read about him, or do we know him personally? It is clear from Scripture that God expects us to have an intimate knowledge of who he is. As he told Moses: "I will take you as my own people and you shall have me as your God. You will know that I, the Lord, am your God when I free you from the labor of the Egyptians." (Exodus 6:7-8) He wanted the Israelites to experience his presence and his power among them so that they would truly know him.

If we keep our minds and hearts focused on the Lord, knowing that God and not this present life is the most important gift, then we also will come to know his presence and power in our lives. Since God revealed himself to the Israelites, he expected them to know him and to love him. That is why for over three thousand years the Jews have prayed their great daily prayer, the *shema*, which says, "Hear O Israel…you shall love the Lord your God with all your heart, with all your soul, with all your strength." (Deuteronomy 6:4-5)

In order to love him, we have to know him.

When a scribe asked Jesus what is the greatest commandment, Jesus quoted the *shema*. Jesus made it quite plain that God wants us to have an intimate fellowship with him. He showed us also that our relationship with the Father ought to be greater than that of Moses. For God said to Moses, "I shall be with you," but to us Jesus said, "I will be in you." (John 14:23)

However, when we live as if this life were the only one, we will not get to know the Lord of Glory. If we do not know him, we will be only half alive. When we entrust our hearts to an ephemeral treasure we are in danger of missing the eternal treasure, the Lord of all creation.

93

"See what love the Father has bestowed on us in letting us be called children of God! Yet that is what we are." (1 John 3: 1) If only we lived up to the truth of that verse. If we spent more time prayerfully contemplating the fact that we are God's children, we would want to become more like him. Then we could begin to love like he loves.

St. John, in his first letter, reminds us that if we really love God, we must love one another. Also he warned us that if we claim to be in the light, and to know the truth, but hate our brother, we are actually in darkness. (1 John 3:10-11) The knowledge in our minds must be subordinate to the love in our hearts. It is not what we believe, or what we say that ultimately matters, rather it is what we do with that knowledge. "For faith without works is dead" (James 2:20) what makes Jesus so compelling a teacher is that his words were always accompanied by action.

As God's children we must imitate Jesus our brother. Our citizenship is with him in heaven, and Scripture clearly states that we belong to his family. (Ephesians 2:19) I doubt whether we have really appreciated the grandeur of that verse...at least our attitude indicates that we have yet to grasp its full meaning. Perhaps our inability to comprehend fully the fact that we are part of the family of God stems from problems inherent in our society. For example, we spend too much time with our things, and not much time with the Creator of all things.

We spend so much time with entertainment and enjoying our material success that we are often spiritually malnourished. As we struggle to shed pounds from our overfed bodies, our spirits are starved for nourishment. That is not the way God intended for us to live. He has provided his word which is "our daily bread," a source of real food for the soul. If we neglect the reading of Scripture and prayer we will eventually suffer from spiritual malnutrition - even starvation.

We are eternal beings; we will never cease to exist. What matters most in this life is how well we prepare for eternity. Unfortunately, we live as if eternity were to be spent on earth. Our possessions take up too much of our time and prevent us from reflecting on our fast approaching face-to-face encounter with God. Jesus understood only too well our propensity to invest all our energies in temporal things. He told his followers not to worry about their lives and possessions, but to seek first the kingdom of God. (Matthew 6:25-34)

Through the prophet Isaiah, God gave all mankind a marvelous invitation to the abundant life. In one unforgettable verse Isaiah prophesied, "Why do you spend money for what is not bread, and your wages for what does not satisfy? Listen diligently to me, and eat what is good..." (Isaiah 55:2)

Surely we should be listening to him?

94

"Out of my distress I called to the Lord, and he answered me." (Jonah 2:3) That's a comforting verse. It becomes an even more powerful statement when we place the stress on different words. For example, if we stress the pronoun "me," it helps us realize that God is personally interested in us as individuals. When we stress the word "answered," we are encouraged by the truth that God really answers our prayers.

If you have never used this exercise of stressing different words in familiar passages of Scripture, I recommend that you try it. You will be surprised by the results. Let me give some examples of well-known verses, and we'll see how they take on new shades of meaning when we emphasize different words. Here is a familiar example, "it is written." They were the first words spoken by Jesus as an adult in the Gospel of Luke. As we emphasize each word individually, we realize how the meaning of the verse changes." *It* is written," does not quite mean the same as "it *is* written;" and "it is *written*," means something else again. When the stress is on each word equally, it carries a different shade of meaning.

A more controversial verse which can have several meanings is "this is my body." If we stress the pronoun "my," we imagine Jesus saying that our body is his body. (Yet we are part of the body of Christ.) Then try emphasizing each word separately. When we stress each word equally it has a powerful Eucharistic meaning.

Lest you think I am splitting hairs, let us examine Matthew 5:8: "Blessed are the pure in heart, for they shall see God." I believe we have often emphasized pure at the expense of heart. Certainly the word pure is important, but the stress must also be placed on heart. Because Jesus was interested in a relationship with the Father which takes place in the heart.

Continuing with the same verse, let us place the emphasis on the phrase "shall see God." It is thrilling to think that when we allow him to cleanse our hearts, we will actually see him! When we meditate for a while on this promise of Jesus we are bound to be filled with gratitude and praise.

Matthew 4:4 is another verse which is enriched when it is read with varying emphasis: "man does not live on bread alone, but on every word that proceeds from the mouth of God." Merely stressing "every" will enable us to meditate for a long time. If we concentrate on "proceeds," noticing it is present tense, we can be captivated by its remarkable implications. You may choose any verse that appeals to you to do the same.

A verse which has greatly helped me is "My grace is sufficient for you, for my power is made perfect in weakness." (II Corinthians 12:9 NIV). When you have the time, just sit before the Lord and slowly emphasize each word in turn as you repeat the verse. It will bless you abundantly!

95

"Come to me all you who are weary and find life burdensome, and I will refresh you." (Matthew 11: 28) Surely this is one of the most comforting of Jesus' promises. Yet it is often overlooked. Everywhere there is pain and suffering, loneliness and sorrow, depression and hopelessness, separation and divorce. Many people are hurting and fearful, and frequently they do not know where to turn for help. This is sad, because help is only a prayer away - even only a word away, Jesus.

When we call out to him and bring our problems to his Sacred Heart, we find him already in our heart. Scripture is full of powerful promises which tell us of his desire to help us and of his closeness to his children. Too often we are not listening. It is no wonder the Lord said through the psalmist, "If only my people would listen to me." (Psalm 81:13) If we listen, he will answer. All through the Bible he tells us of his willingness to help. He says that in our darkness he will be our light; in our sickness he will be our health; in our distress, he is our savior; in our need, he is our deliverer; in our sin, he is our redeemer and forgiver. (See Psalms 18,30 78,91)

Jesus promises to be with us to liberate us from everything that keeps us bound. He destroyed the curse of sin which afflicts us, and he set us free from the law of sin and death. (Romans 8:2) He came to give us life, and his brutal death on Calvary and his resurrection make that life certain. It was not the Roman nails which held him fast to the cross, it was his love. He embraced the cross with a courage and fervor which speaks forcefully of his great love for all mankind.

Jesus loves us with an incomparable love, and his words to us spring from his deep desire to see us live fulfilled lives. Many times in the gospels he urges us to listen to what he says, because his words are "spirit, and they are life." Peter realized that he had nowhere to go but to Jesus, because, as he said, "Lord...you have the words of eternal life." (John 6:63-68) Like his forebears, Peter knew the power of the spoken word.

Jesus wants us to accept what he has said; he also wants us to live by his teaching. He believed we all must live by God's word (Matthew 4:4) He came to earth as the Living Word to give us words we can live by. When the royal official came to Jesus to heal his son, he believed what Jesus said "Return home, your son will live." (John 4:50) The official did not argue or plead with Jesus, he accepted his word and believed. What an example of faith he is for all of us.

In our postmodern society, words are no longer valued as they were in Israel. Jesus clearly spoke to our age when he said, "Unless you people see signs and wonders, you do not believe." (John 4:48) I suspect that even signs and wonders will not be believed by the philosophers of post modernism. Yet Jesus will have the last word for he said, "The heavens and the earth will pass away, but my words will not pass" (Luke 21:33)

To listen to the good news and put ones trust in his word is the greatest wisdom.

96

Perhaps it was easy to see the majesty in Jesus as he rode into Jerusalem. The crowds greeted him with joy, waving palm branches and shouting, "Hosanna! Blessed is he who comes in the name of the Lord." (Mark 11:9) Nor was it difficult to see his majesty as he overturned the moneychangers' tables, showing his anger at the commercial spirit which the High Priest had fostered in the temple area. (The moneychangers occupied the place where Gentiles were allowed to pray, but the commerce going on made prayer difficult, if not impossible.)

The crowds were attracted by his power to heal and his miracles awed them. His ability to cast out demons caused admiration and amazement - though some accused him of being in league with the prince of demons. Wherever he went, the people saw in Jesus a man of great abilities whose words had a majestic power. He was hailed as king by many and they expected him to free them from the might of Rome Even the temple guards saw Jesus as a man with power.

But who could see his majesty and power as he hung on the cross, bleeding, beaten, abused, reviled, and naked? Yet two men, neither of them religious, looked at the broken, lacerated body of Jesus and saw him as the Lord of Glory. The first of these two men to acknowledge Jesus as Lord was the so-called good thief, or Dismas as tradition names him. While the other crucified insurrectionist was reviling Jesus, Dismas rebuked him saying, "Do you not even fear God?"

The good thief defended Jesus, acknowledging he was an innocent victim. Then he turned to Jesus and said, "Lord, remember me when you come into your kingdom" (Luke 23:42) He only asked to be remembered; he asked for nothing more. What was it that he saw in the face of Jesus which led to his great confession? What was it about the dying Galilean which led the good thief to faith? Why did he see glory in Jesus, whilst the chief priests and the elders stood in unbelief and mocked the crucified Christ?

He must have seen love and mercy in the eyes of Jesus which captured his heart. Then, because of his dying defense of Jesus, the Holy Spirit empowered him to see the face of God in the bloodstained face of Jesus. At that moment Jesus looked at him and said those marvelous words we all long to hear, "I assure you: this day you will be with me in paradise." (Luke 23:43) The good thief knew he would not be forgotten.

The second man who saw divinity in the dying Christ was the centurion in charge of the execution at Calvary. As Jesus uttered his last cry, the centurion said, "Truly this man was the son of God." (Mark 15:39) The centurion witnessed the cruel agony inflicted on Jesus. He watched Jesus pull himself up by his nailed hands to speak. He saw Jesus take his last breath so he could shout out, "it is finished." It was a shout of victory. His task was finished. He had done the will of his Father. He had reconciled man to God, and as a silent witness to that truth, the temple veil was torn in two from top to bottom.

How do we witness to the death of the Lord?

97

Zacchaeus was up a tree, and he was enjoying it. Despite his wealth, he was not too proud to climb up a sycamore to watch Jesus pass by. Being small of stature, he could not see over the crowd lining the street, so he had to run on ahead to pick a suitable vantage point. I can imagine his delight when Jesus stopped, looked up, and told Zacchaeus that he would be eating with him that evening.

Now it is not every day that chief tax collectors get singled out for such a compliment. Most of us may prefer to forego the privilege of having dinner with a man from the Internal Revenue, even those of us who have nothing to hide. However, Zacchaeus was a special breed of taxman and was deeply resented, even hated, by the Jews for his collaboration with Rome. Yet Jesus wanted to eat with him, which indicated that Jesus wanted to get to know him. Zacchaeus was so honored by the visit that his life was changed from that very moment.

What Jesus had really said to Zacchaeus was, "Come down quickly. I *must* stay at your home tonight." Jesus knew why he had to go to the chief tax collector's house - he had to seek out the lost. Even lost enemies of the people; for enemies become friends when they are confronted with love. The loving gesture of Jesus prompted Zacchaeus to give half of his possessions away and to repay four-fold those whom he had cheated. That was quite an invitation Jesus made!

And yet, he has invited himself to eat with each one of us: "If anyone hears my voice and opens the door, I will come in and eat with him, and he with me." Revelation 3:20) Just like to Zacchaeus, Jesus asks us to respond quickly because he *must* stay with us today.

It does not matter who we are or what we have done. He came to seek out and save that which was lost - and we are all lost without him.

When, like Zacchaeus, we respond to his invitation we become changed people. Then we can pass his invitation on to others. We can invite them to his banquet because he said that he wants his house to be full. Many people have not been given the invitation; many others do not even know of its existence. That is where we come in. We can be bearers of official invitations to his banquet in the heavenly kingdom. His parables tell us that we can go out into the highways and byways telling all we meet that his banquet is ready and that they are welcome.

When God became man at the incarnation the greatest invitation was given to the human race. In Jesus, God extended to us an offer so great that only God could give it. He invited us to become members of his family and sharers in his divine nature. At the last supper, Jesus offered us his body and blood as a covenant and as a remembrance of his invitation to share in the life of God with him. Who could refuse such a gift?

98

"Life and death are in the power of the tongue." (Proverbs 18:21) This has many meanings. We have power in our tongues to destroy both ourselves and others. Fortunately, we also have the power to uplift and to edify, to ennoble and to encourage. Jesus gave us a solemn promise concerning how we speak. He said that on Judgment Day we would be held accountable for every unguarded word we speak. Yet he also said that our good words would acquit us.

James wrote that the tongue is an unruly evil, full of deadly poison. However, he pointed out that when we allow God's wisdom to govern our tongues, we become pure, peaceable, gentle, lenient, and rich in mercy and kindly deeds. Such is the power of the tongue! It is a small organ, but capable of great good and great harm. The sage Sirach noted that a meddlesome tongue "destroys walled cities and overthrows powerful dynasties." (Sirach 28: 14) Sirach also noted, "Many have fallen by the edge of the sword, but not as many as by the tongue." (Sirach 28:18) St Paul in his letter to the Ephesians wrote, "Never let evil talk pass your lips; say only the good things [people] need to hear, things that will really help them." (Ephesians 4: 29) How often do we say things that help no one, not even ourselves?

One scientist interested in the power of words claimed that the flowers he grew in his laboratory matured according to how he spoke to them: kind words produced abundant and luxuriant blooms; negative words produced stunted and sickly blooms. The report was probably apocryphal...but it ought to be true! Because that is what happens to our spirits, to the garden of our souls, when we speak and hear evil and malicious talk. We languish and grow spiritually weak, and our friendship with God wanes. We become victims of what we hear. We become a wasteland.

That is why it is so important to listen to lovely and uplifting words, words of power and goodness. Words, too, from Scripture which have the power to save us. (James 1:21) Words which renew, restore, remake, and refresh.

Our refrigerators are filled with good food to nourish our bodies with care. Yet we need other food, food of infinitely greater value. We need the word of God, the most enriching of foods. Yet too often our Bibles sit idly on the coffee table and all the while our inner self is starved for nourishment. In the Scriptures we have available the greatest promise ever made: "he who hears my word and believes in him who sent me, has eternal life." (John 5:24) What other food can promise that?

In place of negativity and harsh words, let us plant seeds of eternal life, which will reap a harvest to gladden the heart of God. And we will have an eternity to appreciate the fruit. We will also have an eternity of joy, gratitude, and bliss. "O Lord, set a watch before my mouth, a guard at the door of my lips." (Psalm 141:2)

99

Dear Teenager,

I am writing to tell you that you are more valuable than a million times your weight in precious gems. In God's eyes you are more beautiful than the universe. He made you to be his masterpiece; he carved you out of himself. That is why you are of inestimable worth. Diamonds will one-day turn to dust; you will live beyond time itself.

When God, your Father, made you, he used himself as a pattern and gave you his life force. It is no small thing to have God's life in you - it is an unparalleled and holy thing. You are called to be holy, noble, and filled with all that is good. You are your Father's treasure, his beloved, and his delight! He loves you beyond your ability to comprehend. His love is vast and forever beautiful. You are the apple of his eye, you are his beloved sons and daughters. He loves you as much as he loves his son Jesus.

You see, the Father promised us that if we accept Jesus, he will make us as much his child as Jesus is. Now that promise is given to you. It is a gift from the heart of God himself. Before you were born, he knew everything about you and it pleased him to call you into being. He has a special plan for you, just you, and no one else can give him what he asks from you. He made you irreplaceable: there will never be anyone else like you.

Inside you there is an empty space and he wants to fill it with his love. He cannot do that until you ask him to, for he values you too much to take advantage of you. He will never force you to come to him, but he will never tire of asking you to be with him. He understands your every mood and every thought. He does not think ill of you; but he loves you beyond measure. You are his and he is yours. He loves you so much that he gave his son for you, which means that there is nothing good that he will not do for you.

God is longing to share himself with you, and he wants you to share yourself with him. If you turn to him, he will come to you like the gentle warmth of the morning sun. He will impart his strength to you, and you will no longer be afraid of anything.

Your Father's love is pure and strong and it conquers everything. If you accept his love, you, too, can overcome all things. With such a Father by your side you can become as great as he wants you to be. He gave you life so you could live with him forever. Let him fill the vacuum of your heart with his grace and peace and love and joy. Even if you feel unloved, unlovely, and believe that you are not worthy of his love, he will prove to you that you are his heart's delight. He will show you the path to fullness of life and he will bathe you in his eternal light.

God is waiting for you to make the move and he will even give you the help you need to make the move. (Theologians call it prevenient grace; a grace to help you get grace.) Turn to him now...he awaits you.

100

An Anglo-Saxon poet described life in a most arresting way. He said, imagine a small hut with a fire at one end with open windows on opposite walls. A small bird inadvertently flies through one window, and for the briefest moment is touched by the warmth of the fire, then escapes through the other window. The time it took to fly from one window to the other - barely a second - is our life here on earth compared to eternity. Much of the time we live as if eternity were a mere moment, and life on earth were eternal.

If we are truthful, we have to admit that we spend more time collecting perishable things than we do imperishable ones. Jesus wanted us to realize this when he asked, "To whom will all this piled-up wealth of yours go?" (Luke 12:20) Certainly we won't get to take it with us.

Jesus urged us to store up treasure in heaven. The heavenly bank is thief and depression proof and pays a permanent dividend; yet we often prefer a bank of brick and mortar. Jesus also said, "Lend without expecting repayment." Now wait a minute, that's hardly good fiscal policy! Surely he can't mean it, can he? Some early Christians took him at his word. One lady was described in the following way: "She preferred to store her money in the stomachs of the needy rather than hide it in her purse." That's quite an epitaph.

Scripture has some life-changing instructions on giving to the needy. I am challenged by Proverbs 19:17: "He who is kind to the poor, lends to the Lord, and he will repay him for his good deed." There are also some very difficult sayings, for example, "He who shuts his ear to the cry of the poor will himself cry out and not be heard." (Proverbs 21:13) Then there is Jesus' hard saying, "give to everyone who begs from you." (Luke 6:30) Did he mean me, or the church? We prefer to leave that to others.

I consider Luke chapter six to be the great divide which every Christian has to cross. For not only are we asked to give to everyone who begs from us, but we are commanded to love our enemies. We have yet to obey that commandment. Even Christians do not love fellow Christians who believe differently: we have burned them, hung, drawn and quartered them, and tortured them too many times in the past. We have also murdered our brothers the Jews and treated them as sub-human and thought we were honoring God.

If we remember what Jesus taught, and if we remember the brevity of life and the endless eternity we face, we must not ignore his word. Enemies come and go, but his word lasts forever. With this in mind we can better appreciate Jesus' question, "Why do you call me 'Lord, Lord', but do not do what I tell you?" For the past nineteen hundred years, many of us have called him "Lord" without putting into practice what he taught.

The final word on this must be the Lord's: He told us in the most solemn way that what we do for the least among us, we do or fail to do for him. (Matthew 25)

101

Are you ever sad or depressed or burdened? Do you ever wonder where you are going or what the world is coming to? Have you ever felt alone and somehow out of place. Of course you have! Do you remember how you got rid of those feelings! Probably most of the time they just left. Sometimes, though, they clung to you like an octopus and drag you into the muddy depths of self-pity.

Well, I have a solution. There is a powerful and well-tested way out of those dark moods. It is called a *charaz*. Which means a string of pearls. You use it to praise God and like dynamite it can blast away depression, doubt and despair. Jesus,' mother prayed a *charaz* when she visited her cousin, Elizabeth. We call it the Magnificent, or Canticle of Mary. Zechariah prayed a *charaz* when he was filled with the Holy Spirit and prophesied about his son John.

So what is a *charaz?* It is a collection of verses from Scripture which you put together yourself in any order you wish: thus stringing pearls of praise to the Lord. There are myriads of ways of doing it. The Psalms alone have thousands upon thousands of possible combinations. You can have beautiful and creative prayers as you put together a new psalm of your own.

Allow me to give you an example of how I thread my string of pearls for the Lord:

> Lord, you work wonders for those who love you
> And you always listen when I call on you.
> For you are my hiding place. O Lord,
> And you fill my heart with gladness.
> You brighten the darkness about me.
> You deliver me from all harm.
> In distress I call to you.
> You deliver me from all evil.
> You are close to the brokenhearted.
> And to those who are crushed and dejected in spirit.
> And you keep me in perfect peace when my imagination is stayed on you.
> Amen!

Do you get the picture? It is simple, somehow deceptively simple, but it will lead you into God's presence if you pray it with a trusting heart. You can repeat your *charaz* often, for it is medicine for your whole being. Mix well. Then take it as needed. I recommend that you do it daily, perhaps several times a day. Make up as many as you like and you will find that your mind is being renewed by the power of praising God.

The Bible says, God inhabits the praises of his people. (Psalm 22:3 NKJV) Why not let him inhabit yours.

102

I would like to say more about the *charaz*, or string of pearls. The custom of threading scripture verses together on a string of praise to God has a long heritage. The Hasidic Jews still do it today. Many Jews put a Scripture verse (Deuteronomy 6:4-9) in a metal tube in the right doorpost of their home, so when the inhabitants enter of leave home they touch the doorpost and say a prayer. Some call this superstition, but it isn't. The touching is a gesture of reverence for God's word, and the heartfelt prayer is a love message to the Lord.

So it is with the *charaz*. It is a way of putting Scripture verses together to express praise and love of God. It is a wonderful way of lifting the mind and heart to God. Here is my "second string" which contains some more of the most beautiful verses in the Bible:

Call on me and I will answer you,
And I will tell you things great beyond reach of your knowledge.
For those who seek me diligently find me,
And I am with you always.
I will never leave you nor forsake you and I, the Lord your God,

Teach you what is for your good, and lead you
On the way you should go.
In joy you will go out,
In peace you will return.
No evil shall befall you,
Nor shall affliction come near your home.
Behold I stand at the door and knock. If anyone hears me calling
And opens the door, I will enter his house and eat with him.

Try making a string of pearls for a loved one, or for a friend's birthday. Perhaps you could send one to a sick friend as a get-well card. Your good wishes will have the lasting power of God's word. Scripture is so rich that you will never run out of possible variations. My own rough estimate is that the Psalms alone provide enough verses for many, many millions of variations on a theme. That's food for thought.

My favorite string of pearls is the Beatitudes, the great declaration of dependence on the Kingdom of God. "How blest are the poor in spirit, the Kingdom of God is theirs." We are blest because the minute we see our own spiritual poverty, we find out we have at hand the immense riches of God's word.

And so we can begin to string a new *charaz* on our total dependence on his endless love.

103

"When I found your words I devoured them, they became my joy and the happiness of my heart." (Jeremiah 15:16) Those who love God's word can relate to that. They understand that the Bible is a book of love messages from our heavenly Father where he speaks with love and wisdom to those who listen.

Most verses of Scripture come alive and nourish us when we prayerfully meditate on them. Some verses are so powerful that they are able to lift us from sadness and depression, from sin and self-seeking, and usher us into the very presence of God.

Mary, the mother of Jesus, understood the power of God's word. When the Angel told her God wanted her to become the mother of his son, she said, in effect, "he said it, therefore he will do it." That's great faith. Unlike the rest of us, Mary did not say, "Well, perhaps, possibly, maybe, somehow … he might do it." She knew the nature of God. She knew his word would not return to him void. Like every good Jewish girl she was familiar with Psalm 33: "By the word of the Lord the heavens were made."

The majestic prologue to John's Gospel states "In the beginning was the word … and the word was God … and the word became flesh and dwelt among us." There is great truth here, a truth which ought to encourage us to spend time reading the Scriptures. For the word has the power to save and transform us as James wrote. And Jerome warned that ignorance of the Bible is ignorance of Christ.

One particular verse which I have found to be powerfully effective in prayer is Mark 11:24. It is variously translated, but the literal Greek says: "Therefore I tell you, all things which you pray [for] and ask, believe that you [have] received, and it will be to you" (i.e., you will have it). In verse 22 Jesus literally said "Have [the] faith of God" with which we will be able to move mountains. But how can we have God's faith? And how can we believe that we have already received what we are asking for?

Jesus taught that faith in God is the key to receiving what we need. James urged us to always ask in faith. He said doubters do not get what they pray for, because they are doubting God's goodness. (James 1:17) Jesus reminded us that even sinful fathers give their children good things, so how much more will our heavenly Father give us the good things we need when we ask.

When we consider the nature of the one we are asking, our faith becomes God's faith because the Father gives us his own faith so that we can receive his abundant love. At least, that's how I have come to understand it.

104

"Blessed are the poor in spirit, for theirs if the kingdom of Heaven." (Matthew 5:3 NIV) This first of the Beatitudes is the door through which we enter into a deeper understanding of discipleship.

In order to receive the fullness of God's blessings which Jesus taught us in the Sermon on the Mount, we have to come to God empty handed. It is necessary to realize our own deep poverty of spirit before we can live the Beatitudes. I am struck by the fact that everyone, rich and poor alike, has to be poor in spirit in order to receive the reign or rule of God in their lives. Those who depend on their own resources miss the treasures waiting for the heart which is destitute before God. (In fact the word Matthew used for poor, *ptochos,* really means destitute.)

In Hebrew history, the poor were those who were totally without the means to support themselves. The Hebrew word for them was *anawim*, which often refers to the elderly, infants and the infirm, who were incapable of looking after themselves. They were totally dependent on others for their daily needs. To better understand what Jesus meant by "the poor in spirit" it is helpful to realize the original meaning of *anawim*. Whenever Israel was invaded and its inhabitants were carried off into captivity, the ones left behind to die were the elderly, the infirm and infants. They were the *anawim*.

Jesus said that if we are "*anawim*" in spirit, we will be blessed because the Kingdom of God is ours. This teaching, of course, runs counter to the wisdom of the world which honors the strong and the rich and powerful. (Sadly, even in the church they are often the ones given pride of place.) When we keep in mind what Jesus said about the poor in spirit, we can readily understand what he meant when he said, "Assuredly I say to you, whoever does not receive the kingdom as a little child, will by no means enter it." (Mark 10:15 NKJV) Obviously the poor in spirit are blessed because they recognize their total dependence on God for everything, just as a child must rely on her/his parents.

As long as we rely on our own understanding and try to live the spiritual life using our own resources, we will always be outsiders to the reign of God. The first Beatitude makes it clear that only those who are completely dependent on God for everything are blessed by the kingdom of God within them.

Our pride, self-reliance, and our habit of making God in our own image, are obstacles which prevent us from seeing our true poverty of Spirit. We are conditioned by everything around us to rely on our own strength and abilities. We are like frontier individualists determined to blaze our own trail. Yet if we forsake our own understanding (Luke 14:33), and surrender our lives completely to the Lord, becoming really poor in spirit, we find that in him are "hidden every treasure of wisdom and knowledge (Colossians 2:3).

In our poverty, we will become rich.

105

The common ministry of all Christians is prayer. When we pray, we enter more deeply into fellowship with the Lord, enabling him to drench us with his love. Unfortunately, prayer is the thing Christians generally do the least, when it ought to be our primary spiritual activity. If we want a deep, loving relationship with the

Father, and desire to experience his joy and his peace, we must seek him in prayer.

C. S. Lewis aptly stated, "If we want joy, power, peace, eternal life, you must get close to or even into the thing that has them." Prayer draws us close to God, and his peace becomes an impenetrable force within us. Prayer has incredible benefits. It changes those who pray and empowers them to help others. Prayer reveals one of God's greatest gifts: he imprints his desires on the praying heart, and gives it the gift of being a co-laborer with him in the mission of salvation.

Even before God made the universe, he knew each one of us and chose us to be his instruments of blessing to others. As Pascal termed it, God has given us the "dignity of causality," that is he lets us be creative co-workers with him.

I believe it is through prayer that we become the most creative, for we are united with him who is the creator of everything. It is during prayer that our Father blesses us the most, because he gifts us with his individual attention. We often complain that we are too busy to pray, yet paradoxically, the more we pray, the more time we have available for work. This is in accordance with Jesus' promise that if we put God first in our lives, he will give us everything we need - even more time. (Matthew 6:33)

Another important reason for spending more time in prayer is that God calls us to be intercessors for our nation and our world. In Ezekiel 22:30 the Lord told the prophet that he had searched for someone to stand in the gap and intercede for the nation, but had found no one. I wonder how many intercessors the Lord would find today praying for our world?

It is in intercession that we can fulfill the Christian's most powerful role. When we pray in faith, keeping true to his word and calling on his mercy, powerful forces come to our aid. Our prayers are part of the creative role that the Father has assigned us. As we spend more time with him, he allows us to cooperate with his heavenly will and lets us bring it to earth.

If we become intercessors for the needs of others, for the needs of the world, we will be helping to shape the eternal destiny of those who have no one to pray for them. In prayer we can move mountains of hate and misery and help to renew the face of the world. But if we do not stand in the gap, who will?

106

"If anyone thirst, let him come to me; let him drink who believes in me…from within him rivers of living water shall flow" (John 7:37-38) Of course, Jesus was referring to the Holy Sprit which all believers in him receive. As Jesus told the woman at Jacob's well, those who drink the water which he gives will never be thirsty again. The water he gives becomes "a spring … gushing up to eternal life." (John 4:14 NRSV)

This "living water" is the fulfillment of the great promise of Isaiah 55:

> All you who are thirsty, come to the water!
> You who have no money, come receive grain and eat.
> Come without paying and without cost …

This invitation is for everyone; all of us in our inner being thirst for what is the supreme good. We are all invited to share in the blessings of unending grace.

Sometimes when I think of this "living water" which is the glorious presence of the Holy Spirit within us, I am reminded of the longing David had in the cave of Adullam. He said to his men, "Oh, that someone would give me a drink from the well of Bethlehem." (I Chronicles II: 17 NKJV) David longed for that cool draught of water so much that three of his bravest captains went through the Philistine stronghold at great personal risk to draw water for him from the well by the gate at Bethlehem.

Today there are many brave missionaries who are risking their lives to bring the living water of the gospel into countries where Christianity is opposed. They are ambassadors of Jesus and regardless of personal cost they share the good news of the one who "will lead them to springs of life-giving water." (Revelation 7:17)

Billions of people around the world do not know the Lord. As surprising as it may seem, even in America there are many who are ignorant of the gospel. Therefore, those who love the Lord have a great opportunity to spread the good news of salvation and to bear witness to what God has done in their lives. One of the great promises in Matthew's gospel has to do with witnessing about Jesus: "Whoever acknowledges me before men I will acknowledge before my Father in heaven." (Matthew 10:32)

Hence those who have experienced that life-giving water are obligated to share it with others, either by word or action, as the Spirit leads them. But it is not a burden; rather it is a delight! Telling others about Jesus is full of joy. To see him work in the lives of others, especially those who were burdened by sin and pain, is life's greatest joy.

Let us spread the joy of the Lord by telling others that Jesus lives.

107

Someone has written that "Good Friday was for a day, but Easter is forever." That is because Jesus is alive, and his power, ever flowing from his resurrection, is available to those who seek him.

His resurrection power blinded Saul on the road to Damascus, and instantly converted him. Many years later, Paul wrote to the Philippians that he wanted to know the power flowing from the resurrection of Jesus. (Philippians 3:10) It makes me wonder that after thirty years as an apostle, working in the power of the Holy Spirit, Paul should still be seeking the resurrection power of Jesus.

I am also struck by the fact that he said he wanted "to know" Jesus. This is the same Paul who had met Jesus on the Damascus road, and later was taken up to the third heaven. Surely he already knew the Lord and his power?

But Paul was not satisfied even with a miraculous apparition of the Lord. He wanted to know Jesus in the same way that the Lord knew him - he wanted a deep and intimate knowledge of God. (Like Augustine later on), Paul knew we were called to be Easter people living in the glory of the risen Lord. Paul was aware of what the Resurrection meant for mankind. He knew that Easter is a time of hope reborn, a time of life renewed, a time of faith replenished, and a time of peace restored.

Paul was certain that the knowledge of Christ and of his Resurrection meant knowing it in the heart and not only in the head. He wanted to continually grow in the grace and power of the risen Lord.

He was sure that Jesus lived. In his letter to the Ephesians he wrote of the "exceeding greatness of his power in us who believe." (Ephesians 1:19) It was the power which burst upon the disciples at the Resurrection and at Pentecost. He said that he gloried in "him who is able to do exceedingly abundantly above all that we ask or think, according to the power that works in us." (Ephesians 3:20)

The power which Paul was seeking flowed from the Resurrection. It is the power to conquer sin (Romans 6:6-11); it is the power to bring lasting peace to our hearts and families

(John 20:19); it is the power to quicken our mortal bodies and give them true life. (Romans 8:11)

Certainly Paul wrote eloquently of the Resurrection and what it meant for the world. Yet he sought more and more to know the Lord in his heart who filled him with his love. That is why he could write, "I run toward the prize to which God calls me - life on high in Christ Jesus." (Philippians 3: 14) That prize awaits each of us.

Jesus said, "Go into all the world and proclaim the good news" (Mark 16: 15) that is what Easter is, marvelous good news. Let us proclaim it by the way we live.

108

"I don't want your sacrifices - I want your love. I don't want your offerings - I want you to know me." (Micah 6:6 The Living Bible) That states clearly and succinctly what the Lord expects of us. He wants to be part of our lives so that we can get to know him and thus love what we know.

Scripture gives many examples of just how much the Father wants us to share our lives with him. In his afternoon strolls with Adam, and in his friendship with Abraham, God revealed that he enjoys the company of his children. In his intimacy with Moses, and in his revelations to the prophets, the Lord shows himself eager for our love. In fact, so deeply does he long for his people that he gave his most precious gift, Jesus, as proof of his love. In addition, he sent the Holy Spirit to enable us to love like him.

Even our sinfulness and our inability to live holy lives has not prevented him from reaching into our insensitive hearts. For as he said through Hosea, he knows that we are incapable of turning to him on our own, so he himself heals our unrepentant hearts with his love. This is poetically portrayed in Hosea 14 where he says that he will envelop us like the morning dew and we shall grow in beauty like the lily. Those are tender words of a loving heart. Sometimes I think he loves us too much!

Considering how little we love him in return, how our hearts appear to be far from him, and how are few and feeble are our prayers, it is no wonder that the Lord said through Hosea, "they have not cried to me from their heart." (Hosea 7:14) Do we ever cry to him from our hearts just for his own sake? Have we surrendered our hearts to him in acts of selfless love? Have we cried out to him like Isaiah and said, "Here I am Lord. Send me."

No doubt we have all experienced the tug of his love encouraging us to heroic self-surrender. Perhaps for a while we have even tried to live up to the standard of love set by Jesus. Yet, how quickly we slip back into the world of self-seeking materialism, where Jesus is no longer the great love of our lives.

Fortunately the Lord will not rest until we are back in the favored position he wants for us. Listen to his promise in Ezekiel 34 (NKJV) "I myself will search for my sheep and seek them out ... I will feed them in good pasture ... I will seek what was lost...and bind up the broken and strengthen what was sick." That is a powerful message for our post-modern world. And Jesus underscored the same message in John's gospel, saying that he is the Good Shepherd who has come to give us life and to protect us from the wolves who prey on us.

The Bible clearly teaches that we are loved by God, and if we allow that love to enter into our hearts we will be able to love him in return and to love others in the overflow of his love.

109

"If anyone is in Christ, he is a new creation." (II Corinthians 5:17) So powerful is this truth that St. Paul used the word *kainos* for new, instead of the word, *neos*. *Kainos* means new in the sense of completely new, as something never having existed before. For example, when the Wright brothers flew at Kitty Hawk, they could quite correctly have said that their airplane was *Kainos*, something completely new and original. So when Paul wrote that in Christ we are a new creation, he meant that we become something quite new and different from what we formerly were. That is a profound idea.

In his letter to the Romans, Paul taught that we are baptized into Christ Jesus, both into his death and into his resurrection, which Paul calls new (*kainos*) life. This new life is different from the old one, for it is a life united to the resurrection power of Jesus. (Romans 6:4-5) Obviously, that is indeed a new life.

It is customary on New Year's day to make new resolutions and to decide to give up old unwanted habits; few of those resolutions make it through January. The newness wears off almost at once. But it is not that way with the newness given by the Lord. He has given us the Holy Spirit to lead us into ever new dimensions of his love. (Modern physics has a theory which posits eleven dimensions! However, God's love has unending dimensions and is ever new and fresh.) His word tells us that he makes all things new (*kaina*, the plural of *kainos*). (Revelation 21:5)

When he gives us new life, it is life born of the Spirit. So even though our bodies are growing old, our inner beings are being renewed day by day. (II Corinthians 4:16) This spiritual renewal, according to Psalm 103:5 gives us the power of eagles to soar upwards. Isaiah also promised that if we would sit before the Lord and wait on him, we would renew our strength and soar to the heavens on the wings of eagles. When God renews us, we become truly new.

Jesus came among us to teach us how to live with God here and now. He wanted to restore our relationship with his father and thus enable us to boldly approach the throne of grace in the newness of life. His cross, the old instrument of torture and death, became for us the means of newness of life - indeed for the *kainos* life, which is everlasting. "For Christ suffered once for sins, the just for the unjust, that he might lead us to God, being put to death in the flesh but made alive by the Spirit." (I Peter 3:18 NKJV)

So in him we are made new and empowered to live holy lives by the Spirit.

110

"I had heard of you by word of mouth, but now I see you with my eye." (Job 42:5) Surprisingly, it was only after great anguish and rejection that Job could make such a powerful confession. In his days of prosperity, Job only knew about God (in Hebrew he said by "hearing of the ear"); in his days of sickness and pain he found God face to face: he knew God and rejoiced in his presence.

If we would ask Job whether he though his sufferings were beneficial he would surely say "yes." Although he railed against the injustice of his intense suffering, he came out of his trials with the greatest treasure of all - a deep relationship with the living God. Job discovered that the only lasting joy in life is being in love with God. Even his questions were no longer important after his encounter with God. He had asked God some of the most penetrating and perplexing questions, but when he was allowed to meet the one who knows all things, he no longer needed the answers.

Job did not need the answers any more because he knew the one who has all the answers. Listen to what he said to the Lord: "I have dealt with great things that I do not understand; things too wonderful for me, which I cannot know...Therefore I disown what I have said, and I repent in dust and ashes." (Job 42:2-3)

How much like Job we are in our complaints, but how unlike him in our admission of guilt. Many of us refuse to admit that we are angry with God, and unlike Job, we fail to face up to the fact that we really don't know God at all. We only know about him, or as Job said, we have only hearsay knowledge of him.

A sure test of our relationship with the Lord is how we deal with difficulties. When beset with tribulations do we believe that God is with us in our pain and that he is master of the situation, and we can rely on his love. Or do we give in to our circumstances and blame God for being absent? Difficulties either draw us closer to God or pull us away from him. It all depends on our attitude.

Countless books have been written about suffering and pain, and the struggles which humanity is heir to, and there is nothing I can add to those volumes. Yet, when I examine what Job said, I believe there is an important truth to be highlighted.

When Job said, "I have seen you with my eye," he could also have meant, "I have seen you with my affliction," because *ayin* in Hebrew means both eye and affliction. So Job found out God was with him even in his misery and his crushing loss of all that he had. In fact, it would be permissible to say that without Job's terrible afflictions, he would never have met God and known his wonderful love and mercy.

111

"Do not sorrow, for the joy of the Lord is your strength." (Nehemiah 8:10) Not only is that good advice, but it is true. The joy of the Lord is a powerful force. In fact, the word for strength could be translated fortress, or stronghold, indicating that his joy fortifies us against "the slings and arrows of outrageous fortune." (Shakespeare)

To be a Christian means to be joyful, for joy is a fruit of the Holy Spirit. We are expected to spread joy and to foster its growth. Joy grows by prayer, and when we pray we enter the presence of God where there is fullness of joy, where he turns our sorrow into dancing for joy. (Psalm 30:11) For some of us, it has been too long since we danced for joy.

David prayed that God would give him back the "joy of salvation." (Psalm 51:12) How often do we equate the word joy with salvation? Jesus assured his followers that his own joy was available to them, a joy that is full and unending. It seems to me that joyful Christians are in the minority - some even consider them to be strange or even fanatical. One joyous Christian I know was accused of living in his own bubble going blindly through life unseeing. I wonder what they would say about Francis of Assisi?

A lovely verse on joy is I Peter1: 8 (JB). It says that even though we have never seen Jesus, we "are already filled with a joy so glorious that it cannot be described." As another translation puts it, we rejoice with joy inexpressible and full of glory." (NKJV) How many of us have experienced such joy?

But if we haven't, there is no need to lose heart; there is a way to receive that "unutterable and exalted joy" (I Peter I: 8 RSV) the way is Jesus. Scripture says, "with joy you will draw water at the well of salvation." (Isaiah 12:3) Salvation in Hebrew is *yeshuah*, which also is the name of Jesus. So Jesus is the fountain of joy, and our fellowship with him means lasting joy.

St. Paul taught that joy was a natural ingredient in the Christian's life. Even though he was whipped five times, beaten with rods three times, stoned, imprisoned, and shipwrecked three times, he could write that our lives were to be peaceful and joyful in the Holy Spirit (Romans 14:17) Surely Paul knew something about letting joy overcome adversity! Our problem is that too often we let our difficulties extinguish our joy. We grumble about our problems and tell others about them instead of talking to the Lord - the true problem solver.

The Rabbis had a saying: "there is no joy without wine." Perhaps that is one of the reasons why Jesus changed 180 gallons of water into wine at Cana. He was saying "when I am in your life, there will surely be great joy."

112

"It is he who is our peace." (Ephesians 2:14) What does it mean that Jesus is our peace? That depends on the meaning of the word. In Greek the word means cessation of hostilities, to be in harmony with someone. In some circumstances in can mean welfare, or union after separation.

For the first century Christian, it also meant health, spiritual and physical well-being, to be whole, which is the original meaning of *shalom* in Hebrew. So we can say that Jesus is our welfare, our well-being, our health and our union with the Father. This peace of Jesus is so important that after his resurrection he made a point of emphasizing it three times to his followers. (John 20:19-26) It is the peace which garrisons hearts and minds and gives them calm in the midst of turmoil. (Philippians 4:7) When we receive such peace we are safe from the ravages of evil. (See Psalm 91)

The peace which Jesus gives is a peace with God and the peace of God. When we receive such a gift we are safe the from ravages of spiritual evil. In the preamble to every one of his letters, St. Paul gave to his readers the blessing, "grace and peace to you from God our Father and the Lord Jesus Christ." He knew how vital they were. Not only must we be at peace with God, but we must be at peace with our neighbors and be at peace within ourselves. The presence of Jesus guarantees such a three-fold peace.

Isaiah called Jesus, "The Prince of Peace" and prophesied that he would bring lasting tranquility. (Isaiah 9:5-6) At his birth the angels sang of peace, and at the last supper before he died he gave peace to his disciples. The peace he gave made us friends of God as well as his children. On the cross, by his transcendent gift of love, he became our peace and reconciliation. With outstretched arms he offered heaven to the whole world and no one is beyond his reach. All are called to be the children of the Father.

So we are God's children, with all the rights and privileges that being in God's family entails, but how lightly we accept such an invaluable and wondrous gift. How poorly we often live our daily lives in his family. Do we ever think about what Paul said to the Athenians about the Lord, "In him we live and move and have our being." I think if we understood what it means "to live in Christ" we would live at peace with everyone and bring the light of Jesus to shine in the darkness of hatred and prejudice.

As St. Paul said, "let the peace of God rule your hearts," and thus allow it to change us, "for God has called us to peace." (I Corinthians 7:15) When we allow God's peace to penetrate our hearts we can begin to let his peace flow through us to others. We are called to be peacemakers and reconcilers, promoters of justice and truth. Peace on earth has to begin within us, before can we help others to know the peace of the Lord.

113

"Thy kingdom come." Many people think that this refers to God's kingdom which is to come at the end of the world. Others believe it is a prayer to hasten the Millennium. Some of us see it as asking God's rule to come now in our hearts. The kingdom of God is not a place; it is wherever he is honored and worshipped and loved.

In his letter to the Colossians, St. Paul assured Christians that the Father had already "rescued us from the power of darkness and brought us into the kingdom of his beloved son." (Colossians 1:13) That is powerful good news. In addition, Paul wrote that in baptism we were not only buried with Christ, but that we were also raised with him. The Greek is very specific, saying we were "co-raised" with him. The implications of that for the church are awe inspiring. It is no wonder that Paul wanted us to "attain full knowledge and spiritual insight" (Colossians 1:9), for without that insight we are unable to grasp the full meaning of God's word.

The Bible assures us that we can enter God's presence whenever we wish, that his kingdom rule is in our midst, but how reluctantly we take advantage of such a truth. We are also too often forgetful of the privilege Jesus gained for us. He has made us members of the household of God we are citizens of heaven, or as James Moffat translated it, "We are a colony of Heaven." When I first read that I was startled by its implications.

Many times we fail to live up to the grace which is so freely lavished on us as heirs to the kingdom of God's son. We forget that the Lord can do "exceedingly abundantly above all that we can ask or think." (Ephesians 3:29 NKJV) Furthermore, he will supply every need fully "in a way worthy of his magnificent riches in Christ Jesus." (Philippians 4:19) Is it any wonder St. Paul said that he had "accounted all things rubbish" in order that Christ could be his wealth.

Surely he is our wealth, too? But as the New American Bible notes, "Everyone is busy seeking his own interests rather than those of Christ Jesus." (Philippians 2:21) When we spend more time with mundane matters than we do seeking the kingdom of God, we are bound to adopt the attitudes of this world rather than those of the Kingdom.

Jesus warned us that we cannot serve two masters, we cannot swear allegiance to two kingdoms. He said quite clearly that we are to "seek first the kingdom of God." (Matthew 6:33) Isn't it sad that we behave as if he had said seek his kingdom second...or last! He taught that the kingdom or rule of God is within us, and that his Father and the Holy Spirit, and he himself would live within us when we are true to his word. On the Mount of Transfiguration, we were told to listen to Jesus. We know we should, because he has the words of eternal life.

But how often do we really listen to what Jesus says?

114

"Yes, I have loved you with an everlasting love." (Jeremiah 31:3) If we let that verse penetrate our whole being, we will be greatly blessed. For we will allow the Father's love to soak into our hearts, we will get rid of fear and doubt, since his perfect love casts out all fear. Furthermore, his love enables us to love others without conditions. For as the prophet Malachi powerfully reminds us, we all have the same Father and consequently we must deal lovingly with one another. (Malachi 2:10)

However, all too often we ignore God's love, living as if there were no such thing and we become insensitive to his gentle tug on our hearts. It is then easier to judge our neighbor rather than love him. But the Lord has commanded us to love our neighbor as ourselves. In John's gospel he made loving one another a demand. (John 15:12) At least it can be translated that way. Which indicates how reluctant we are to love some of our "unlovely" neighbors.

The prophet Hosea noted that we are often cold hearted when it comes to returning God's love. Poignantly he speaks of God's tenderness towards us:

> I drew them with human cords, with bands of love;
> I fostered them like one
> Who raises an infant to his cheeks;
> Yet, though I stooped to feed my child,
> They did not know that I was their healer. (Hosea 11:4)

In a similar vein, the Lord complained through the prophet Micah asking what had he done to us that we are weary of him. The Lord said that he only required of us to act justly, do what is right, and walk humbly with him in love. (Micah 6:8) When we do walk with him he gives peace to our agitated hearts with his loving presence, as Zephaniah said. According to the same prophet he made an unusual promise - he said that he would sing for joy over us as one would sing at a wonderful festival. (Zephaniah 3:17) What an incredible thought, that the Father would sing for us with joy!

It is no wonder that Psalm 119 says "My heart stands in awe of your word" for his word brings hope and beauty to an aching heart. The psalmist then says, "I rejoice at your word as one who finds great treasure." (Psalm 119; 162 NKJV) How true that is: his word is full of precious nuggets. Here is one gem we can hang on our heart: "The Lord takes delight in his people" (Psalm 149:4) How seldom do we realize that our Father delights in us. Finds pleasure in us! If we realized the extent of his love we would run to him and share in his delight.

Jesus told us it was his Father's "good pleasure" to give us the kingdom. What are we pleased to give him? If we give him our hearts, even though they may be tarnished, and if we rejoice in him, he will grant us our deepest desires. (Psalm 37:4) Who could wish for anything more?

115

"His emblem over me is love." (Song of Songs: 2:4) Emblem can be translated banner, pennant, or flag. There is a delightful meaning here. When the Lord unfurls his flag, he is waving his love over us; it is not a standard for battle, rather it is an ensign of peace and good will, because his love is without self-interest. He loves us without expecting a return. (But he wants us to return his love, also without self-interest.)

His love for us is so great that "while we were still sinners" he died for us. (Romans 5:8) Such love impels us towards the lover; it attracts us with its purity and truth. When we accept the gift of his death incredible things happen to us, not the least of which is that we experience the Father's love, which is exactly the same love the Father has for Jesus. (John 17:23) If we let this message penetrate our being it will transform us; the love of God will melt our hearts and give us the ability to love others without expecting anything in return.

Indeed, his banner over us is his love and grace which he has lavished on us. His emblem on that banner tells us that "the gift of God is eternal life in Christ Jesus our Lord." (Romans 6:23) It tells us that we were beloved of God even before the foundation of the world (Ephesians 1:4) His love is everlasting and will never diminish. He delights in his children and longs to fill us with his gifts of grace. As a perfect lover, God wants us to live in peace and joy so we can relish the transcendence of his love, which is freely and bountifully given.

Now that is a flag which we could gladly wave.

I have wondered what colors God's flag would have, but I am unable to decide how multi-hued it would be. Yet I am sure it would be radiant and translucent and dazzle the eyes with its splendor, and stir our hearts with its noble coat of arms. It is a pennant we can carry with unflinching patriotism.

I have wondered what size and shape his flag would be. Perhaps pennant-shaped with a bold border, or maybe a grand rectangle bordered with the stars of heaven. Of this, though, I am sure, it would outshine all other flags with its beauty and truth.

What I have written sounds fanciful, yet it has a deep message within it. As a flag represents a country, so would God's flag represent him. Since he is love, it is altogether fitting that his banner over us is love, and once unfurled will remain with us forever.

116

"Come to me all you who are weary and find life burdensome, and I will refresh you. Take my yoke upon your shoulders and learn from me, for I am gentle and humble of heart. Your souls will find rest for my yoke is easy and my burden is light." (Matthew 11:28-30) These are comforting words for our troubled world. They contain the sure promise of rest and peace; the two things most needed in our fast-paced restless society. In addition to his promise of rest, Jesus offers us a real treasure: he promises to take our burdens and give us in exchange his own yoke, which is light and easy to carry; it is a perfect fit. Actually the word easy could be equally translated as benevolent, or pleasant, or even beneficial.

His burden is beneficial because he his yoked to us and we carry it together with him. Actually, he balances the load and takes upon himself the things we are unable to carry. (In the rabbinical writing around the time of Jesus, the yoke was the *tefillim* and the *shema* which every Jew recited daily. They took on the yoke of Torah. We are invited to take on the yoke of Jesus, the living Torah.) In Jesus we have a partner who wants to carry our burdens. St. Peter understood this perfectly, for he wrote "cast your cares on him because he cares for you." (I Peter 5:7)

There is great comfort in Peter's words. Yet all too often we grumble and complain and look for someone to blame when we are troubled. We often fail to take our problems to the Lord for his solace. I suspect the reason why many people are slow to seek the Lord is because they have given up the habit of prayer. I use the word habit advisedly: prayer must be as natural a part of our day as getting dressed or eating dinner. (How often do we forget to get dressed or to eat dinner?)

Prayer should be as natural as breathing. We tend to make it a chore, or something we <u>have</u> to do, when prayer should really be very easy: it is acknowledging and thanking God for his love and asking him to bless all we meet with the same love. At least that's a good start. As we pray more we find that God is an ever-present help in time of need and an ever-present friend in whom we can confide. In this way we come to know God, rather than merely know about him. To know God is the greatest blessing of all, and we experience that blessing in prayer. We will no longer be satisfied knowing about God; we will have a deep hunger to know him more and more.

Job learned that lesson well. He had heard about God, but when he met God he was stunned to silence - he realized that he had never really known what God was like. His understanding of what God was like had been learned from others who also did not know God. That can be said of many of us. But if we pray often and earnestly, we will have a real encounter with God. We will be transformed by him into his friends. Every day he will be yoked to us in joy or sorrow.

The Living Bible translates Matthew 11:28-29, "Come to me and I will give you rest - all of you who work so hard beneath a heavy yoke. Wear my yoke - for it fits perfectly." His yoke fits because he fashions it individually for each one of us.

117

"Praised be the God and Father of our Lord Jesus Christ, who has bestowed on us in Christ every spiritual blessings in the heavens." (Ephesians 1:3) I am thrilled and amazed by the power of that verse. It says that when we are in Christ, we have everything. The one who has God, in truth, does have everything.

The question which comes to mind is "what are we doing with such incredible blessings which have been given us?" Are we using them to grow in love and service as the Lord wants, or are we ignoring those blessings altogether? Indescribable blessings are available to us whenever we ask for them in faith. (Psalm 68:19 NKJV) Incredible blessings are available to us so we can grow in service to others. As God told Abraham, he blessed him so he could be a blessing to all nations. St. Paul said we are blessed so we can be "imitators of God as dear children." (Ephesians 5:1 RSV)

How is it possible to imitate God? We can begin by forgiving one another as he has forgiven us. In fact, we are commanded to forgive, and Jesus said that if we do not forgive, we will not be forgiven. Jesus made it plain that being forgiven by God depends on how we forgive others. We have to work hard on that.

We can also imitate God by loving one another. Jesus said that love is the fulfillment of the law. He expects us to love others and to do good to them, even though they may not be loveable or good. As he said God let his sunshine on the just and the unjust alike.

In what other ways can we imitate God? Scripture says we must be perfect as our heavenly Father is perfect. How is that possible? It depends on what Jesus meant by perfect. In Matthew 5:48 the word for perfect is *teleios*, which means "having attained the end or purpose for which it was intended." Now that makes Jesus' statement much more understandable. It means, imitate God by being true to his design for you. Another way of putting it is, "be a complete whole person as your Father meant you to be,"

I pray that we can obey that word.

Each one of us in Christ has the grace available to be a whole person. In reality, we have more than enough help available, for the Bible says, "My God will supply every need of yours according to his riches in glory." (Philippians 4:19 RSV) Those two promises, "he will supply every need" and that we have "every spiritual blessing" are wonderful and life-changing truths. They will enable us to live as God calls us to live in Christ Jesus our Lord.

118

"What are you looking for?" Those are the first words spoken by Jesus in the Gospel of John. They are the words we all must take to heart in our search for meaning in life. We have to know what we are really looking for; if we are not looking for the truth we will surely lose our way.

When Jesus asked Andrew and his companion what they were looking for, they replied, "Teacher, where do you live?" Jesus answered, "Come and see." Isn't that the same invitation he offers us? He says come and see where I dwell; come and see who I am; come and see what I have to share with you.

That has been the heart cry of God throughout the ages: come to me that you may have life. He calls come to me, come and eat of my bread and of what is good and what will delight you with abundant joy. (Isaiah 55:1-2) How often we turn down the invitation to dine with him! We refuse to have supper with the Lord of glory Too often we prefer the fast-food which the world has to offer.

Taste and see how good the Lord is, the psalmist exhorts us, but we have little desire for his banquet; he may ask something of us that we are unwilling to give to him. However, God is patient and long-suffering. He continually beckons us through his prophets, through his word, and through his church. He repeatedly calls us to seek him that we may find rest in him.

If only we would hear him and place our trust in his love, we would have the strength to change, and thus to help change what is wrong in our society. If we surrender to him, he will enrich our lives in such a way that we will bring hope to those who experience sadness and despair. We will be able to bring to him the suffering so that he can give them peace of mind. So that he can give them rest. Those who are hurting long for relief from pain, from heartache, from loneliness, from want, from guilt and from sin.

He wants us to work with him in rescuing the lost. He esteems us in such a manner that he asks us to be co-laborers with him in his vineyard. How often we ignore his call or refuse to answer it when we hear it. He told us to go out into the whole world and bring the lost to him. We have glorious good news which we are keeping to ourselves. When someone hears that God loves them right where they are they begin to have hope They can see the possibility of change. If we love God, we will surely share the joy we have found with anyone willing to listen.

How long is it since you asked someone to come and worship the Lord with you? When did you last invite somebody to "come and taste the goodness of the Lord" in the church where you worship? You see, if you have found him, you know where he lives. Tell them to" come and see."

119

`I have treasured the words of his mouth more than my necessary food." (Job 23:12 NKJV) Job's reverence for God's word is worthy of imitation. What Job said can be understood on two levels. On the one hand it can mean skipping a meal to study Scripture. On the other hand, it means that God's word- our spiritual food - is more important than food for the body. For his word teaches about his will for us.

Jesus made it clear that God's will was paramount in life when at Jacob's well he told his disciples, "I have food to eat which you do not know." Of course, the disciples misunderstood and thought someone else had given him something to eat. So he explained to them: "Doing the will of him who sent me and bringing his work to completion is my food." (John 4:31-34)

In addition to being our food and his will for us, God's word is also our light. Psalm 119 aptly states that God's word "is a lamp to our feet and a light to our path." The same psalm also teaches us that when God's word enters our heart it brings with it light, understanding and revelation, even to "the simple."

Perhaps no one in the last thousand years was as simple as St. Francis of Assisi. He prayed earnestly that the Father would enlighten the darkness of his mind with the light of his word. How wonderfully the Lord answered Francis's prayer, and how Francis became truly simple when he understood and lived the words of Jesus!

As well as shedding light, God's word gives life and healing. (Psalms 107 & 119) And as James tells us, God's word saves us. (James 1:21) No wonder Job believed that God's word was more desirable than the choicest food. (Scripture teaches us in many places that the word of the Lord is sweeter than the honey in the honeycomb, and it satisfies the deepest desires of the heart.)

The most luminous revelation of what God's word is, can be found in the majestic prologue to the fourth Gospel: "In the beginning was the Word, and the Word was with God, and the Word was God." It is Jesus himself who is the living word of God and he satisfies the greatest longings and fills the deepest voids in the human spirit.

The Word became flesh and "we have seen his glory, the glory of an only son coming from the Father, filled with grace and truth." (John 1:14 RNAB) The word of God became flesh so that mankind could see the message of God's heart in all its glory. In Jesus we see the word of power, the word of light, the word of healing, the word of salvation, and the word of renewal and restoration. He is the fullness of God's word to us; he is the perfect embodiment of the father's love. (John 14:9)

His word discerns *the* thoughts and intentions, of the heart - allow him to pierce your heart with his word of truth and love, to lay bare all the areas where without him our thoughts are futile. (I Corinthians 3:20)

120

Do we believe that we have been created to be God's treasure? In Isaiah 43:7 the Lord said that everyone called by his name had been created for his glory. The word glory used in this verse comes from an ancient Hebrew word meaning riches. In other words, God considers us to be part of his treasure. That is a humbling thought, but also wonderful when we consider that God made us to enrich himself (Some theologians will probably have trouble with that idea.)

I know one theologian, however, who would accept that thought, because he teaches that the Pearl of Great Price is really each one of us, for whom Jesus gave up everything, even his life, which puts a very high value on our lives. Human life is sacred and highly esteemed by God. For example, the Lord said, "you are precious in my eyes, and glorious... and I love you." (Isaiah 43:4) John's Gospel states that God loves us so much he gave his only begotten son to set us free.

So what does that make us, the ones for whom God gave so much? It means that we are more than priceless. God's gift of the Holy Spirit is a further indication of our value in his eyes. That should enable us to live amazingly blessed lives.

But we are very slow to accept the truth that God does indeed love and value us, and that he made us to share his blessings. We struggle with the idea that he wants us to be close to him and to be blessed so we can bless others. We never feel worthy of him and find it difficult to accept that he loves us unconditionally. His good news seems too good to be true.

Psalm 103:2 says, "Bless the Lord. 0 my soul, and forget not all his benefits." What great advice! If we think often of the blessings which the Father has given us and we are thankful for them, we become joyful and gracious people. Just as soon as we understand how he has blessed us, we become eager to bless others.

When we accept the truth that we are his beloved, we become free to love others and free to share with them his surpassing goodness. We no longer harbor prejudice and hatred, rather we give up being judgmental in order to get rid of the beam in our own eye. Such is the power of his love.

When we survey the life of Jesus and see how he loved and cared for people, we get an idea of the Father's love for his children. Jesus is the "exact representation of the Father's being," (Hebrews 1:3) therefore we see the Father at work in the miracles of Jesus. We hear the Father's voice in the words of Jesus. And above all, we see the Father's love in the sacrifice of Jesus. How can we not believe that we are God's prized possession?

121

"What do you want me to do for you?" How would you answer if Jesus asked that question of you. What would you ask for?

Blind Bartimaeus knew what to ask for and he received it. The father of the possessed boy knew what he wanted, and he also received it. So did the lepers, the blind, and the lame who came to Jesus. The four men who lowered the paralytic through the roof of the house in Capernaum saw Jesus grant their friend's request for healing before they had a chance to ask for help. The Syro-Phoenician woman delighted Jesus by her reply about the little dogs eating crumbs under the children's table and got what she was looking for.

She was a remarkable woman, because she understood better than some of the Pharisees what bread on the children's table meant. She knew that the bread Jesus talked about was the blessings of the covenant which God had provided for his people. She believed in God's promises even though she was not a Jew. We can learn much from her faith. We. too, can approach the table of the New Covenant with her kind of trust and receive all that has been promised.

The Syro-Phoenician woman was not put off, she pressed ahead with her desire to have her daughter set free. She knew what

Jesus could do; she knew what God had promised, and she knew what she wanted. I am encouraged by her simple understanding of who God is. She believed God heals and delivers, so she expected that he would heal her daughter.

Jesus did not ask her what she wanted as he did Bartimaeus because she did not need to be asked - her persistence spoke for her. She was determined to have her daughter restored and she would not give up. She is an excellent model for us of how to pray, She asked, she believed, and she received. (In Mark 11:23 Jesus made the amazing statement that if we are prepared to believe that we have already received what we ask for, it will be given.)

Her approach to Jesus was direct and simple. How unlike her we are. We have become so sophisticated and so aware of modern psychological ideas that we have almost intellectualized away the Gospel. We have forgotten that the gospel is truly good news. Jesus said that we have been given the Kingdom and that all its benefits and blessings are ours. But we write volumes wondering just what kingdom really means.

When Jesus said, "Ask and it shall be given to you... for everyone who asks receives.", (Matthew 7:7-8) he meant it. God's children are constantly asking and are constantly receiving, for God is what his word says he is: he is provider, healer, restorer, redeemer, forgiver, savior and Father.

Listen and hear him say, "What do you want me to do for you?" (Mark 10:51)

122

"Do not be afraid, little flock, for your Father has been pleased to give you the kingdom." (Luke 12:32 NIV) When we understand and believe this saying of Jesus, our lives become transformed by the power of its truth. We realize that the kingdom is already ours and fear no longer has a place in our lives. Love, peace, joy, faith, are all gifts, and they are given to us when we surrender our hearts to the Lord and receive his kingdom.

God's gift of the kingdom is not some unattainable prize which a capricious master holds out to those who do his bidding. Rather it is a free, undeserved gift, which only a heart of love could give. One of our difficulties in accepting such love is that we feel unworthy. All our lives we have been told that if we want to be accepted we must conform to certain expectations. As children we learn that gifts are earned, and if we are very good, we receive the best Christmas presents.

We sometimes bring this attitude to our relationship with God. We play at pleasing him, and we bargain with him; we even try to bribe him. Obviously, all to no avail. What our Father is asking of us is to approach him with a sincere heart. He wants us to be transparent before him so we can be transparent to ourselves. He asks us to return his love, and he does not bargain or play games with us.

In his sublime letter to the Ephesians, St. Paul summed up the immensity of God's love for us when he wrote that God had given us every spiritual blessing in the heavens. "Every blessing" is an enormous gift, and we could spend a lifetime contemplating the implications of that verse. We have received all we need to live out the New Testament's commandment to imitate Christ in our daily lives and to serve the needs of others.

I suspect that many people cannot accept the truth that we have been given all those blessings because it sounds too good to be true. Perhaps others refuse to believe it because they think it defies reason, They ask themselves how could God have given the kingdom and his spiritual blessings to believers who are weak and uninspiring. But it is the weak who need God's grace more than the strong. God comes to those who depend on him and want him and cannot live without him.

The truth of the matter is that in our weakness there is great power, for Jesus himself said to St. Paul that his power reaches perfection in weakness, and in consequence Paul could say, "when I am powerless, it is then that I am strong." (2 Corinthians 12: 8-10) In truth, it is much better to be weak so that Christ can be our strength.

Such is the power of truth that when we admit our failings and weaknesses we can have the Lord Jesus Christ as our strength.

123

The beginning of wisdom is fear of the Lord." (Proverbs 1:7) I once read a very appealing translation of that verse: "The choicest part of wisdom is reverence for God." I do not remember who translated it, but it captures the meaning of the Hebrew word *reshith* which is usually translated as beginning and can also mean first or principal thing. So I prefer to think of it that way because true reverence for God is among the choicest of blessings.

Fear of the Lord, that deep and reverential awe, respect and love of almighty God is a gift to be sought after and esteemed. Scripture gives many examples of the blessings bestowed on those who stand in awe of the Lord. For example, in Psalm 25 we read this about it:

> Who is the man that fears the Lord?
> Him shall he teach in the way he chooses. He himself shall dwell in prosperity,
> And his descendants shall inherit the earth.
> The secret of the Lord is with those who fear him,
> And he will show them his covenant. (Psalm 25: 12-14 NKJV)

Those few lines speak volumes.

Psalm 19 teaches that fear of the Lord "is pure, enduring forever." (NIV) This reminds me of what Jesus said in his Sermon on the Mount: "Blessed are the pure of heart, for they shall see God." (Matthew 5:8) If we want to see God, we must be pure of heart, and in order to be pure, we must have fear of the Lord. We are shown in Psalm 34 how to fear the Lord. Among the several amazing promises in that psalm is the statement that those who fear the Lord will want for nothing.

A wonderfully encouraging word for parents is Proverbs 14:26, which promises that if we fear the Lord he will be a refuge even for our children. Through fear of the Lord St. Monica rescued her son Augustine from a life of immorality and he became one of the church's greatest theologians. St. Bridget of Sweden reverenced and loved the Lord so much that she saved her son Charles from a dissolute life. So, too, countless other mothers whose love of God brought salvation to their offspring.

The prophet Isaiah observed that fear of the Lord is a man's treasure. (Isaiah 33:6) It surely is! When we seek to serve him in heartfelt reverence and love, we are taught by the Holy Spirit how to venerate and worship the Lord. Then we find the pearl of great price and the buried treasure of God's kingdom.

In addition to leading us into authentic worship and love of God, fear of the Lord enables us to love one another as the Lord commanded. That's what Paul learnt on the Damascus Road. For him, his new found reverence for God was indeed the choicest part of wisdom.

124

"The river of God is full of water." (Psalm 65:9 RSV) That is a refreshing verse to those suffering a drought. It is even more refreshing to those suffering from spiritual dryness and aridity.

Happily, God's river is not the only thing that is full. His storehouse is full, and so is his heart. There is nothing but fullness in him. He is full of peace, full of love, full of beauty, full of glory, and full of grace and truth. Isaiah said that all the earth is full of God's glory. (Isaiah 6:3) And of that Glory ours is a share in its fullness. (John 1:16)

That is a wonderful truth. We have been called to share in the glory of God. Jesus said everything the Father has is his, and Jesus has given us a share in his fathers blessings. He has imparted to us a share in the fullness of his light; the true light which dispels the darkness of our minds. It is a light which darkness can never apprehend or overcome.

We ought to rejoice over such knowledge. How can we not be joyful when we consider the loving kindness with which the Father blesses us every day. It is no wonder that Isaiah urged us to shout out with joy, because God is great among us. (Isaiah 12:6) He is among us and within us, and beside us and above us. He surrounds us with the majesty of his presence. His fullness permeates everything if only we have eyes to see.

When we begin to look, Isaiah says, we will see the splendor of God and we "shall be radiant at what we see." (Isaiah 60:5) The desert of our hearts will burst into flower and the dry river beds will run with water. His spirit will fill us with divine love and he will renew us in that love.

The fullness of God's holiness is not a prize we earn; rather it is a gift to be received. Jesus told us how we can become holy. In his Sermon on the Mount, he solemnly assured us that if we hunger and thirst for holiness, we would be filled with it. (Matthew 5:6)

Thus we become partakers of the divine nature as Peter taught. (II Peter 1:4) We get a marvelous portion of God's love, and as Paul wrote we receive with that love "the immeasurable scope of his power" when we believe. (Ephesians 1:19) So let us rejoice! For we have been promised the fullness of God.

But in return, the Lord asks for our fullness. He wants us to offer him everything that we are and hope to be. As someone said, he wants our heart, because the heart of religion is the heart. If that is so, then we have the heart of God in our midst from which flows an endless torrent of his love.

125

Every time we consider the love and goodness of God we ought to be overwhelmed by his kindness towards us. He has freely given us "exceedingly great and precious promises" which, when we receive them, enable us to live lives of spiritual beauty and power in the midst of our day to day lives. (II Peter 1:2-4 NKJV)

Often, however, we do not spend any time meditating on those surpassing gifts and promises of God. We pass over them lightly as if they were promises of mere men. We fail to realize the integrity and power which stands behind those words.

For example, Jesus gave us his solemn word that the one "who has faith in me will do the works I do, and greater far than these." (John 14:12) Have you ever wondered what he meant by that? Have you ever considered that to be true and that it was meant for all of us who follow him? Only rarely has a believer dared to live by those words of Jesus.

Again, have we ever considered the promise of God which says that when we obey his word we become his "special treasure?" (Exodus 19:5) Equally worth contemplating are the words of Jesus which promises us his very own peace and joy. There does not seem to be a lot of peace and joy around these days. It seems we do not take Jesus literally at his word.

In an earlier reflection I wrote about Brother Lawrence, a man who took Jesus at his word. He believed that "all things are possible to him who believes," and he had no doubts that joy and peace were his "for the receiving," So he opened his mind and heart many times a day to receive what Jesus had promised. Before long Brother Lawrence was filled with peace and joy which never left him. He died at the age of eighty, full of the joy, peace, and love of Jesus (If you have not already read it, I highly recommend his book, <u>Practicing the Presence of God.</u>)

There are hundreds of promises in the Bible, each one of them is backed by the honor and majesty of God. Each word, as Jesus taught, is worthy of our wholehearted allegiance. Like Brother Lawrence, we can put into daily practice the living word of God.

Those who are not in the habit of thinking about God and his promises on a daily basis could change their lives by taking up the practice. You could start by reciting a few times a day the powerful verse, `Any who did accept him, he empowered to become children of God." (John 1:12) Or you could consider these startling words, "Call to me, and I will answer you: I will tell you great things beyond the reach of your knowledge." (Jeremiah 33:3,which one preacher referred to as God's telephone number) The Living Bible translates that verse in this way: "Ask me and I will tell you some remarkable secrets."

Do you believe he will answer your call?

126

"Be still and know that I am God." (Psalm 46:10 RSV) If we can do that, we will be greatly blessed. Unfortunately, we are in danger of losing the ability of sitting still before God in loving worship. We are too busy, people of action, and prayer that requires silence and contemplation seems foreign to our materialistic and assertive age. We hate to "waste time," even for God.

Yet if we want to let God into out lives, we have to learn to find him in silence. C. S. Lewis said that God will only shout at us in our tragedies. Most of the time he waits for us in silence. Too many people wait for disaster before they will hear him. Elijah's experience is helpful here. Elijah experienced the storms and noise of life, but he had learned to find God in silence. On the Mountain of God he heard "a still small voice, or a "whisper" as one translation says. But I like the translation which says he met God "in a sound of gentle stillness." (I Kings 19:12 ASV) The Lord stood before him in silence.

Yes, Elijah found out the beauty of silence, and when he did, "he hid his face in his cloak," in other words, the experience overwhelmed him.

Isaiah, too, understood the need for silent waiting on the Lord of all creation, for he wrote, `By waiting and by calm you shall be saved, in quietness and in trust your strength lies. (Isaiah 30:15) We need calm and quiet in our lives because noise meets us almost everywhere we go. Unrest is rampant throughout society and we desperately need to be quiet and alone with God. We need the peace of God which refreshes and renews us.

Perhaps the most striking example in the Bible of the significance of silence is found in Revelation 8:1. "When the Lamb broke the seventh seal, there was silence in heaven for about half an hour." It is interesting what followed the silence: "from the angel's hand the smoke of the incense went up before God, and with it the prayers of God's people" (Revelation 8:4) If heaven treats our prayers that way, how much more ought we to offer the Lord our silence?

If we spend five minutes a day waiting on the Lord in silence before we speak to him, we will find that "doing nothing" for God has great rewards. As we grow in the ability to silently be present to the Lord, we will find peace and rest in him. His love will permeate our whole being. He will silently impress on our hearts his words of love. We may never hear a sound, but we will know that we have been with God.

127

As Jesus was on his way to the house of Jairus to heal the synagogue leader's daughter, a woman in the crowd reached out and touched the tassel on the corner of his garment. Immediately power went out of him, and "the feeling that she was cured of her affliction ran through her whole body." (Mark 5:29)

Approaching Jesus she said to herself, "If I just touch his clothes, I will be healed." (Mark 5:28 NIV) She received according to her faith, and Jesus honored her faith by acknowledging it in front of the whole crowd. Jesus knew, of course, that many people had touched him, but he also knew that only one touched him with faith. Despite her condition, which made her ritually unclean and subject to punishment for appearing in public, she had approached Jesus. Her faith was greater than her fear of punishment.

I am impressed by her powerful trust in the Lord. She went to him fully convinced that by merely touching his clothing she would be healed. Her faith was rewarded. But she received more than physical healing: Jesus gave her salvation and peace.

Every day we have the opportunity to touch the Lord in faith and be made whole. Every day he is among us and within us waiting for our response to his call on our lives. Like Samuel in the temple at Shiloh we can hear the Lord call us by name, and like Samuel we can respond, "Speak, Lord, your servant is listening" (I Samuel 3:10) Or we can pray like Isaiah saying, "Here I am, send me." (Isaiah 6:8) Perhaps we can quote Psalm 40 and say, "Behold I come... To do your will, O my God, is my delight." God will not spurn our reaching out to him.

Each response, is pleasing to the Lord, for the Bible clearly teaches that God responds according to our faith. (Matthew 21:22 and Hebrews 11:6) Our faith, as Scripture shows, "is the substance of things hoped for, the evidence of things not seen." (Hebrews 11:1 NKJV) In other words, our faith is a concrete, tangible gift we combine with prayer to reach out and touch the heart of God. The woman who touched Jesus believed that.

A noted preacher once remarked that the woman's faith was especially noteworthy "because she wasn't even baptized." By that I think he was saying that we who are baptized ought to have at least as much faith as she had.

Her kind of faith is contagious, because in the next chapter of Mark we read of others imitating her boldness. Mark laconically put it like this. "All who touched him got well" (Mark 6:56) Do we ever reach out to touch him ... with faith?

It is common today to belittle such "fundamentalist" faith, for intelligent people know better, they say. But I have encountered such people who, when suddenly struck with some cruel change of fortune, then turn to those with faith asking for prayer. In their heart they know that faith is more than contagious, it is effective.

128

What would you do if God suddenly said, "You are my delight! I love you"? That is exactly what he has said through the prophet Isaiah. He also said that we are his joy, and that he would exult in us. Furthermore, he is so eager to hear from us that he promised to answer us even before we begin to speak (Isaiah 65:18-19,24) It seems incredible, but I believe it.

I would like to share with you how I came to "experience" the truth that God loves me. It happened some years ago while I was feeding the birds in my garden, something I did every day. On that particular day I was worried about several things and my usual optimism had temporarily deserted me. As I threw some seed on the ground for the sparrows, the thought struck me that despite my troubles I had not forgotten to feed my friends. Then I remembered the words of Jesus, "Look at the birds of the air: they neither sow nor reap nor gather into barns, and yet your heavenly Father feeds them," and he does it with prime birdseed.

I asked myself why was I feeding the birds. It was because I loved them and delighted in them and I never tired of their antics - I even overlooked their squabbling and their territorial feistiness. They were my friends and I cared for them. Even when I had problems, they were not forgotten. It was this realization that I had not forgotten them which triggered that moment of new understanding, that moment of great joy and peace. With a flash of insight, I knew that the Father would never forget me either. (Isaiah 49:15)

I stood in the yard, overwhelmed by the fact that the creator of the universe cared for me. Even though there are over six billion people on earth, he knows my name and cherishes me. I am his, and he is pleased to care for me, despite my squabbling and territorial feistiness. (That is my religious affiliation and doctrinal defensiveness.) Then I recalled the words of Jesus, "Do not live in fear little flock, it has pleased my father to give you the kingdom." He has, he has given it to all of us. Every good thing we have comes from him, even my birdseed.

Suddenly my optimism returned. I knew I was loved and worth more than a whole flock of sparrows - as the Lord had said. I was certain that The Lord would help me in my need, for if I who am sinful had given good seed to his sparrows, how much more would the heavenly Father give me the good things I need when I ask. (Matthew 7:11)

So I asked him, and he gave.

129

Almost twenty years ago I witnessed something truly remarkable. I was at my friend's house when a dove flew into his porch door, breaking a wing and it's beak The bird was bloodied and incapable of flight. My friend picked up the bird and asked the Lord to heal it. Nothing happened. Then in a moment of spontaneous honesty, he shouted out to God, "Father, if I could help this bird and you asked me to heal it, I would do it for you. Why won't you do it for me?"

What happened next astounded me. As soon as my friend had spoken, the dove flew away, none the worse for its encounter with the door. The man was awe-struck by God's immediate response, and he was humbled by the way the Father responded to a prayer of the heart.

There are some powerful lessons to be learned from my friend's experience. Perhaps the most important one is how the Lord responded to a heartfelt prayer. Sometimes our "praying:" gets in the way of our encounter with God: we can often be caught up in the words we are using and forget to whom we are talking. Another valuable lesson I learned that day was my friend's honesty and openness to God. He blurted out his prayer from the heart without thinking. He said to me later that it was the best prayer he ever said.

As I thought about that dove and God's providence, I was reminded of the Lord's own words about the birds of the air and how our Heavenly Father cares for them. I thought, too, about the psalmist who asked the Lord to "hide me in the shadow of your wings." That is the image Jesus used when he wept over Jerusalem. He said he longed to gather the children "as a hen gathers her chicks under her wings, but you were not willing." (Matthew 23: 37) Surely that is a marvelous picture of the way God wants to care for us? But are we willing?

I think we often reject some of the Lord's most delightful advances. While the Lord is trying to protect and comfort us in our moments of grief or doubts or hopelessness, we are stubbornly clinging to our emotions and refuse to seek his consolation.

Our problem is that we prefer to rely on our own understanding of things. We want to keep God at a safe distance and we want him to be the God we want him to be, rather than who he really is. That is why in Proverbs 3:5 we are told not to rely on our own understanding. God knows how faulty it can be. However, when we give up our preconceived ideas of who God is, and of how we want him to act, we are ready to let the Lord show us who he really is.

When we do that, and pray from a heart humbled before him, he reveals himself, and we are never the same. We are truly in the shadow of his wings.

130

In psalm 81 the Lord told Israel that if they would hear him and follow his counsel, he would feed them with the finest wheat and fill them with honey from the rock. Since all of us have been grafted onto the vine of Israel (Romans 11), we, too, if we heed the Lord will share in the finest wheat and honey from the rock.

I understand that promise to be a spiritual one in addition to its obvious meaning. The finest wheat is the Eucharist which the Lord instituted at the Last Supper. The honey is the words of Jesus, the rock of our salvation. Like the rock which Moses struck to save the Israelites from dying of thirst, Jesus, the rock, gives us food and living water with his very words.

Psalm 81 continues the metaphor with a life changing verse: "Open wide your mouth and I will fill it." (Psalm 81: 11b) He will fill it with physical as well as spiritual food. Jesus fulfilled this verse in several ways. In the sixth chapter of John's Gospel Jesus had fed the five thousand with five barley loaves and two dried fish. The next day the crowd went to find Jesus who had gone across the Lake to Capernaum. He said they were looking for him because they had eaten their fill of the bread he gave them, and admonished them for seeking "perishable food." He tol them to seek "for food that remains unto life eternal, food which the Son of Man will give to you." (John 6:27)

When he told them that he would give them heavenly bread, they said, "Sir give us this bread always." (v.34) Jesus then said, "I am the bread of life." But when he claimed, "I am the bread that came down from heaven," they protested and began to murmur against him. Yet Jesus went further. He told them that he indeed was the bread from heaven and whoever eats that bread will live forever. The people murmured again and asked, "how can he give us his flesh to eat?"Jesus replied: "Let me solemnly assure you.,if you do not eat the flesh of the Son of Man and drink his blood, you have no life in you. He who feeds on my flesh and drinks my blood has life eternal life and I will raise him up on the last day. (John 6:53-54)

John went on to say "From that point on many of disciples broke away and would not remain in his company any longer." They just could not believe it.

Somewhat later in Rome many Christians were put to death for believing that the Eucharist was Jesus truly present. They were called cannibals. Such was the controversy raised by the adoration of Jesus in the Eucharist.

Two thousand years later those words of Jesus still cause disagreement.

131

The Roman crucifixion was a brutal and terrible way to die. Those who saw men die that way never forgot the experience. One Roman writer said the memory of a crucifixion he had witnessed haunted him for more than twenty years.

Before crucifying a condemned man the executioners would first "soften him up" with the *flagellum,* the Roman cat-o'-nine-tails. Cunningly intertwined with bits of bone and lead, the Roman whip would tear out pieces of flesh when it was applied. Some executioners were so adept with the *flagellum that* they could tear off an ear or gouge out an eye, yet making sure they did not kill the victim. Even so, some did die under the whip.

After the whipping, the prisoner would be forced to carry the *patibulum* or crossbeam to the place of execution. They would make the prisoner walk the longest route, often through winding, crowd-filled streets. They did this to demonstrate Roman power and to show condign punishment to those who brooked Rome's edicts. In Jesus' case, little did they realize that it was a demonstration of God's power, the power of love.

When they reached the place of execution the condemned man was nailed to the crossbeam and then hauled screaming onto the upright, which had been left there since the previous execution. His feet were nailed to the upright, and he was left to die a slow, cruel death, which when it came was a blessed relief. Such was the terrible death Jesus endured for us. What kind of love would lead a man to die like that? What kind of man would suffer excruciating torture for ungrateful sinners? What kind of Father would let his son be brutalized and degraded like that? Have you ever wondered why?

Obviously, mankind was in such a serious state of rebellion and denial of sin that only the perfect obedience of a perfect man could restore the breach between mankind and God. Jesus was that perfect man. Yet to his countrymen his death was a stumbling block, and it was foolishness to the Gentiles. Even today it is a stumbling block and often brushed aside as folly. A crucified God can only be perceived by faith and love. Reason can explain, but love believes. Reason can persuade, but love convinces, "For love bears all things, believes all things, hopes all things, endures all things." (I Corinthians 13:7)

That love which emptied itself out on the cross- yet it can never really be emptied out - is offered to us at this moment. God lavishes his love in a constant outpouring and asks us to let it soak in like the spring rains on a parched earth.

His love cries out down through the ages saying, this is my beloved son look at him; this is my beloved son, listen to him; this is my beloved son, follow him; this is my beloved son. imitate him. We have the power to do it, the empty tomb and Pentecost are proof of that.

132

"And Enoch walked with God." (Genesis 5:24) Could that be said of you and me? Are we joyfully walking up the road with the Lord like Bartimaeus, or are we walking away from Jesus like the rich young man who went sadly away?

John the Baptist urged his followers to prepare the way for the Lord and to make straight his paths. He repeated the prophecy of Isaiah concerning the Lord's highway upon which the redeemed would walk. Isaiah said that once we walk on "the highway of holiness" gladness and joy would overtake us. He said we would experience blessings, and sorrow and mourning would flee away. (Isaiah 35:8-10)

Isaiah painted quite a picture for those who follow the Lord. He said God would make a highway in the wasteland, and he would renew their lives so powerfully that they would soar like eagles. (Isaiah 40:31) He urged them to go up to a high mountain and cry out the good news that God is their midst. That commission was renewed by Jesus who told all of us to proclaim that the kingdom of God is among us. Thus we would fulfill the prophecy of Isaiah: "How beautiful on the mountains are the feet of him who brings good news... announcing salvation and saying to Zion, "Your God is King." (Isaiah 52:7)

The prophet said our comings and goings would be filled with joy and peace. (Isaiah 52:12) He said we would rise up in splendor and the glory of the Lord would shine upon us. We would be anointed with the oil of gladness, and be clothed in the garments of praise and be wrapped in the robes of justice and salvation. Furthermore, Isaiah proclaimed God's promise that he would create us anew to be his joy and his delight. He promised that we would be greatly blessed, and that God would answer our prayers just as soon as we begin to pray. (See Isaiah 60, 61 & 65)

Do we believe that?

Have we begun the journey on the highway of holiness? If we follow Jesus we are already well on the road. It is a journey of love and praise and prayer and exultation; a journey of renewal and restoration. It is a pilgrimage of faith in the majesty and goodness of God. Those who travel on that highway are destined to encounter the beauty of God and to experience his all-encompassing love. Those pilgrims will hunger and thirst for justice and will seek to help the poor and the marginalized and the downtrodden. They will have compassion on the weak and the sick. They will feed the hungry and have concern for those suffering injustice and want. In a word, they will follow the lead of Jesus who pointed out the way by his life.

He said that he is the way, and that he is the real way to the Father. He is the way that leads to the heart of God. Those on the highway of holiness are called upon to point it out to others by the way they live. All those who find the Lord's highway take the greatest journey of their lives.

133

Have you ever watched a seed germinate? Have you noticed how it grows in two directions at once. One part grows into the earth whilst the other part reaches up to the light. The seed of God's word does the same.

A seed is such a small thing, yet from one seed there can spring up countless others. As Emerson put it, "There are a thousand forests in an acorn." So it is with the seed of God's word. Jesus said the kingdom of heaven is like a mustard seed. It is tiny, but packed with the potential for amazing growth. Like a regular seed, God's seed grows in two directions at once: it reaches up to heaven for light and power and it also holds tenaciously to the earth.

Jesus taught that his word is like a seed., pregnant with a powerful life force within it. He illustrated an amazing truth: as large plants come from miniscule beginnings, so, too, does the kingdom of God. The seed begins small in our hearts when we receive his word of truth. Then, if the light and soil are right, the ensuing growth is inevitable and abundant. As more seeds are planted, the harvest of love, peace, and joy is prolific and healthy. In a parable found only in Mark's gospel, Jesus preached on the mystery of growth in his kingdom, and he indicated that the increase would be sure and vigorous. (Mark 4: 26-29)

So if you are experiencing a time of spiritual dryness when nothing seems to grow, or perhaps you feel that God is not close to you, take heart! He has promised that his word will take root within you and lift you heavenward. He is the light you need for growth, so persevere in seeking him.

The seed which grows within is an incorruptible one which guarantees eternal life. Let us imitate the psalmist who proclaimed that he had hidden God's word in his heart so that he would not sin against his Lord. (Psalm 119:11) St. Paul said, "The word is near you, on your lips and in your heart (that is the word of faith which we preach.)" The word of God is a light and a lamp showing the way we are to live. It teaches us "to be" before we can "do."

When we water the seeds planted in us by prayer they grow and burst into bloom to brighten the life around us. His word has limitless riches which enliven our homes and our work. We can share with others the blessings he gives us; and share the joy and the glorious good news that Jesus is alive in our midst. We can take that news wherever we go, planting seeds of joy and power.

Sadly, the word of God is in danger of slipping into disuse. Almost every Christian has a Bible, but many do not read it regularly. St Jerome wisely said, ignorance of the word is ignorance of Christ. After all, Jesus is called the Word. In the postmodern Europe few believe in the Bible and fewer believe in Jesus. Unbelief for a generation destroys the seeds of faith. Who will sow them anew? Will you?

134

"Out of the depths I cry to you 0 Lord; Lord, hear my voice!" (Psalm 130:1) How often have we cried out from the depths of our distress to receive mercy and kindness from our God.? His mercy is always forthcoming and he does not delay in quieting the anxious heart.

Psalm 127 teaches the surest way to live at peace without the stress of modern living:

> It is vain for you to rise early,
> or put off your rest,
> You that eat hard-earned bread,
> For he gives to his beloved in sleep. (Psalm 127:2)

In the Sermon on the Mount Jesus taught us to trust our heavenly Father for all our needs and not to worry about the future. "Look at the birds in the sky. They do not sow or reap, they gather nothing into barns, yet your heavenly Father feeds them... Which of you by worrying can add a moment to his life-span... Seek first his kingship over you, his way of holiness, and all these things will be given you besides." (Matthew 6:26-33) For two thousand years countless Christians have found that to be true. In my opinion, the greatest modern believer who lived that truth was Mother Teresa. Her trust in the providence of God to supply the needs of her thousands of sisters and the poor they cared for was unshakeable. And I had the opportunity many times to witness it.

Our modern way of thinking looks askance at such "naive" faith. We are too realistic and intelligent to trust that we will receive all we need merely by seeking and trusting God. We are sure that it will be by our own efforts and shrewdness that we get what we need (even all that we want). To leave our future to a far-away God seems uncertain at best, and unrealistic at worst. No, we are responsible for our own well-being and we alone have the power to make our future.

But trust in Divine Providence is the greatest cure for many of our contemporary neuroses. Too many people are afraid of loosing their jobs, of sickness, of financial collapse, and a host of other fears. They are worried and stressed out. The cure is sure and simple, yet it seems too good to be true. It is the wonderful middle verse in the Gospel of Luke:" Do not live in fear, little flock. It has pleased your Father to give you the kingdom." (Luke 12:32) Trust in the Lord is the most comforting and stress-relieving medicine we can take, it is free and the only side effect is peace of mind.

Unfortunately, even many church-goers only pay lip service to the truth that God will take full responsibility for a life fully surrendered to him. On Sunday we sing and place our trust in him; on weekdays we grumble and place our trust in money. What a wretched trade-off, to exchange the love of the Father for a debased currency. It is written on our money that "In God we trust." But is it written on our hearts?

135

"The message of the cross is complete absurdity to those who are headed for ruin, but to us who are experiencing salvation it is the power of God." (I Corinthians 1:18) St. Paul was so convinced of the power of the cross that he told the Corinthians as long as he was among them he would only speak of "Jesus Christ and him crucified." He must have preached some powerful sermons.

In Athens, Paul using philosophical arguments tried but failed to convince his listeners of the truth of Christianity. The other teachers and philosophers called him a seed picker, or rag-picker, hinting that he had plagiarized someone else's ideas. Rather quickly Paul gave up "wise argumentation" and instead clearly portrayed the crucifixion of Jesus(as he had to the Galatians) and then he gained some converts. (Acts 17:16-34)

It is no different today. The cross speaks powerfully of God's love, and as Jesus promised, when he is lifted up, he will draw us to himself. But he does more. As the prophetic action of Moses with the brass serpent predicted, those who look on the crucified Lord with eyes of faith are made whole.

The Apostle Peter knew first hand the healing love which flows from the cross of Jesus. That is why he repeated the prophecy of Isaiah, reminding us that we are healed by the stripes of Jesus. (I peter 2:24)

Before Jesus died, he told his followers that unless they take up their cross and follow him, they were not worthy of him. (Matthew 10:39) Those are stark words. Yet, the Lord promised great blessings to those who were not offended by his message. (Matthew 11:6) Jesus promised life to those who would shoulder the cross. That is the life we need today - God's life. With his life in us we can deny our egocentric behavior and courageously take up the cross and follow Jesus. The only way to the resurrection power of Jesus is through the cross.

Almost six hundred years before the crucifixion, Ezekiel found out the saving power of the cross. The Lord showed him that those marked with the Hebrew letter *taw* on their foreheads would be saved. (Ezekiel 9:4-6) In Ezekiel's day the letter *taw* was shaped like a cross!

The cross is a constant reminder of God's love. It is a sign of his desire to reconcile us to himself, and a sign of his deep desire for fellowship with us. Also, it is proof that the Father wants to give us everything we need to live lives pleasing to him. (Romans 8:32) As Jesus hung on the cross, he abolished in his flesh the enmity which separated us from God. How tragic it is that billions do not know the way to peace. They do not know the crucified Lord of Glory who brings reconciliation to those who seek him. If we do not tell them, who will?

136

During the persecution of Christians by the Roman Emperor Nero, two friends were confronted by the authorities and ordered to forsake Christ in favor of Nero. If they refused, they would be burned to death. One of the friends was so afraid that he denied the Lord and agreed to call Nero divine. The other friend remained faithful to Jesus and was condemned to death.

Nero was fond of fires, especially when it meant burning Christians whom he blamed for the great fire of Rome. He had them chained to pillars, daubed with pitch, and set them alight using them as grisly candles to light up his palace gardens during nightly revelries. It was to such a fate that the friend loyal to the Lord was led away. The soldiers tied him to a pillar, covered him with pitch, and set him alight. From a safe distance the apostate friend watched in horror as the executioners brutally put his friend to death.

As he watched his friend's agony, he saw a strange light coming from the dying man's countenance. It was as if the life ebbing from the burning martyr was brighter than all the flames burning in that infernal palace garden. In a matter of seconds the man who had turned his back on Jesus and on his friend repented of his cowardice. He ran towards his dying friend and shouted, "Nero is a tyrant! Jesus is Lord!" He said he would rather die than live under the evil Nero. He got his wish. Quickly the guards fastened him to a pillar and he died a martyr alongside his friend.

What had he seen in that strange light emanating from his burning friend? Others saw it too and believed that it was caused by a sudden updraft of air which fanned the flames with a bright intensity. But he believed he had seen the light of Christ. As he died he bore testimony to the Light.

I am persuaded by ancient writers that the incident was probably true. Eye witnesses, who later accepted the Lord, gave their account of what happened. The persecutions by other tyrants, such as Diocletian, Valerian, and Trajan, record similar heroic deaths of believers for the sake of Jesus.

So many Christians were put to death in the early centuries of Christianity that it became a truism to say that the church flourished on the blood of martyrs. But what of the recent past? Well, church historians say that more Christians died for the faith in the Twentieth Century than in all previous centuries.

If that is so, then we can expect a wonderful harvest of conversions, for that is what happened in the Roman Empire. The more Christians that were put to death in the Empire, the more people turned to Christ. And Jesus had promised growth and persecution: he also said that a seed had to die in order to bear fruit.

This makes me wonder if my commitment to the Lord is strong enough to bear that kind of fruit? Is yours?

137

"When you discover the door of your heart, you discover the gate of heaven." So wrote St. John Chrysostom, the Fourth Century Patriarch of Constantinople. He is absolutely right. For when we love Jesus, the living God comes to reside in our hearts, and sets up a dwelling place within us. (John 14:23)

Whenever we open the door of our hearts we enter into a glorious communion with the Lord. Writing about fellowship with God, St. Paul told the church at Ephesus about its sublime mystery: "And I pray that Christ will be more and more at home in your hearts, living within you as you trust in him. May your roots go down deep into the soil of God's marvelous love... to experience this love for yourselves, though it is so great that you will never see the end of it, or fully know or understand it. And so, at last, you will be filled up with God himself." (Ephesians 3:17-18 The Living Bible)

But how is such a thing possible? It is brought about by faith, love, and prayer. Jude's letter expressed it this way: "But you, beloved, grow strong in your holy faith through prayer in the Holy Spirit." (Jude v.20) We grow strong in faith as we pray in the Spirit, seeking God's will rather than our own. When we understand that his will for us is greater than any desire we may have for ourselves, and when we willingly accept the truth that his will is perfect, and when we submit ourselves to his lordship, we are indeed knocking at the gate of heaven.

All of us are called to that life of faith and prayer. Sadly, though, we do not give the Lord enough time to flood our hearts with his love and power. Yet his door is ever open, as his word promises. (Revelation 3: 8) If we really examine ourselves and see just how much we need his presence in our lives, we will readily open our hearts to him. If we sit before him daily, allowing him to impress his love and his perfect will on our hearts, surely we will be changed and empowered to live joyful lives for him.

As we enter into this life of love and prayer, we will experience the truth of this promise: "All of us, gazing on the Lord's glory with unveiled faces, are being transformed from glory to glory into his very image by the Lord who is the Spirit." (II Corinthians 3:18) That is a marvelous description of prayer. We sit with unveiled faces and look at the goodness of the Lord. Then he pours out on us an ever increasing portion of his glory, and he does not stop until we are changed into his very image.

Jesus promised that he would give us life, life in abundance. Such abundance is our inheritance, granted us by the power flowing from the resurrection of Jesus. Let us open wide the doors of our heart to receive the indescribable presence of God's ineffable love.

138

Some twenty years or so ago, a Rabbi wrote a book about why bad things happen to good people. It was a best seller, because people have pondered the problem of innocent suffering for thousands of years seeking an answer. One of the oldest recorded attempts to answer the question is the book of Job which deals extensively with the problems of evil and suffering. Its conclusions are profound and uplifting.

The one result of Job's questioning that I found the most rewarding is patterned after the wisdom found in Genesis 50:20, which clearly states that what is meant for evil God turns into good. For when all of Job's trials were over, and they were many and severe, he could say that he had found God in the greatest way. Before his greatest hardships he had only known God by hearsay; after his terrible ordeal he said, "I have seen God." In other words, he had previously only known about God; after his suffering, he had a relationship with God.

One reason for the problem of suffering often cited has to do with free will. Since God gave us the power to choose between good and evil, he cannot intervene and thwart our freedom of choice when we decide to do something wicked. Our transgressions may also inflict pain on others. For example: the free will of promiscuous adults can result in a child being born with aids. God cannot be blamed for that...and certainly the child is innocent of wrongdoing.

But ultimately, there is no satisfactory human answer to the problem of innocent suffering. So perhaps it might be more appropriate to rephrase the question and ask, "What should good people do when bad things happen to them?" After all Jesus warned us that we would experience such things. (For example, John 16:33) He has also given us the power to overcome them. (The scriptures to support this are many, but one important example is John 1:12)

The life of St. Paul offers a marvelous example of how to overcome suffering. He was whipped five times; three times he was beaten with rods; he was stoned and left for dead. He was shipwrecked three times, imprisoned without cause and greatly mistreated in many places. Yet in all this, he said. "we are more than conquerors." (Romans 8:37; II Corinthians 11: 24-28) Paul knew where his strength lay for he wrote, "when I am powerless, it is then that I am strong."

Of course, the greatest example of innocent suffering was the crucifixion of Jesus. The Son of God was reviled, cursed, spit upon, whipped, and brutally crucified - surely the greatest act of injustice in the world. Yet God turned it to good, into amazing grace. God will not let evil triumph over good, that is why Scripture says, "conquer evil with good." (Romans 12:21) In the same vein, St. Peter asked, "who indeed can harm you if you are committed deeply to doing what is right." (I Peter 3:13) No one! Nothing can ultimately prevail over God's love. Neither tribulation, nor trial, distress, persecution, war, famine, or disease, not even death.

139

"God so loved the world…" What a sublime truth, and how powerfully Jesus stated it. He said the Father loves us so much that he gave us his beloved son to save us from sin, and condemnation, and self-destruction. He gave the treasures of heaven to enrich his children.

God has such love and mercy for us that he came in human flesh to redeem us and set us free from the weakness of the flesh. His compassion is so deep that he got into our skin in order to suffer with us and for us. Surely that's true compassion! He came as a child in order to fulfill one of the great promises of the Bible, that God himself would take away our guilt and heal our sinfulness. The word of God promised, "I., even I, am he who blots out your transgressions for my own sake; and I will remember your sins no more." (Isaiah 43:25) That is complete forgiveness.

Yet not only did Jesus become man to bring God's forgiveness, but he also became human to bear the sin of the world and to expiate its evil. Actually, not only did Jesus bear our sins, but he became sin as he hung on the cross so that sin could be destroyed, and in him we could become the holiness of God. (II Corinthians 5:21) This is a great and humbling mystery, too full of the purest love for me to grasp completely, but I believe it. And with St. Paul, I ask for the grace to share in the fellowship of his suffering so that I can know him and the power flowing from his resurrection. (Philippians 3:10)

That power was already evident in the stable at Bethlehem. The angels sang of glorious good news, and the shepherds were transformed. The Magi gave kingly gifts, and in return found a new way to go home and a new way to live. For the glory of the Lord had shone - and still it shines today.

On that first Christmas, God's love came and dwelt among us. The Word became flesh and "we beheld his glory" full of grace and truth. (John 1:14) The sovereign of the universe, to show his love, came as a baby, vulnerable and weak. The creator lay in the arms of his creature, and she beheld his glory.

He did not come to be a voice in the wilderness as John the Baptist was, rather he came as the living Word of God, the word of love and restoration from the heart of God. He came as the voice of truth and beauty, the voice "of rejoicing and salvation." (Psalm 118:15) But many refused to listen to him; many today still will not hear him.

However, to those who listened he gave incredible gifts. He gave them light to obliterate darkness; he gave them love to overcome hate; he gave them his Holy Spirit to make the church alive with the works of his heavenly Father. If we hear and answer his call, he will lead us to Bethlehem, to Galilee, to Golgotha, to glory. For "God's gifts and his call are irrevocable." (Romans 11:29)

140

The angel of the Lord said to the shepherds in the fields at Bethlehem, "You have nothing to fear! I come to proclaim good news to you - tidings of great joy to be shared by the whole people. This day in David's city a savior has been born to you, the messiah and Lord." (Luke 2:10-11) One translation says, "I have glorious news of great joy." Glorious it is, and marvelous, because it is for all people.

In his overwhelming goodness, God sent us Jesus as his most precious gift to lift our thoughts and hearts heavenwards. "For unto us a child is born, unto us a son is given…and his name will be called Wonderful, Counselor, Mighty God, Everlasting Father, Prince of Peace." (Isaiah 9:6NKJV) Yet how inauspicious were his beginnings.

We, who love our creature comforts, quickly pass over the fact that he was born in a cave used for sheltering animals. Or we romanticize the scene of his birth by making pretty cribs with gaily painted angels and loveable animals in attendance. We ignore the fact that Jesus was born in conditions that we would call deplorable. We also romanticize the supposed inn which refused Mary and Joseph a place to rest. It was a caravansary, a rough circle of stones where camel drivers stayed at night with their beasts. Even in such a place, there was no room for Jesus. And so the Lord of Glory was born like the poorest of the poor.

So, how do we celebrate the birth of the Son of God, the Word made flesh? Do we honor a baby sleeping in warm, clean hay, surrounded by adoring shepherds and the Magi adorned in exotic garb. Or do we stand in wonder at such a God who came to us destitute of worldly comfort, sharing his birthplace with beasts of burden?

He came as one who would be so gentle that he would not break the bruised reed nor extinguish the smoldering wick. (Isaiah 42:3) However, his coming among us was so stark and bereft of comfort that the prophet exclaimed, "There was in him no form of comeliness; and when we see him, there is no beauty." (Isaiah 53:2 NKJV) Therefore, he was despised and rejected by men…and so it is today.

The world rejects the truth of Jesus in the same way it rejects the truth of his birth. It sanitizes his message to make it palatable to a world that will not accept a God born among the refuse of animals. As one academic has said, it is absurd to expect intelligent people to believe such ancient myths and stories of wonder-working heroes born in squalor. Like Pilate, he wouldn't recognize the truth if it stood before him.

But the angel was right. It is exceedingly great and glorious good news. God came to us as the weakest and humblest child so that the weakest among us could identify with him. He drew close to us in lowliness, so that we could draw close to him in our brokenness.

141

"See what love the Father has bestowed on us in letting us be called children of God. Yet that is what we are." (I John 3:1) When we believe in Jesus we are "born of God," and have received the matchless gift of membership in God's family. (I John 5:1) In pointing out the majesty of the Father's love, St. John used an expression in Greek which expects a positive response to his statement. The response could go something like this: "Yes, I do see the Father's great and magnificent love, and I am overwhelmed by it!" Could we say that in reply to John's assertion?

John could write of God's love so powerfully because he had seen and heard and had touched Jesus, the visible manifestation of God's love. He had lived and eaten and walked with the love of God made flesh. The impact of that love changed John forever. Another person miraculously changed by encountering God's love was St. Paul. A few words from his letter to Philemon will illustrate the depth of that change. When Paul wanted Philemon to forgive the runaway slave, Onesimus, he wrote this timeless line: "If he has wronged you or owes you anything, put it on my account." (Philemon v.18)

Paul had learned from Jesus how to reconcile others ; by taking their burden as his own. That's what Jesus did. He interceded for all of us, and God laid our offenses on Jesus' account. Like Jesus, Paul deliberately chose to "put on love," which he knew was the bond of perfection. (Colossians 3:14 NKJV)

It is important that we, too, should make the decision to love others and be willing to overlook their failings. In fact, we are commanded by God's word to love one another. The one who refuses to love others, John wrote, "abides in death." (I John 3:14 NKJV) But in practical terms, what does it mean to love one another? It means that we are to care for others and help them in their need. We are to love others as a sign that God is in our midst, and to share his blessings as we are able.

A simple story will illustrate the point. A traveler once saw hundreds of hungry children begging for bread. They were filthy and wore rags and their smell made him feel sick. He was very disturbed by their plight and wondered why God had not done anything to help the children. Suddenly a thought came into his mind: "I did do something to help them, I sent you!"

The letters of both James and John teach us that if we ignore the needs of others, the love of God is not in us. Our faith, in effect, is dead if we ignore the crushing poverty of the many millions around the world. As John wrote, "Whoever has this world's goods, and sees his brother in need, and shuts up his heart from him, how does the love of God abide in him?" (I John 3:17 NKJV) If we are unable to help, we know the one who can. Let us draw on his account, for the word says, "My God will meet all your needs according to his glorious riches in Christ Jesus." (Philippians 4:19 NIV)

142

Why does God want our cooperation in order to accomplish his will on earth? The simple answer is that he loves us and created us for good works. He loves us so much that in a divine, wondrous, and almost unbelievable way, he has given us a co-equal share in his labor of love among us. His love for us is so great that he has allowed us to become partakers of his divine nature. (II Peter 1:4) He has commissioned us to be co-workers in his vineyard. What a pity so many of us do not believe it!

Oh, we believe it intellectually, but we seldom believe it with our hearts. We really believe in the new birth, and in the power of the Holy Spirit in our lives, yet we mostly seem to demonstrate that belief in church.

God's word has many examples of men and women who were just like us in their narrow vision of God's power in their lives. Many people in Scripture demonstrated a singular lack of faith when it came to believing the presence of God in their daily lives. For example, Moses told the Lord that he was completely inadequate for the task God had given him. But God ignored his complaint, and encouraged Moses in a most amazing way: he said to Moses, "See, I have made you as God to Pharaoh." (Exodus 7:1) It is not recorded what Moses thought, but I suspect he flatly refused to believe it.

Not long afterwards, God told Moses to tell the Israelites that he wanted them to be his special treasure. (Exodus 19:5) They did not accept this, because shortly thereafter they were grumbling and blaming God for their difficulties, and would later choose to worship the golden calf in preference to the Lord. Like us today, they just could not accept the truth that God esteemed them as his prized possession. And like the Israelites, we readily run after the golden idols of our age.

Another example in Scripture of someone failing to see himself as God sees him, is Gideon. He was hiding in fear from the Midianites, afraid that they would plunder his freshly ground wheat, when the Angel of the Lord appeared and said to Gideon, "The Lord is with you, O champion!" (Judges 6:12)

Gideon utterly rejected the messenger's estimation of him as being a man of valor and a champion and said, if the Lord is with us, why are we in such a mess, (sound familiar?), and where are all those miracles that the Lord worked in bringing our fathers out of Egypt? Then Gideon said something which we can all identify with: he said to the Lord that he was the least and the weakest in Israel, therefore he was totally unfit to be the Lord's servant. But we know that Gideon did indeed become a mighty champion, despite his excuses.

And we, too, in spite of our weaknesses and failings, can become the Lord's servants and share in his labors of love. Since it is his work, he will supply the grace to accomplish it. All he requires of us is our willingness to try.

143

"I am my beloved's and my beloved is mine." (Song of Solomon 6:3 NKJV) In this simple, yet beautiful way, the Song depicts the relationship between God and man. In Hebrew, the Song is called *shir hashirim*, the Song of Songs, which means the "greatest song." It is a fitting title for a poem which extols the love relationship between God and his people.

The Song of Songs is a love poem honoring the depth of God's love for us as individuals and as a church. The poem illustrates the yearning God has for intimacy with his beloved: it also tells of the love which each soul will have for God once it understands how much it is loved.

But often we experience great difficulty in understanding the majesty of God's love. We know in our heads, but our hearts remain far from him. This is surprising, for the Lord has given us his written word declaring his everlasting love for us. Then he sent his only begotten son to prove his eternal love. Finally, he invaded our lives with his Holy Spirit and made us his dwelling place. What more could God do?

So it is perhaps understandable why God chided us through the prophets. It is no wonder that he called out to us through the prophet Micah saying, "O my people what have I done to you, or how have I wearied you? Answer me!" (Micah 6:2) What can we say? How can we remain unmoved when we know that the Lord wants to set us as a seal upon his heart?(Song of Songs 8:6) All through Scripture God tells us in the clearest terms that we are his special possession and that he holds us close to his heart. Tirelessly he sent us the prophets and holy men and women to proclaim his care for us, and his desire to be close to us.

From the very beginning he poured out his blessings on all those who received him and who had faith in his word. Whenever his people cried out and turned back to him with sincere and repentant hearts, he restored them to fellowship with him. Then he blessed them and saved them from their enemies.

Sometimes we are so busy with our own lives, with amassing things and seeking pleasures, that we forget to ask the Lord for the good things he wants to give us. And what are those good things he wants to give us? They are love, joy, peace, goodness, kindness, his abiding presence - the very things the world is hungering for but seeks them in all the wrong places. They can only come from God, and they can only live in a heart surrendered to God's love.

As the Song of Songs illustrates, the love of God is so strong that he is unable to hold back from any soul that loves him. With great love he repeats our name and tenderly tells us of his love. His name is poured out on us as the finest anointing, and we become whole because we are loved. It is no wonder that the Song of Songs is read every Friday in the Synagogue. It is the holiest book in all of Israel, and as one great Rabbi said, "the whole world is not worth the day when the Song was given to Israel." (Blaise Arminjon. <u>The Cantata of Love</u>, Ignatius Press, 1988, p.35)

144

"We are God's artistic masterpiece." That's how one scholar translates Ephesians 2:10, and I agree with him. We are indeed "fearfully and wonderfully made." (Psalm 139:10) He made us that way in order that we may know him, and love him, and enjoy him.

Most people balk at the idea of enjoying God. But listen to St. Peter:" Though you have not seen him, you love him: and even though you do not see him now, you believe in him and are filled with an inexpressible and glorious joy." I Peter 1:8 NIV) that kind of joy is pretty rare these days.

A few Christians in every century have walked in the Father's love and have experienced transcendent joy - and they have insisted that such a relationship should be enjoyed by everyone. They knew the Lord as a "consuming fire," (Hebrews 12:29) and they exulted to be the fuel in the flames of his love.

Our problem is that we are so caught up in our daily lives that we think such intimacy with God is beyond us. So we leave such relationships to the "saints." Yet Jesus showed in the parable of the prodigal son that his Father longs to share his love with even the worst of us. In fact, that is the reason why Jesus came - to demonstrate the Father's love for all, even the lost. The prodigal son found that love, and his joy was so great that he even danced for joy. (It is the only example in the New Testament of anyone dancing.)

Now just what did that young man do to experience such joy? He came home and said that he was sorry. That is how we, too, can share in that glorious joy Peter wrote about. We have only to come home. It is so easy that we reject it off hand, even before we try it. We are so used to earning our way through life that we think we have to earn our way into the Father's heart. Nothing could be further from the truth.

He loves us with an everlasting and unshakeable love, regardless of what we have done. He has shown his love in the most exquisite way: "God so loved the world that he gave his only begotten son…" And as St Paul pointed our in his letter to the Romans, since God gave such a gift in Jesus, wouldn't he give us "all things besides?" Scripture promises us that we will be "filled with the very fullness of God himself." (Ephesians 3:19) Every time I read that verse I am overwhelmed by the generosity and love of God.

So a joy inexpressible and glorious is a gift God wants all of us to receive. It is a free gift from the heart of God to all who sincerely seek him. We spend so much time seeking things which fail to satisfy that it is time we sought what really fulfills the hunger of the human heart. The ones who hunger for God will never be disappointed; they will never hunger again.

145

"Draw close to God and he will draw close to you." (James 4:8) Note that it is we who have to make the first move. (Although I believe prevenient grace is involved in our search.) If we desire a deeper relationship with the Lord, we are the ones who determine the extent of that fellowship.

If all we want is a Sunday acquaintance with God, we will never experience the majesty and grandeur of his love and our worship will be shallow and weak. But if we seek him every day and spend time in his presence, we will experience the truth of David's advice to Solomon: "If you seek him he will let himself be found by you." (I Chronicles 28:9b) His closeness will be an ever present blessing.

When we call to him for help he will answer, "In distress you called and I delivered you." (Psalm 81:7) When we sing to him in joy, his word assures us that he will rejoice over us with gladness and he will sing joyfully for us as ones sings at a festival. (Zephaniah 3:17-18) Have you ever imagined God singing with joy over you?

In addition to the joy of his closeness, we also receive power to live productive lives. The Psalms attest to how God values our being close to him, and about his concern for us. Psalm 127 says "He gives to his beloved in their sleep." (Some translations say only, "he gives sleep.") Many, many Christians have fallen asleep reciting that verse and trusting in his providence - they were not forsaken, To show his deep concern for us he said, "Open your mouth and I will fill it." (Psalm 81:10)

There are many verses of Scripture which extol the beauty of having a personal relationship with the Lord, and which tell of his desire for intimacy with us. When we respond to his love, he puts gladness into our hearts…and as soon as we lie down, we fall peacefully asleep." (Psalm 4:7-8) Millions of sleep deprived sufferers could benefit from reading this psalm which promises security and rest to the fearful.

In the Song of Songs we see the longing of the father to share his love and presence with his people. While on one level it is possible to read the Song as a lyrical poem on human love, it is really a deep spiritual lesson on the sublime love God has for us who are his beloved. (The rabbis and the Church Fathers all saw it as a spiritual message on God's love.) In the Song he tells us how he longs to hear our voice which is lovely to him.

With such a Father, why do we keep him waiting to hear from us? Let us call out to him and ask him to set us "as a seal on your heart" (The early church saw this seal as the Holy Spirit) Then for us his name will indeed be "oil poured out", and we will rejoice in him and be glad as the Song of Songs says. How comforting is to know that we are his beloved…is he ours?

146

"If the son sets you free, you will really be free." (John 8:36) So far, most of us have never had to risk our lives for the sake of freedom. Like me, you may wonder whether you would have the courage to risk all for freedom's sake. Our freedom has not been put to the test. But I know of many people who in spite of terrible ordeals, remained truly free. Here are a few examples.

A Jewish victim of Nazi atrocities was forced to strip naked then he was beaten, humiliated, and reviled as a sub-human. Through it all he refused to hate his torturers, for he had seen what hatred had done to the Nazis and he refused to become like them. He was free not to hate.

Dietrich Bonhoeffer, the Lutheran pastor and theolgian, demonstrated freedom to an extraordinary degree. Like the Apostle Paul, Bonhoeffer was imprisoned as a menace to society, and like Paul, Bonhoeffer had an incredible impact on his jailers. Even hardened Nazis saw something in Bonhoeffer which made them marvel, and his free spirit in the midst of such evil was a beacon of hope to his fellow inmates. He prayed and sang hymns with such courage that even his guards were affected. The S.S. moved him from prison to prison to prevent him from gaining converts In spite of his imprisonment, Bonhoeffer was a free man in the midst of hatred and unprecedented evil.

Perhaps one of the greatest apostle of freedom in the twentieth century was Raoul Wallenberg, the Swedish diplomat in Hungary who rescued over 100,000 Jews from the jaws of death during the Second World War. Wallenberg, at great personal risk, outwitted Eichman and his henchmen and shepherded to freedom an incredible number of people marked for extinction.

Wallenberg died in a Soviet prison, a victim of Stalin's demonic paranoia. Those who met Wallenberg in the Russian jail say that he was an incredibly free person in the midst of torture and slave labor. Another hero in the hell of a soviet prison camp was Fr. Walter Cisek, S.J. Fr. Cisek survived 24 years of forced labor with incredible courage and endurance. His faith and love for Jesus has had a deep and powerful effect on all those who know his story.

Finally, there is the Russian poet Julia Voznezenskaya, who was sent to Siberia for writing a poem about God. As she left the courtroom for her frozen prison, she was heard to say, "You can put me in prison, but you cannot imprison God."

What amazing people; what noble and courageous witnesses they are to freedom. Perhaps their courage is best summed up by the beaten and bloodied prisoner who refused to kneel before his captors. Then he was kicked so savagely that he fell to his knees. "So," his torturer said, "we finally have you on your knees. "My body may be kneeling," came the answer through swollen lips, "but my spirit is still standing."

147

"If anyone loves me he will be true to my teaching. My father will love him, and we will come and make our home with him." (John 14:33 NIV) Restated, it says the if we love Jesus and are true to his word, we become the dwelling place of God. What an incredible promise.

Our minds cannot grasp that truth, for the mind, unaided is incapable of understanding how the Creator, who holds the whole universe in existence, could possibly live inside us. Nor can we understand another breathtaking promise of Jesus, which says that if we obey him, he will reveal himself to us. (John

14:21)In Greek it literally says "I will become visible" or "I will show my self." Let that sink in for a minute...

I suspect you may be puzzled by the implications of Jesus' promise. Did he mean it literally? If he did, how can he actually become visible to us?" I believe he did mean it, and I also believe that millions have seen him made manifest.

There are different ways in which Jesus chooses to reveal himself. We see him in his Church, we encounter him in the lives of those who love him, and we see him in his word. But I also believe that he comes to people in a visible way as he promised. Since he appeared to the two disciples on the road to Emmaus, he has be seen by people in every age and every nation. The one I find most moving is his apparition to St. Faustina Kowalska telling her of his immense and inexhaustible mercy.

No doubt the most common revelation of Jesus is in his word. Every book of the Bible reveals him and the Gospels are, of course, power-packed with his presence. Yet many of us allow his word to sit on a table or in a bookcase unread.

He is visible all right, but unseen.

Could that be said of our lives? Have we failed to see him in what we do? Have we become so preoccupied with the world or with self that we have missed the Lord of Glory. Have we forgotten that he who made the universe only lives where he is offered a place. Even though his glory fills the cosmos, he will not enter a heart which has no room for him.

He is standing at the door of all hearts asking to come into our busy lives to give us peace. If we hear him and open up to him we will be radiant with joy and enjoy the banquet he wants to give us.

But listening is like looking, it must be developed. Jesus warned us that it is possible to be looking and yet not see; he warned that it is possible to be listening and yet not hear. The key to hearing and seeing him is obedience; to actively seek him in love and to take his mother's advice: DO WHATEVER HE TELLS YOU TO DO.

148

The Bible has numerous examples of people praying in desperate situations and getting remarkable answers. One of my favorite examples is the prayer of Hezekiah when Jerusalem was under siege by the Assyrian army. Sennacherib, King of Assyria, sent Hezekiah a letter insulting the God of Israel and boasting that the Lord would not be able to withstand Assyria. Sennacherib had placed himself above the God of Israel.

Hezekiah knew that without the Lord's help the Assyrian king would make good his boast, for he had already captured all the fortified cities of Judah. So Hezekiah went to the House of the Lord and spread out Sennacherib's letter before the Lord. He opened his heart to God and prayed for the salvation and peace of Jerusalem.

Meanwhile, Sennacherib was boasting that the God of Israel would end up defeated like all the other gods Assyria had fought against. He also bragged that he had shut up Hezekiah like a "caged bird." (But that caged bird knew how to sing to the Lord.)

Now as Hezekiah was praying and asking the Lord for help, the prophet Isaiah received a word from the Lord concerning Sennacherib. Through Isaiah the Lord said to Sennacherib, "I will put my hook in your nose and my bridle in your lips, and I will turn you back by the way you came." (II Kings 19:28)

The outcome was swift. As the historians relate it, thousands of the Assyrian troops died of the plague and the decimated Assyrian army with Sennacherib at the head returned home to

Nineveh. Sennacherib was murdered by his scheming sons as he was worshipping in the temple of Nisroch. He reaped what he had sown.

Hezekiah, who was a good king, was remembered as a leader who "prospered wherever he went." His goodness and victory were a result of his prayer life. He knew the power of prayer. When he prayed, the Lord heard him. That is borne out by the fact that when Isaiah told him he was about to die, Hezekiah prayed and the Lord spared him giving him fifteen more years of life. The Lord said to him, "I have heard your prayer, I have seen your tears: surely I will heal you." (II Kings 20:5)

When we pray, we can expect to be answered. For we have the authority to pray in the name of Jesus, which is the real prayer of power. Furthermore, Jesus promised that whatever we ask in prayer, if we believe we have already received it, it will be ours. (Mark 11:24 JB) Of course, the Holy Spirit will guide us to pray for what we really need. (Romans 8:26)

.
So let us believe in him, and ask the Holy Spirit to lead us in prayer, and we will receive the promises of God and everything we need besides.

149

"Delight in the Lord, and he will grant you the desires of your heart" (Psalm 37:4 NIV) If you think that sounds too good to be true…try it, you'll be surprised!

The word of God is full of such promises, In jeremiah, the Lord said, "Call to me, and I will answer you: I will tell you things great beyond the reach of your knowledge." (Jeremiah 33:3) Finding our true heart's desire is one of those things beyond the reach of our knowledge. We all too often delight in the wrong things and end up in a mess of our own making. God, of course, knows this so he warned us that the only way we can experience peace, joy, and delight is to make him the center of our lives. When he becomes our delight, he also becomes our heart's desire.

The path to sharing our lives with God so we can delight in him, is prayer. Prayer is talking to God and asking him for our daily needs, but it is also letting God's presence saturate us with his silent beauty. Being present to God, and asking him to be present to us is the beginning of prayer. Often our greatest prayer is when no words are exchanged, just love. Naturally, as our Father, God wants to shower us with his love. He wants us to "experience this love which surpasses all knowledge, so that [we] may attain to the fullness of God himself." (Ephesians 3:19) That is an overwhelming promise!

Jesus told us that our Heavenly Father's love is so great that he wants to help us in all our needs. He said if human fathers know how to give their children gifts, how much more will our Father in Heaven give us the truly good gifts we all need. He said that when a child asks his father for a fish he is not given a snake, so why do we think that God will not be more generous than our earthly father. In Matthew's Gospel Jesus says *"How much more will your heavenly Father give good things to anyone who asks him."* (Matthew 7:11 Italics added.)

The greatest of these gifts is the Holy Spirit which God will give to all those who ask him. (Luke 11:13) This is perhaps the most wonderful promise Jesus ever made. Not only did he promise the gift of the Spirit, he promised to lavish it upon us. He wants to pour into us an ever increasing stream of love and to give us a power to live for him which can do "immeasurably more than we can ask or imagine" (Ephesians 3:19)

How could we ever refuse such an offer? We must not think that humility requires us to accept scraps when God wants to give us a feast. By all means let us realize that we are not worthy of his gifts, but we must not refuse them on that account. After all he is our Father, and it is his good pleasure to give.

Who could not delight in such a Father?

150

One of the titles of Jesus is Rose of Sharon. It is an epithet I especially cherish. Some years ago I was reminded of that title in a beautiful way. It was Easter Sunday morning and I was welcomed to a new church in a most touching manner by one of the congregation. He left the church so quickly that I had no time to thank him.

On his way out of church, just as the service was coming to a close, he stopped at my pew, took a gorgeous pink rose out of his lapel, and gave it to me saying he was happy to see me in his church. I was deeply moved.

What my welcomer did not know was that for many years I had a request for the Lord concerning roses. Whenever I need to know his will for me concerning a new direction in my life, I have always asked him to confirm my choice by sending me a rose. I adopted this modern Gideon's fleece from St. Therese of Lisieux.

One winter in a severe northern climate with deep snow covering the ground, my wife found a rose bud growing in our garden. The sign indicated to us that our planned move to a new area was the right change for us.

There is no way that my new friend could have known of my predilection for roses, or of my prayer asking for a rose to confirm a difficult new decision. But what his gesture illustrates is just how wonderfully the Lord uses each of us to encourage and affirm others. Obviously, my new friend was listening to the Lord.

Jesus said, "He who welcomes you, welcomes me." (Matthew 10:40) My Easter Sunday greeter had put that word of Jesus into practice - he welcomed me as if he were greeting the Lord himself. I was overwhelmed by the impact of this stranger's act.

How marvelous it would be if everyone of us took the time to welcome visitors to our churches, and extend to them the same love that was shown to me. The impact would be incalculable!

I am sure I will remember that rose, and the person who gave it to me for as long as I have a memory. He touched a cord deep within me: he became the hand of the Lord extended to me in love. Isn't that what the Lord wants us all to be?

Twenty-seven hundred years ago Isaiah prophesied that the desert land would rejoice and bloom like a rose in the days of the Messiah. (Isaiah 35:1 NKJV) We live in those days, for Jesus the Resurrected One, the Rose of Sharon, is in our midst. Although I did not need the gift of a rose to believe in Jesus, that man's loving token said quite clearly to me that Jesus is risen and is among his people.

151

"Do whatever he tells you." (John 2:5) With these words at the wedding in Cana the mother of Jesus showed her unshakeable faith in the mission of her son. When she told Jesus that the wine for the festivities had run out, he replied, "Woman, how does this concern of yours involve me. My hour has not yet come." (John 2: 4). But his mother went ahead and told the waiters to follow Jesus' instructions. Thus did a humble woman of Nazareth inaugurate the mission of Jesus, the Messiah and Son of God.

Mary, who prophesied that all generations would call her blessed, was so loved by Jesus that he began his public ministry prompted by her faith and trust. Her power of intercession is so great that she went ahead with her desire to help the newly weds without waiting for Jesus to let her know that he would acquiesce to her petition. Her faith is so great that she is indeed "blessed" among all women.

What is puzzling to me is how in so many churches her faith is ignored and her prophecy is made void. Many church leaders will preach about Gideon, Ishmael, Jabez, Enoch, and a host of other ancients, but never a mention is made of the "Blessed Mother" of Jesus, nor is her faith ever admired. Perhaps a cursory mention in passing, but her faith is seldom held up as something to be emulated. After all, God chose her to be the living temple of his son - such a choice should tell us something about her incomparable worth. Above all women, Mary alone was asked to bear the child who would redeem the world. Even the Angel Gabriel called her *kecharitomene* (filled with the *charis*, or grace, of God). She is highly favored by the Living God, but ignored by millions of those who love his son.

After Jesus rose from the dead he told the disciples to wait in Jerusalem until they were imbued with power by the Holy Spirit. As the disciples waited and prayed in the upper room they were accompanied by some women and "Mary, the mother of Jesus." (Acts 1:14) Her role would be as mother of the church. Since the church is called the body of Christ, then his mother is *ipso facto* our mother. Even many of the reformers in the sixteenth century did not refute that.

Perhaps excesses of misplaced devotion to the Blessed Virgin have made people afraid to honor her lest they be thought giving her worship which is God's alone. However, those same people will honor, and rightly so, Abraham, Moses, and the prophets and pay no respect to the mother of Jesus, their Lord and Savior.

I think it is time for all Christians to give Jesus' mother the honor which is her due. For when we cherish her memory, we are giving praise to our Heavenly Father, the Holy Spirit, and to Jesus her son. The Triune God was completely involved in her life and remained with her until she was called to her eternal home. As the mother of God's only begotten Son her role in Christianity is second only to that of her son. Her role in heaven is as queen, since her son is King of Glory. So let us rejoice in the grace given to Mary, the Queen of Heaven.

152

Psalm 139 teaches us that God is ever- present and knows us perfectly. Reading that psalm helps us to meditate on God's word and to be open to his probing of our heart. To pray this psalm it is necessary to allow God to be fully present to us and to empty our heart of self and selfish desires. To seek God for his own sake and to be thankful for his love is at the very center of true prayer. As the previous psalm says, "I will give you thanks, O Lord, with all my heart." because you listen to my words. (Psalm 138: 1)

"Even before a word is on my tongue, behold, O Lord, you know the whole of it." (Psalm 139:4) So it is often better to sit in silence before the Lord and let him put into our hearts what he wants to give us, for he already knows what we want That is why St. Paul urged us to let the Holy Spirit guide our prayer, because we are weak and "do not know how to pray as we ought." (Romans 8:26). When we pray in the will of God as led by his Spirit we are sure of the Lord's "Amen" to our words.

Psalm 139 reminds us of a wonderful truth:

Truly you have formed my inmost being,
You knit me in my mother's womb.
I give you thanks that I am fearfully, wonderfully made.
Wonderful are your works. (vv 13-14)

And we are told that even before one of our days existed, God had set their allotted time. That is what the Lord said to Jeremiah, "Before I formed you in the womb I knew you." (Jeremiah 1:5) Even before we saw the light of day God loved us and called us into being. Even before the creation of the universe he knew us and wanted us to be born. That is why abortion is so tragic, because it thwarts the love and will of God.

After a long meditation on the omnipotence of God, the psalmist realizes that he needs to know himself as God knows him. So bravely he asks God to shine the light of truth into his heart to reveal his inner life.

> Probe me, O God, and know my heart;
> Try me, and know my thoughts;
> See if my way is crooked.
> And lead me in the way of old. (vv 23-24)

He now wants to obey the word of God in its entirety. Would that our age had such a desire.

Praying the psalms is a marvelous way of getting close to the Lord, for they are redolent with the odor of incense, which is the prayer of God's children and pleasing to our Father who longs to share his love with us.

153

After Jesus fed many thousands in the wilderness, those who had witnessed that miracle searched for him the next day and found him at Capernaum. If he were the Messiah, they believed that he would perform some mighty sign to authenticate his mission. Surprisingly, the multiplication of the loaves and fish was not a powerful enough sign for them, even though they wanted more of the loaves and fish which Jesus had given them. Jesus told

them not to be seeking perishable food, but for the food of
eternal life which he will give.

Now the crowd wanted to know what works of God they had to
perform in order to be acceptable to God. Jesus' answer is very
revealing: in effect, he said it is not "works," but only one thing
above all is required: "This is the work of God: have faith in the
One whom he sent." (John 6:29) When we believe in Jesus, we
perform the act which precedes all the others. As St. Paul wrote,
citing the prophet Habakkuk, "The just man shall live by faith."
(Romans 1:17) And again he noted, "For we hold that a man is
justified by faith apart from observance of the law." (Romans
3:28) This was expressed poetically in the psalms:

> Yet in no way can a man redeem himself,
> Or pay his own ransom to God;
> Too high is the price to redeem one's life;
> He would never have enough
> To remain alive always and not see destruction.
> (Psalm 49: 8-10)

As Fr. Raniero Cantalamessa noted in his excellent book, Life in
The Lordship of Christ, "To want to pay God his price through
our own merits is another form of the never ending effort to be
autonomous and independent of God, and not just autonomous
and independent but actually God's creditors." That is exactly
what the crowd believed when they asked about works.

Of course, we are not so direct in our dealings with the Lord, but
often our behavior seems to indicate that we believe we can earn
salvation by works. We know that faith without works is dead,
but faith in what? Not only do we have to believe in Jesus, but
we must also believe everything he said. That's where it
becomes tricky. Because there are some words of Jesus which
we ignore and choose not to believe. For example, "Do not
worry about your livelihood, what you are to eat or drink or use
for clothing." (Matthew 6:25) Or, "Do not lay up for yourselves
an earthly treasure." (Matthew 6:19). If that is not sufficient to

prove the point, what about this one: "Love your enemies, do good to those who hate you." (Luke 6:27)

There are many, many more of the sayings of Jesus which most Christians choose to ignore. So when Jesus said that the main "work" of his followers is to believe in him, he meant it.

154

"Who do you say that I am?" This question which Jesus asked is in the very middle of mark's Gospel. Since it is in the very heart of the Gospel of Mark, it is obviously a central and pivotal question - one which we must all answer, as I have written earlier.

We cannot be his disciples until we have faced the probing gaze of Jesus and have responded to his inquiry. Our answer will say much about our relationship with him. Is he just a good man, or a prophet, or a patriot-rebel? Or is he the Word made flesh and the Son of God.? Is he our Redeemer whom we love with all our heart?

Unless we encounter him on his terms and allow the Spirit to reveal him personally to us, we cannot say who he is. We may have heard who he is from others, but we can only know who he is for ourselves by experiencing his life within us.

St. Peter's response to the Lord's probing question was, "You are the Messiah, the Son of the Living God." (Mathew 16:16) Jesus then told peter that he was blessed by having such knowledge. The word blessed was only used in Classical Greek to describe the happiness of the gods. Peter had become the recipient of divine favor because the Father had revealed to him who Jesus really is. Like Peter, when Job finally understood who God was, he made a profound observation: "I had heard of you by word of mouth, but now I have seen you with my eye." (Job

42:5) It is interesting to note that once Job knew God and not merely knew about him, he no longer needed answers. To know God is all the answer we ever need.

Later, the disciples of Jesus understood the same thing as Job. They told Jesus that they were convinced that he knew everything, and they no longer needed to ask him anything. (John 16: 29-30) Knowing God is sufficient: in his presence all things are answered.

So who do you say Jesus is? Have you met him like Paul on the Damascus Road? Or are you still kicking against the goad? Is there still an "if" in your relationship with the Lord, or has he removed it as he did for the leper in Matthew 8:2-3? Can you say without doubt that you know Jesus personally?

If we are not sure of our relationship with Jesus we can ask him to reveal himself to us. He solemnly promised that he would. (John 14:21) It is worth noting that the Greek word for reveal in that verse actually means "to become visible." So John 14:21 could read, "I will love him and become visible to him." Now that is a verse to meditate on for a lifetime.

Even if we think we already know the Lord, it is important to ask ourselves the question which Jesus asked Peter and the disciples. Our answer will tell us the immediate state of our spiritual health.

"And you, who do you say that I am?" (Mark 8:29)

155

"The Lord is my light and my salvation." (Psalm 27:1) So begins one of the most comforting and powerful prayers in the Book of Psalms. This psalm is a cry from the heart rejoicing in the truth that God takes care of those who completely trust in his goodness. Like other psalms and passages of Scripture, psalm 27 teaches us that those who wait on the Lord will experience his bounty and goodness "in the land of the living," which means we do not have to wait until heaven to know the blessings of God.

Jesus knew this psalm and summed it up in one life-changing message: "So do not worry, saying, 'What shall we eat?' or 'What shall we drink?' or 'What shall we wear?' For the pagans run after all these things, and your heavenly Father knows that you need them. But seek first his kingdom and his righteousness, and all these things will be given you as well." (Matthew 6:31-33 NIV)

Psalm 27 continues with the life-changing message, adding one which Jesus also knew and taught, and that is how to pray. "Of you my heart speaks; you my glance seeks; your presence, O Lord, I seek." (Psalm 27:8) The psalmist knew that being in God's loving presence was true prayer and he longed for the Lord to point out to him the path of light and peace. St Paul summed up psalm 27 in this way, "…Put on the armor of light…Rather put on the Lord Jesus Christ, and make no provision for the desires of the flesh." (Romans 13:12-14) Prayer must reflect, in the end, total confidence in God's love.

The psalmist urges us to have courage in addition to trust. Both are gifts of the Holy Spirit without which our witness to the truth would soon wilt and die. Psalm 28:8 says that "The Lord is the strength of his people, and the saving refuge of his anointed." Since we have been anointed by the Spirit we have God's strength to live lives of real witness to his power. For we are, "'a chosen race, a royal priesthood, a holy nation, a people he claims for his own to proclaim the glorious works' of the One who called [us] from darkness into his marvelous light." Sadly, we do not always live up to that high calling.

But we must not lose hope. The mercy and compassion of God are endless and his love for us is beyond measure. So we can always begin anew, confident that the Lord is our light and salvation and that we do not need to be afraid. He will restore us as soon as we glance his way. As Isaiah proclaimed:

> Though your sins be like scarlet,
> they may become white as snow;
> though they be crimson red,
> they may become white as wool.
> If you are willing and obey,
> you shall eat the good things of the Land. (Isaiah I:18-19)

The Word of God tells us repeatedly that when we turn to him with all our heart we find him in our heart, and he will care for us as only he can.

156

"Your word is a lamp to my feet and a light for my path." (Psalm 119:105 NIV) When we live believing that God's word is the light we need to walk in his presence, we gain a deeper insight into the wisdom of the Bible, and in consequence draw closer to the Lord.

When Job was confronted with the enormity of his situation, he realized how much he needed God's word and how faithfully he had tried to live it: "I have treasured the words of his mouth more than my necessary food." (Job 23:12b NKJV) Jeremiah, also suffering, could exclaim, "When I found your words, I devoured them; they became my joy and the happiness of my heart." (Jeremiah 15:16) But like Job, he would find obeying God's word to be sometimes burdensome, even painful. The initial joy in encountering the Living Word only becomes lasting joy when like Mary we can say, "I am the servant of the Lord. Let it be done to me as you say." (Luke 1:18) And then put it into practice.

Obedience to God's word is the guarantee for a life well spent. Jesus said that those who listen to his word and live it would be his friends. John's Gospel calls Jesus the Word, the *logos*, which is the eternal wisdom of God. That is why Jesus said that his word would remain always, and would never be obsolete. (Matthew 24:35) But his word is only a living word to those who receive it in faith - for many, the Bible is a dead letter, or a work to be studied alongside other "myths." I have read scripture scholars who do not believe much of what they are experts in. I understand why Jesus said, "I offer you praise, O Father, Lord of Heaven and earth, because what you have hidden from the learned and the clever you have revealed to the merest children." (Luke 10:21) In fact he rejoiced that it was so.

Jesus told his disciples that his words "are spirit and life," and those who believe in his message have experienced the life-giving spirit in what Jesus said. St. Peter, speaking for all of us, said to Jesus, "Lord, to whom shall we go? You have the words of eternal life. We have come to believe; we are convinced that you are God's holy one." (John 6:68-69) That, I think, is the central point: to believe that Jesus has the words of eternal life is essential for a true understanding of the Gospels. To water down his words, or to explain away his teachings, or to modernize Jesus in light of contemporary scholarship offers no help to anyone seeking the truth of who Jesus is. It seems that in Jesus' day and ours, the experts are often those who do not recognize who he is.

Jesus came to give us life and to give it in abundance. The way to receive that abundant life is to accept his word and live it. He said, "If you make my word your home you will indeed be my disciples, you will learn the truth and the truth shall make you free." (John 8:31-32 JB) But we must make his word a home, we must be living in his word and let his word live in us. It is important to read the word prayerfully in faith. His word is our spiritual food, our bread from heaven. As St. Jerome remarked, if we are ignorant of his word, we are ignorant of who Jesus really is.

157

"I am the good shepherd; the good shepherd lays down his life for the sheep." (John 10:11) To the Scribes and Pharisees listening to Jesus, what he said sounded blasphemous. They would be familiar with the great passage of Ezekiel which prophesied that God himself would come among them as shepherd and he would seek out the lost and those that had strayed, and "bind up the injured" and heal the sick. All because the shepherds of Israel had not cared for the flock. (See Ezekiel 34)

Psalm 23 tells us that the Lord is a shepherd who takes care of his flock The psalm also points out that the Lord as shepherd will lead us on the right path. Jesus said that he himself was the right path, "I am the way, and the truth, and the life." (John 14:6) Based on the Psalms, Proverbs, and the Prophet Isaiah, the idea of the "way" had an ancient history. In proclaiming himself the way, Jesus let his disciples know that he was the fulfillment of God's promise to Israel.

As the good shepherd he was not only the way, but he was also the truth that God will lead his people into all that is right, and good, and holy. Jesus embodies God's way and truth and gives God's life to all who seek it. Since he is the way, he opens the door to his Father's home and thus all who find God, find him by virtue of Jesus being the way to the Father. Those who use Jesus' statement that no one comes to the father except through him to deny access to heaven to non-Christians misunderstand what Jesus meant He opened the door to his Father's house and he alone will decide who enters. His sacrificial death opened up heaven and for that reason he is the way to the father. He said, "In my Father's house there are many dwelling places" which I take to mean that there is room for all who want to come. (John 14:2)

One of the wonderful sayings of Jesus is that the sheep "recognize his voice." Once on a mission trip in Romania I saw a perfect example of what Jesus meant by recognizing the shepherd's voice. I saw two groups of sheep coming to drink at a small, shallow body of water, each led by a shepherd. In short order the sheep were all mixed together and I wondered how they would ever get the two flocks separated. After the two shepherds had spoken to each other for a while one of them moved away and shouted out a few words. Suddenly half the sheep at the watering place quickly moved to follow him. They recognized his voice (they are short sighted and perhaps couldn't tell the two shepherds apart, except by sound of their voice.)

I realized at that moment the truth of Jesus' statement - we, who are sometimes short-sighted- can recognize his voice since he is the Good Shepherd. Just as the sheep did not follow the other shepherd, but recognized the voice of the one who cares for them, we, too, will recognize the voice of our shepherd who is the way and the truth and the life.

But of course, we can only recognize his authentic voice when we know him. When his words, his love, his life, his promises, and his presence are part of our lives. To know him is to love him and to love him is to serve him. Let us seek the shepherd who wants us all to be one flock that he will lead to his Father's house.

158

The Apostle Paul was preaching in Iconium with Barnabas when opposition to their message became so hostile that they were on the verge of being stoned by a mob. So they left the town in a hurry and went to Lystra to proclaim the good news. As Paul was preaching he saw that a man crippled from birth was listening to him intently. He noticed that his listener believed his message and had the faith to be healed. He told the invalid to get up and the man jumped up and was healed.

The townspeople believed Paul and Barnabas were the gods Zeus and Hermes, because in Lystra there was a myth that Zeus and Hermes had come disguised to their area and were well received by an old couple whom the gods rewarded for their kindness. Seeing the miracle they believed that the gods had returned. Despite their protestations, Paul and Barnabas were being hailed as gods and a local temple priest was ready to sacrifice oxen to them.

At that very moment, men came from Iconium, the very ones who had tried to stone the apostles earlier, and turned the people against Paul and Barnabas. These people who moments earlier had wanted to worship the apostles as gods, were now ready to stone them. Such is the fickle nature of faith based on myths. Inexplicably, only Paul was stoned and left for dead. His disciples formed a circle around him and prayed. After a brief interval, Paul got up and went back into the town. That's apostolic courage! (see Acts 14)

It seems that Paul attracted trouble all his life. By his own admission he had frequent brushes with death and suffered at the hands of fanatics who hounded him from town to town. He was scourged five times; beaten with rods three times; shipwrecked three times; lost at sea; suffered untold hardships involving the weather, hunger and thirst. He also said he had many other sufferings that he would leave untold. (See II Corinthians 11:24-28) How is it possible for a man so harassed in the performance of his calling that he could continue on for over thirty years?

The answer is not hard to find. In his letter to the Philippians Paul offered advice on how to overcome all adversity: "Dismiss all anxiety from your minds. Present your needs to God in every form of prayer and in petitions full of gratitude. Then God's own peace, which is beyond all understanding will stand guard over your hearts and minds in Christ Jesus." (Philippians 4:6-7) In other words, the Lord will garrison our hearts in prayer and enable us to withstand the tribulations we are bound to encounter. But even Paul had his moments of great doubt and weakness, but the Lord sent Titus to sustain him. (II Corinthians 7:5-6)

The moral is that we can be like Titus and uplift even the greatest among us. We can also imitate Paul and pray full of gratitude because the peace of God is available to us every day.

159

"Trust in the Lord with all your heart, on your own intelligence rely not." (Proverbs 3:5) This is an example of Hebrew parallelism, where the same thing is said twice. It is a parallelism because heart in Hebrew was believed to be the center of intellectual activity, so the poet in Proverbs is saying it is essential to trust God's word and wisdom in preference to relying on our own understanding. That sounds obvious, but quite often we ignore its advice.

The author of Proverbs had much to say about the heart (i.e. mind). He said we should keep words of wisdom in our minds to guide us, because they give life and health to those who contemplate them. (Proverbs 4:20-22) In sum, he wrote, "With closest custody, guard your heart, for in it are the sources of life." (verse 23) Remarkably, there is a double meaning here, for both mind and heart are essential for life and learning.

Jesus taught that our hearts follow what we esteem as our treasure (Matthew 6:24). So to check the health of our spiritual lives all we have to do is think of what captivates us. What have we dedicated our lives to; what motivates us the most? Since the Lord said that we cannot serve two masters, and we cannot give ourselves to God and something else, then we can easily discover who or what has captured our heart. I am surprised by how many of us have never examined our lives to find out where the real treasure lies.

If we take the time to make an inventory of our lives to date and find that we have placed other things ahead of what is truly important for our spiritual well being, then we are blessed, because the Lord is at hand to renew us in his love. He promised that if we seek to live in him and open ourselves to his presence we will live abundant and productive lives. (John 15:5-8) Somehow we always think that if we seek the Lord he will make demands on us that we cannot fulfill. We are afraid of losing our freedom and having to live a life of difficulty. But the opposite is true. When we give him our heart and mind his love so fills us that all we want to do is his will - and his will for each one of us brings freedom, peace, joy, and blessings. Who would refuse such a life?

Unfortunately, millions refuse to seek the Lord because they see those who profess to believe in him often do not live as if they truly loved God. That's why Gandhi, who had read the New Testament, could not become a Christian, because as he said, he had never met anyone who lived the message. What a shame he died before he could meet Mother Teresa! How sad that so many believers live half-hearted lives and are ignorant of the glorious joy the Holy Spirit wants to lavish on the Lord's disciples. For it is his love which triumphs over all difficulties. (I Corinthians 13:7)

If we live in the love of Jesus we will find our hearts and minds renewed and empowered to live abundant and grace-filled lives. In his last discourse Jesus promised nothing less. (John 15)

160

"Nothing is impossible with God." (Luke 1:37) That is axiomatic for all who believe in God. But what does it mean for the lives of those who follow Jesus? The literal translation of Luke 1:37 is helpful here. Luke wrote that "every word" of God will "not be impossible." The double negative serving as an emphatic positive. In other words, every word of God is backed by the power of God.

The prophet Isaiah summed up the power of God's word in this poetic verse:

> So shall my word be that goes forth from my mouth;
> It shall not return to me void, but shall do my will,
> achieving the end for which I sent it. (Isaiah 55:11)

Jesus echoed the same thing when he said that the heavens and the earth would pass away, but his word would remain forever. (Matthew 24:35) He promised that the one who lives in him and keeps to his word may ask "what you will- it will be done for you." (John 15:7) Jesus also said that even if his followers' faith in him was as small as a mustard seed, they would be able to say to a mountain "Move from here to there," and it would do as it was commanded, because "Nothing would be impossible for you." (Matthew 17:20) Metaphorically speaking, we all have mountains in our lives which need moving, and Jesus gave us the authority to remove them. It is all a matter of faith.

It is also a question of humility. As psalm 119:130 says, "The revelation of your words shed light, giving understanding to the simple." The word translated as simple, is really "infant," or "minor." It takes spiritual grace to see oneself as a mere child who needs to rely on the word of God. Our age is too sophisticated to accept what it sees as simplistic faith; it is also too egocentric to accept what it does not want. But to those who are committed to the truth, the word of God is the plumb line to true peace and wisdom. And Jesus said as much. (John 18:37d)

He also said that we do not live on bread alone, but on "every word that comes from the mouth of God." (Matthew 4:4 NIV) God's word being the superior food we need to live each day in tranquility and joy. Of course, Jesus knew that living his way would bring opposition, and for many, it would result in harsh treatment and even death. But even in the midst of pain and suffering he promised that his Father would give us words to live by, words which opponents could not refute. His words would bring comfort and strength to uphold even those facing a cruel death, for his word does not return to him void, it is full of love and compassion to those who believe in it.

"Indeed, God's word is living...it judges the reflections and thoughts of the heart." (Hebrews 4:12) The living word is like a mirror which reflects back to us the condition of our lives. It is by reading Scripture that we come to know how to live and to discover how near or far we are from the Kingdom of God in our midst. Ultimately, however, when we keep God's word we are truly brothers and sisters of Jesus. (Luke 8:21)

161

"As the Father has loved me, so have I loved you." (John 15:9) We wonder how Jesus can love us just like the Father loves him. How is it possible? We who are sinful, quarrelsome, self - seeking, and proud, are loved with a divine intensity. We are loved by the Lord because he can see beyond our weaknesses and he knows what we were created to be. He also sees the place in heaven he has ready for us - and the faith we have in him, be it ever so little.

Love is not given in order to get something in return. Love is the very nature of God. He cannot stop loving us. No mater what we do, he loves us just the same. He made us for himself, and like a true mother he cannot turn his face away from us. St, Paul has written a sublime panegyric on love which powerfully illustrates the depth of love's perseverance and beauty.

"If I speak with human tongues and angelic as well, but do not have love, I am a noisy gong, a clanging cymbal...If I give everything I have to feed the poor and hand over my body to be burned, but have not love, I gain nothing. Love is patient, love is kind...It is not self-seeking...There is no limit to love's forbearance, to its trust, its hope, its power to endure. Love never fails... There are in the end three things that last: faith, hope, and love, and the greatest of these is love." (I Corinthians 13: 1-13)

While St. Paul is speaking of human love, it is a love implanted in the believer by the Lord, and therefore has some of the attributes of divine love. The love which grows in us for God, for his people, for creation, is the work of the Holy Spirit. As we seek to love God and to serve him with our lives, the Spirit fans the flames of love within us which enables us to do things that we could not do on our own. The Holy Spirit is the Sanctifier who gifts us with the necessary abilities to live for the Kingdom of God.

Jesus promised that he would send the power of the Holy Spirit on those who believe in him. (Luke 24:49 and Acts 1:8) He said that the Spirit would be the comforter, the advocate, the one who enables his disciples to preach the Good News to the whole world.

Scripture teaches that to "each person the manifestation of the Spirit is given for the common good." (I Corinthians 12:7), which means that the Holy Spirit's gifts can be seen in every believer. The gifts of the Holy Spirit are manifestations, or public demonstrations of God's presence among his people.

St Paul wrote that each believer must seek to discern what gifts has been given by the Spirit, and then use them for the common good. Hence we cannot say that we really have no gift and do nothing. We are called to follow Jesus and to show his love and concern for others as the Spirit leads - surely that is everyone's gift. The other gifts follow on from love…

162

"The heavens declare the glory of God." (Psalm 19:2) To look at the sky on a clear night is to see incredible wonder. Billions of stars, countless galaxies, and planets move in a stately dance across the firmament year after year. The spiral galaxies have the identical shape of the Nautilus shell on earth, which indicates that both were designed by the same maker. The vastness of space moves in a predictable pattern - no mere accident fashioned this celestial dance.

The amazing pattern of the DNA molecule, made up of only four elements but with intricate complexity, indicates the handiwork of a master intelligence. In fact, even hardened atheists after studying the latest findings of modern biology and chemistry, readily admit that the universe reflects a creative intelligence. Saints like Francis of Assisi, poets like William Blake, and musicians such as J.S. Bach knew that intuitively all along. And psalm 104 for over two millennia has cried out, "How manifold are your works, O Lord, in wisdom you have wrought them all…" (Verse 24)

Today, however, the danger is that we no longer wonder about the majesty of creation and seem to care little for the beauty of the earth. Ironically, as onetime atheists begin to see the hand of "God" at work in all that came to be, some believers seem to ignore God's handiwork and readily plunder it for material gain. The Lord made us stewards of the earth, we are only caretakers and we need to listen to the teachers in our midst who decry what we are doing to despoil the earth. They are reminding us that when God created the heavens and the earth "he looked at everything he had made and he found it very good." (Genesis 1:31) Our task is to help keep it that way.

But our more urgent task is to care for God's greatest creation: man whom he made in his own image. Every day over 17,000 children die because no one has provided for them food, or fresh water, or medicine. Billions cannot afford even the most elementary health care. Billions eke out an existence on pennies a day while the affluent nations squander most of the world's resources. And the great tragedy is that the rich nations could eliminate most of the problems of the third world if they gave a tithe to help economic development. When we examine just what aid we do give, it is surprising to see that we give only a miniscule amount of our GDP to poor nations.

Scripture teaches us that we who love God must also love his children. When we consider how generously the Lord has given good things to us, how can we refuse to give generously to others? Each of us knows what we can do to help, and each of us must do it in a spirit of thanksgiving to God for his love. When we do, he will say, "When I was hungry you gave me food. I was thirsty and you gave me drink. I was a stranger and you welcomed me. Naked and you clothed me. I was ill and you comforted me....I assure you, as often as you did it for one of my least brothers, you did it for me." (Matthew 24:35-36; 45) As we help the needy we will begin to see their lives improve and understand what St. Irenaeus meant when he wrote, the glory of God is a human being fully alive.

163

"I set the Lord ever before me; with him at my right hand I shall not be disturbed." (Psalm 16:8) By keeping the Lord at the forefront of our lives we gain immeasurable graces and blessings. When we seek the presence of the Lord every day and call to mind his love and seek his help, we grow in love, joy, strength and peace. Recalling the goodness of the Lord as often as we remember it, is a sure way to lead tranquil lives.

It is also very helpful to call to mind the power of the Holy Spirit who is the one who fills us with the fire of God's love. When the Lord sends forth his Spirit we are created anew and through believers he renews the face of the earth. (Psalm 104:30) His word promises that as we seek him we will experience "fullness of joys" in his presence now, and eternal delights forever. (Psalm 16:11) As the Holy Spirit reveals the wisdom of God to the believer, they accept the truth of what Scripture says concerning everlasting life: "Eternal life is this, that they should know you, the only true God, and the one whom you sent, Jesus Christ." (John 17:3) Knowledge of God is imparted by the Holy Spirit through Scripture and prayer.

Jesus promised that he would send the Holy Spirit from the Father to empower us to live holy and productive live, and that the Spirit would instruct us and bear witness on Jesus' behalf and give him glory. The Holy Spirit would be the Paraclete, the one who stands along side us to help, to advise, to strengthen, to intercede, and to lead us into the truth. (See John chapters 14,15,16, and John's first letter.) The Holy Spirit is so evident in the Acts of the Apostles that it could easily be called "The Acts of the Holy Spirit through the Apostles."

Since Scripture speaks so often of the Holy Spirit's role in the life of the People of God, how is it that not all Christians are acquainted with the Spirit's work within them? Obviously, they are not being reminded that the Holy Spirit is the giver of the gifts needed to live a Christlike life and is the giver of the gifts of power to evangelize the world. Happily, though, there is a growing awareness of the Spirit's presence in the lives of believers, and millions of Christians are committing their lives to the Holy Spirit's leading. By setting the Holy Spirit ever before us we can be assured of living vibrant and faithfilled lives.

Realistically, what does it mean then to "set the Lord ever before" us? Is it possible to do it? It is, if we allow the Holy Spirit to to be our helper. When we commit our lives daily to the inspiration of the Holy Spirit we are able to grow close to God and to lead the life which we were created for. Since the Spirit will guide us "into all truth" we can safely seek the Holy Spirit's presence at all times. (John 16:13) Allowing the Paraclete to be our advocate enables us to grow close to God, who in turn draws closer to us. Since it is the greatest way to live, and assures us of divine guidance, our lives are impoverished if we ignore the help of the Spirit, because "the Spirit gives life." (II Corinthians 3:6b)

164

"Out of the depths I cry to you, O Lord; Lord, hear my voice." (Psalm 130: 1) I have prayed that psalm often in moments of pain, spiritual difficulty, or aridity. This psalm brings relief and comfort to a soul which sees the evils of this world and cries out to God for help. The psalm promises that God will redeem sinners from their iniquities because of his great kindness. It is a prayer we can offer for the conversion of sinners (including ourselves) as we intercede with the Lord for the whole world.

Many psalms bring comfort and help to those seeking the Lord in difficult moments. One such verse is a powerful word against temptation: "That you love me I know by this, that my enemy does not triumph over me." (Psalm 41:12) God's loving presence overcomes all the blandishments of the Devil. The psalmist confesses that the Lord has hold of his right hand so he is secure. He admits that he had almost lost his balance and fallen, but when he understood what it would mean to forsake the Lord, he remained loyal. As he said: "But for me, to be near God is my good; to make the Lord God my refuge." (Psalm 73:28)

The Lord is our refuge and "an ever- present help in distress." (Psalm 46:1) Scripture clearly reveals God to be the source of help and compassion, to be the source of all that is good and who rejoices and delights in his people. (Psalm 149:4) Jesus said that his Father wants to give "good things to anyone who asks." (Matthew 7:11) If we ask for faith, love, peace, joy, forgiveness, grace, and the myriad of things we need to live in God's presence they will readily be given, because Psalm 55 says, "Cast your cares upon the Lord, and he will support you;" for he will never allow the just person to be disturbed. (Verse 23)

It is no wonder that the Letter to the Hebrews says "God's word is living and effective." (4:12) Living things give life and God's word gives life eternal, a life filled with hope and tranquility. It is the living word for the living people of God. It is a word which brings comfort, compassion, and the wisdom needed to grow in love and service to others. By reading the Bible every day we receive the bread from heaven, the bread of God's word, which nourishes us in the spirit and leads us closer to the heart of God.

He has sent his word to heal us and to rescue us from destruction. (Psalm 107:20) His word enlarges our heart and guards us from evil and sin. When we rely on his word it saves us from having a divided heart - we are his alone. His word gives light and direction for our lives. God's word, which endures forever, gives us a deep understanding of God's love. (See Psalm 119)

In the end, it is the heart of the believer which penetrates Scripture with the help of the Holy Spirit. As Antoine de St. Exupery said, what is essential is invisible to the eye; it can only be seen with the heart. And as St. Cyril of Alexandra pointed out, "The Holy Spirit enables us to see things beyond the range of human vision."

165

In the first half of the nineteenth century in France there was a remarkable parish priest by the name of Jean Vianney, known familiarly as the Cure D'Ars. In his lifetime he is credited with converting thousands of sinners and working extraordinary cures. He was a man of deep prayer, great humility, and selfless service as a profound spiritual director. Hundreds came daily to seek his advice and prayers. To read his biography is to be astounded by the fervor and holiness and self-sacrifices of this wonderful saint.

The secret of his power to draw sinners back to God was his lifelong intercession for those who had walked away from God. He preached fervently on the mercy of God and would often say that our sins are as dust compared to the mountain of God's mercy. He understood the power of the cross and moved many to repentance by his love for Jesus crucified. He counseled, "You must accept your cross; if you bear it courageously it will carry you to heaven" (Thoughts of the Cure D'Ars, Tan Books, p.9) Like St. Paul, he experienced the opposition of his contemporaries to his preaching of "Christ crucified." In an age of immorality and irreligious spirit he was a voice of truth and reconciliation calling the wayward back to God.

Even though St. Jean Vianney lived in a small remote town his fame spread throughout France and people came from all over the country seeking his spiritual help. His life is an example of what one person can do who is fully committed to serving God and neighbor. Our age needs more people like him, who will give themselves totally to God and be led by the Holy Spirit in their daily lives. It needs servants who will put the needs of others ahead of their own, for as Scripture teaches, each of us must "look to others' interests" rather than our own. (Philippians

2:4) Only with God's grace are we able to serve with such sensitivity.

Prayer is the way we obtain the grace we need to be servants. It does not matter what our occupation is, we are all called to serve others. By frequent prayer, and recalling often the mercy and love of God, we will be able to live the high calling we have as a "royal priesthood." (I Peter 2:9) We can make intercession for the lost. The Cure D'Ars remarked how readily God answers even the smallest prayer when it is heartfelt for others. Intercession is often regarded as a calling for the few, but it is really the duty of all. We are called to make intercession for others even as the Holy Spirit makes intercession for us.

Prayer is being with God and loving him with praise and worship. Prayer is also being alive and breathing and working. As Paul said, "Give you service willingly, doing it for the Lord, rather than for men." (Ephesians 6:7) That, too, is prayer. When we do everything for the Lord, we have a special joy when we meet him in our prayer time - for everything leads us to him and he blesses us with a special blessing: but remembering the advice of the Cure D'Ars, "To pray well we need not speak much."

166

God's ultimate desire for all his children is that they become sharers of his divine nature. He has given us "great and precious promises" and he enables us through his love to achieve the end for which we were created. (II Peter 1:3-4) As St. John wrote. "See what love the Father has bestowed on us in letting us be called children of God. Yet that is what we are." (I John 3:1) In the next verse St. John says something truly amazing: he reiterates that we are indeed God's children, but adds that our final destiny is to be like God, "for we shall see him as he is."

Only the overwhelming love and power of God could make us like him.

Jesus also taught that we were destined for greatness when he said, "you must be made perfect as your heavenly Father is perfect." (Matthew 5:48). It is God who will enable us to be perfect to the extent in which we cooperate with his grace. The word perfect in this verse is the Greek, *teleios*, which does mean perfect, but also means complete, mature, and in the moral sense, fully developed. It can also be translated as having attained the purpose for which it was created. Again, it is God who will enable us to attain our destiny when we are in a relationship with him.

Sharing our lives with God is the greatest adventure we could ever experience. St. Paul described it this way: "All of us, gazing on the Lord's glory with unveiled faces, are being transformed from glory to glory into his very image by the Lord who is the Spirit." (II Corinthians 3:18) The Holy Spirit will enable us to come before the Lord so that we can be transfigured by his love. St. Paul insisted that we are an entirely new creation when we are in Christ. "God made him who did not know sin to be sin, so that in him we might become the very holiness of God." II Corinthians 5: 16-21)

The overwhelming truth is that God made us to enjoy his love forever. The experience of that love begins in this life and is enkindled by the Spirit when we pray. The Lord wants us to grow in love every day as we wait in joyful hope for the fulfillment of his promises. As St. Paul expressed it: "May he enlighten your innermost vision that you may know the great hope to which he has called you." (Ephesians 1:18) In that letter to the Ephesians St. Paul wrote to ordinary people outlining the glorious inheritance which God has given to the members of his church. All too often, believers are unaware of the transcendent gifts God wants to bestow on his children.

His first and most precious gift is his love which he has lavished on us. He has also forgiven us, so there is "no condemnation for

those who are in Christ Jesus." because we have been freed from
the law of sin and death. (See Romans5: 5 and 8:1-2) Guilt and
self-condemnation have plagued mankind since the beginning.
To be set free from shame and remorse so we can share God's
life within us is an inestimable gift. Let us tell this good news to
those who are burdened under the weight of unbelief and sin.
How many people pay therapists huge sums to get rid of guilt
and regain their innocence but to no avail? Usually all they
needed to hear is that the mercy of God is everlasting, and that
Jesus will turn no one away who comes seeking forgiveness and
peace.

167

"Listen that you may have life." (Isaiah 55:3) Perhaps the most
common command of the Lord in the Bible is to listen. The great
prayer which the Jews prayed every day, the *shema*, is a
commandment to listen to God, to love him, and to take to heart
his words. (Deuteronomy 6:4-6) This prayer is Judaism's great
confession of faith which the devout place in phylacteries on
their forehead and left arm, and place in the mezuzah (doorpost)
of their homes. It was this confession of faith that Jesus told a
scribe was the greatest commandment, and the second
commandment he said is, "You shall love your neighbor as
yourself." (Mark 12:28-31)

Listening is an art. Obeying is a grace. Of course when the
Lord's word tells us to hear, or listen, it is really saying, obey.
But it also means to make listening a habit in prayer. Listen to
what you are reading, listen to how you are praying, and listen in
reverent silence to allow the Lord to flood your heart with his
peace. It is difficult for many of us in the West to sit and do
nothing. We fill our days with doing and even our leisure is often
filled with noise and activity. To obey Psalm 46 by being still in
order to know God is a great trial for many. To seem to be doing

nothing, indeed sitting idly waiting upon the Lord, seems un-American. But to know God is the main purpose of our existence and we are unfulfilled until we have encountered the one who is the source of all that is good.

Listening requires practice, patience, and above all humility. We have to know that we are totally ill prepared to serve God, completely unworthy of his attention, but expecting it because he made us to share in his mission of love to the world. We must realize that on our own we can do nothing, and that we are dependent completely on his grace and mercy. To seek him in this way is to elicit his response, because humility is truth and God, being the source of all truth, will respond to our cry for help.

A good prayer to prepare ourselves for silence is to repeat often," God be merciful to me a sinner." Asking often for mercy. is like a child asking his father for bread - it is as natural for God to give mercy as it is for a father to give bread. When we have asked as many times as we feel comfortable with, we can then sit in silence and wait for the Lord. Even if nothing seems to happen, God will flood the heart with his love. But often the Lord's presence is experienced by a deep sense of peace and love. When we have made a practice of this type of silent, attentive listening to the Lord, we will notice a change in our lives. Perhaps patience increases unexpectedly, or we are no longer angry, or we have learnt to forgive someone, or we find joy in prayer. No matter what it is, the Lord will implant his mark on our lives and we will be different.

So, the next time you read the word hear, or listen, in the Bible, check to see how you are listening to the Lord. Take a mental inventory of how you are or are not listening and resolve to do better. Keep on expecting the Lord to help; keep on expecting him to act; and keep on expecting his love to grow in your heart, Remember, if we are not growing in love and service we are actually regressing in them - for no one stands still in the spiritual life.

168

"A herald's voice in the desert, crying, make ready the way of the Lord, clear him a straight path." (Luke 3:4) John the Baptist's experience of crying out in the desert to proclaim the coming of the Lord did not fall on deaf ears. People came to him and repented in response to his words and asked how they were to live a life pleasing to God. John told them to share generously with those in need and be peaceful and satisfied with what they had. Jesus built on John's message and warned his hearers to "avoid greed in all its forms. A man may be wealthy, but his possessions do not guarantee him life." (Luke 12: 15)

Jesus taught his listeners to trust in God and to live tranquil lives secure in the providence of his heavenly Father. He said "Which of you by worrying can add a moment to his life-span? If the smallest things are beyond your power, why be anxious about the rest?" He told them to stop worrying, for it is only the unbelievers who are anxious about possessions. (Luke 12:25-30) Well, it seems that today his words are falling on deaf ears. Even people of faith are anxious and are eagerly seeking to amass the things of this life. Sadly, even churches are in the race to amass wealth, numbers, and "the good life." For many in our age, both John and Jesus are really voices crying in the wilderness, the wilderness of self-seeking and desire for the things of this world.

Jesus said that we cannot give ourselves to God and money…"What man thinks important, God holds in contempt." (Like 16:13-15) (It says literally, "what men highly value, is an abomination before God.") We protest and say, yes, but we have to have money in order to be happy. That is the mantra of western consumerism. In all the poor countries that I visited, I witnessed a great trust in God, and a willingness to share what they had with those who had nothing. Without romanticizing the poor, I have to admit that in spite of their hardships, they had more joy than most of us experience.

I think that the great gift the very poor have is faith. They believe that God will provide because they have nothing else to trust in. Those of us in the rich nations have forgotten how to trust in God and believe that we are the sole providers of our needs and wants. Faith is lacking. Jesus wondered about that when he said. "When the son of man comes, will he find any faith on the earth?" (Luke 18:8) Remember, Jesus taught that even faith the size of a mustard seed is enough. How poor we are when we do not even have that much faith!

Yet there is a remedy for the lack of faith. It requires those who have faith to pass it on to others. As simple as that sounds, it does work. When we encounter someone with genuine faith it puts in us a longing to have the same trust in God. Faith is passed on in concrete ways; by praying for someone to have faith; by standing with another in difficulty all the while expressing a deep faith in the goodness of God. Remembering that Jesus said everything is possible to one who has faith - even bringing an unbeliever to faith merely by believing is possible A simple prayer, said with child-like trust, can bring faith to the most hardened heart.

169

"Mercy triumphs over judgment." (James 2:13) This verse epitomizes the forgiveness God has for sinners. The word translated as triumphs, (*katakauchaomai* in Greek), was used of a gladiator exulting over a defeated foe. Jesus, by his death on the cross, has triumphed, and exulted over the defeat of Satan. He told his disciples to take heart because he had overcome the prince of this world. Jesus rejoiced that mercy was available to all.

The divine mercy is infinitely greater than all of mankind's sins. Scripture repeats dozens of times that the mercy of God endures forever and his mercy overwhelms those who repent. God's mercy is an integral part of his covenant which in a sense means he is obligated to forgive those who turn to him for mercy. As Jesus promised at the Last Supper when he took the cup, "this is my blood, the blood of the covenant, to be poured out in behalf of many for the forgiveness of sins." Forgiveness is guaranteed to all who sincerely seek God with a repentant heart.

We read in the Beatitudes, "Blest are they who show mercy; mercy shall be theirs." (Matthew 5:7) Since we have received such transcendent mercy we, too, are obligated to show mercy to others. In fact, if we refuse mercy to others, Jesus said that we would be refused mercy. (See Matthew chapter six). The Hebrew word behind the idea of mercy is rich in meaning. In addition to its meaning of mercy the Hebrew word means favor, kindness, loving kindness, pity, and goodness. Appearing first in the book of Genesis, *chesed* (mercy), it is used in many places in the Old Testament, but it is used most abundantly in the psalms where it appears almost one hundred times, thus giving the psalms some of Scriptures' most beautiful prayers. Also in the psalms, another word for having mercy, is to be gracious, and to have pity, thereby making the psalms redolent with God's mercy.

St. Paul, who had received great mercy, understood the power and all-encompassing nature of God's mercy. He wrote, "God has imprisoned all in disobedience that he might have mercy on all." (Romans 11:32) While that may sound paradoxical, it really indicates how much God wants to forgive and heal, and how he can even use sin and rebellion to further his compassion: "We know that God makes all things work together for the good of those who love him..." (Romans 8:28) After all, God foreknew our sinfulness, but he did not refuse to create us, rather he planned to send Jesus to redeem us from sin and death. Such is the compassionate love of our heavenly Father.

For the sake of his son's excruciating passion, God poured out on mankind a universe of mercy, yet tragically that mercy is spurned by countless millions, many because they have never been told of God's free gift of mercy, but many, also, refuse the crucified one because it seems to have no relevance to post-modern thinking. Then there are those who ignore mercy for the sake of their sinful desires. Yet the canopy of God's mercy can shelter all, if we who believe will venerate his divine mercy and intercede for all who are lost. Thus we become sharers in the redemptive love of God, and co-laborers with Jesus in his Father's vineyard.

170

"Let the morning bring me word of your unfailing love." (Psalm 143:8 NIV) If we pray, we will experience his steadfast love every morning. Sometimes, however, as the poet wrote, "the world is too much with us..." We get lost in the busyness of life and fail to contemplate the reason for our existence - which is love. We were created out of love for love. But even the word love has been corrupted by the world which really is "too much with us."

If we on waking develop the habit of thanking God for life, for his love, and for the myriad wonders of his creation we will grow in joy and gratitude. Our lives will be centered on the one who created all that is good and our days will have meaning and purpose. Not only will we be blessed, but we will be a blessing to others. To be a sign of God's love in our daily lives is the most fulfilling and enriching way to live. As Christians we will be made joyful by the presence of Jesus as he promised.

One great problem that we must overcome is the fear of silence. We fill our lives with. noise and entertainment because we do not want to be alone with God. We won't admit that it is the reason why we are occupied with doing, but in truth, we are reluctant to let ourselves just be. We do not want to face the vast emptiness we sometimes feel, nor are we willing to expose the inner recesses of our being to scrutiny. But that is because we have yet to experience the fire of divine love. Exposed to God's gaze we encounter love and not condemnation; forgiveness and mercy, in place of judgment. An inner life open to God's love is the greatest journey we can ever make. Yet not too many are willing to try.

Perhaps the greatest reluctance to be still before God is that we do not know how to do it. How do we, the creature, understand the creator, "who lives in unapproachable light." Will we say with Job, that when we expected to see light, there was only darkness? (Job 30:26) Have we tried and only given up in confusion and failure? Have we said that contemplative prayer is only for those who live in monasteries? Or worse, do we believe that such prayer is harmful as I have heard people say.

Being still before God is not difficult. We just need to be patient and let God be God. Since we are his children, and each of us is a unique individual, God will lead us along the path of prayer perfectly suited to our temperament and situation in life. Not knowing how to pray is a benefit, for the Holy Spirit can then lead us to the light. Sometimes it is best to say nothing; at other times we pour out our hearts like water before him. (Lamentations 2:19) But above all, since the Lord knows what is in our hearts and knows all that we want to pray for, being quiet before him in loving adoration is sometimes the greatest prayer. "I have stilled and quieted my soul like a weaned child, like a weaned child on its mother's lap." (Psalm 131:2)

Just by saying "Our Father" and stopping to ponder the enormity of the truth that he is our Father can lead us into the throne room of prayer and adoration.

171

"This is the day the Lord has made; let us be glad and rejoice in it." (Psalm 118:24) That is wonderful advice, which if followed, leads to peace and happiness. But our problem is that we are either living in the past where things were better than the present, or we are waiting for some future prospect to bring us happiness. Contentment and peace of mind seem to be just out of reach and we can see it like a mariner in the crow's nest can see land ahead. We are convinced that if we just wait out the present discontent we will surely attain some future boon yet to be realized. Thus we miss the blessing of the moment.

Scripture tells us to shout for joy now, because the Lord is in our midst. (Isaiah 12:6) The blessings which we seek are available every moment of the day and they are found by those who seek them. Unfortunately, we are habitual procrastinators, always putting off till tomorrow the search for the heart of God. Somehow, we think that the real life of the gospel is waiting ahead for us to catch up to it, when it is already at hand. In this we seem incurable, unable to grasp the happiness of the Lord in the present moment. We feel unworthy, unready, for the love which God's word says the Lord wants to pour into our lives. That is the trap laid by the enemy: for no one is worthy, no one is ready, but the Lord gives it to us anyway - such is his love.

He loves each one of us so much that if we were the only person created, he would have made the whole universe for us and then sent his son to rescue us when we sinned with our hubris and idolatry of self. Even knowing this, we still resist the grace of the present moment for we find prayer painful and unrewarding. This is because we pray wrongly, seeking our wants instead of God's will. When we are ready to seek God for his own sake, and are ready to surrender our will for his, we come to realize that the beginning of wisdom is fear (reverence) of the Lord. We fall on our knees and worship him in spirit and truth. Then the Lord meets us in the present moment and we encounter the Kingdom of God within. Prayer becomes joy and a way of life.

But the tempter is always ready to remind us that we are deluding ourselves and that our prayers are falling on deaf ears. He insinuates into our thoughts the idea that what we believe is the presence of God is really our own imagination. Or more often, he persuades us to believe that all of our thoughts are from God and that we are really people of prayer who are close to God. The way out of this dilemma is humility, making sure that we are not "wise in our own estimation." (Romans 12:16c) As St. Bernard said, the greatest virtues are humility, humility, humility and humility.

By remembering that we are always novices in prayer, that we are beginners who need constant "practice" in learning to pray, we will realize the truth that prayer is a gift each day - it is daily bread provided for us by a loving Father. When we know that each day is an opportunity to speak to the Lord, we will be sure to spend it wisely. "Today, if you hear his voice…" (Hebrews 3:15)

172

"Their amazement [at Jesus] went beyond all bounds." (Mark 7:37) Can this be said of us? We who know the whole story of Jesus as revealed in the Scriptures should be even more amazed than those who saw him in the Decapolis. We know he rose from the dead and that he is the Son of God. We have the witness of two thousand years of Christianity with its countless heroic lives of missionary and evangelical zeal. We of all his followers should be astounded by the work of God's grace flowing from the resurrection of his Son. But we live as if we are not in the least amazed.

The astonishing truth that God became man to share our lives in a very human way should render us speechless. We should fall down on our knees before such a God who loves us and became one of us to bear witness to that love. Yet we live as if we are oblivious to that truth. We do not live vibrant lives of thanksgiving and joy which would make unbelievers wonder what motivates us. Modern paganism is the result of Christian Luke warmness. For we, too, are seduced by technology and materialism. The words of Jesus and the witness of the faith of our forefathers are silenced by our mundane lives. We have almost swallowed the myth that we are free to live as we please instead of living to please God by loving all of his children.

Where is the fire of God's love which he poured out at Pentecost? Have we so institutionalized and symbolized it that it no longer burns in the hearts of many baptized believers? Of course there are exceptions, and in many places there is a growing witness to the truth that Jesus is the same yesterday, today, and forever. (Hebrews 13:8) There is living proof that the Holy Spirit is still pouring out God's love into the hearts of those who seek it. But even as it is astonishing to those who are experiencing it, there is a simultaneous denial of its authenticity by many church leaders and clergy. Even worse, there is indifference to the Spirit's work by those who should know better: indifference on a large scale to the Spirit of God is the great sin of our acquisitive age.

In modern technological societies the percentage of people who profess to be believers is shrinking rapidly. The fast-paced lives of millions mitigates against their seeking the time to discover the things of the spirit. In an age of labor-saving devices, we find ourselves enslaved even more by work and the hectic pace of life. We seek relief in entertainment and a myriad forms of leisure, but we do not find peace or contentment. Like caged mice in the treadmill, we eagerly seek ever new and enslaving means of recreation. Ultimately, society cannot continue following that path. It will end like ancient Rome in disillusion and dissipation.

The remedy is Jesus. He alone can save the Western World from its downward spiral into paganism and spiritual malaise. The Holy Spirit is still revealing the majesty and power of grace available through the Son of God. The Spirit will reveal the gifts of God to anyone who sincerely seeks the truth. The Christians' task is to live in the joy of the Spirit which will entice the unbelievers to discover Jesus for themselves.

173

"Your rebirth has come, not from a destructible but from an indestructible seed, through the living and enduring word of God." (1 Peter 1:23) The seed of God's word, planted in the fertile soil of a believer's heart, grows and matures into a harvest of heavenly mana. The daily bread of God's word, new every morning, gives life and hope to those who receive it, for the word "endures forever." (Isaiah 40:8)

But to receive the word in this way requires a humble and simple heart. In fact, the word can only be revealed in depth in a heart receptive and malleable to the work of the Holy Spirit. A Francis of Assisi, receiving God's word and instantly acting upon it. A Thomas Aquinas, brilliant but child-like, explaining God's word with clarity and great depth, yet with simple faith. Or a Blaise Pascal writing his understanding of the Gospel on a piece of paper and sewing it into the lining of his coat close to his heart. "The heart has its reasons…"he said. Such a simple gesture by a most brilliant mind; but a mind converted by the power of the Gospel.

"Indeed, God's word is living and effective, sharper than any two-edged sword. It penetrates and divides soul and spirit…it judges the reflections and thoughts of the heart." (Hebrews 4:12) But hearts closed to the truth, or hearts blinded by pride and the opinions of men, are impervious to the Scriptures. Actually, they are incapable of understanding the spiritual messages contained in the Gospels. But Jesus who gave sight to the blind can heal their spiritual blindness if they turn to him. However, the change of heart they need is not very often manifested in their lives - perhaps in death they see the light.

The wonderful thing about the Scriptures is that they contain the power to save us. (James 1:21) The Gospels have immeasurable depths which continually surprise and delight those who seek them. The words of Jesus are truly food for the soul, a food that is ever fresh and alive. We can read or hear a certain message of Jesus countless times, then suddenly, like a flash, we perceive a new and breathtaking meaning. Suddenly a whole new way of seeing is opened to us and we understand what the Lord meant when he said, "See, I make all things new!" (Revelation 21:5) Then the daily bread of his word is fresh indeed.

But for this to happen, of course, we need to make a habit of reading the Bible every day. Also, before we begin to read we should ask the Holy Spirit to help us understand and live the message we are reading. Even passages we know well will elicit deeper meanings when we seek the Spirit's help. Jesus promised that the Holy Spirit would be with us always and would guide us to "all truth." (John 16:13) He said that the Holy Spirit would bear witness on his behalf, (John 15:26) and would glorify him. (John 16:14) Then we will be able to testify to the life of Jesus within us and glorify Jesus by proclaiming him by word and action.

With such a need in our hearts for truth and peace, we can no longer refuse the daily bread of God's word in our lives.

174

Daniel had a problem. As intelligent and spiritual as he was, he could not fully understand what Jeremiah meant when he prophesied concerning the Babylonian captivity of seventy years. However, through prayer, Daniel received the revelation that the period of seventy years was really seventy weeks of years, that is 490 years. (Daniel 9:1-27)

What impresses me about Daniel's attitude is his humility. Thirty-two times in his prayer he associated himself with the sins and disobedience of the people. As he interceded he said, "we have sinned...we have not obeyed." Daniel did not exclude himself from blame. And the moment he began to pray, the angel Gabriel left heaven with Daniel's answer. There is a great lesson here. Effective intercession is a matter of the heart. And in chapter 10 of the Book of Daniel we learn the secret.

Daniel had been given a vision by God which he did not understand. So he fasted and prayed for three weeks seeking understanding. At the end of the period, the angel Gabriel came to him to explain the vision. However, he told Daniel that "from the first day that you set your heart to understand, and to humble yourself before your God, your words were heard; and I came because of your words." (Daniel 10:12 NKJV)

Gabriel came because Daniel prayed from his heart. We can expect the same thing. (See Hebrews 1:14) Furthermore, God's word promises us that those who humble themselves get heard. (II Chronicles &:14) And as the seer Hanani said to king Asa, "The eyes of the Lord run to and fro throughout the whole earth to show himself strong on behalf of those whose heart is loyal to him." (II Chronicles 16:9)

Undoubtedly, prayer is an affair of the heart. But how do we get our hearts prepared for God? I think psalm 33 gives us a wonderful idea of how it is done:

The Lord looks from heaven…on all the inhabitants of the earth: He fashions their hearts individually. (Psalm 33: 13-15 NKJV)

So he fashions our hearts individually. What a beautiful word! When we spend time with him, letting him penetrate our darkness with his light, he molds our hearts into the shape of his son's, so our hearts are no longer hard and cold. They will become, new hearts, as Ezekiel foretold, and they will replace our hearts of stone. (Ezekiel 11:19)

Jesus must have the last word: "learn from me, for I am gentle and humble of heart." (Matthew 11:29)

Printed in the United States
100315LV00002B/289-291/A